URBAN LIFE AND URBAN LANDSCAPE SERIES

HISTORY IN URBAN PLACES

The Historic Districts of the United States

David Hamer

OHIO STATE UNIVERSITY PRESS

Columbus

Library of Congress Cataloging-in-Publication Data
Hamer, D. A. (David Allan)
History in urban places : the historic districts of the United States / David Hamer.
p.   cm. — (Urban life and urban landscape series)
Includes bibliographical references and index.
ISBN 0-8142-0789-8 (alk. paper). — ISBN 0-8142-0790-1 (pbk. : alk. paper)
1. Historic districts—United States.   2. Cities and towns—United States—History.
3. Urbanization—United States—History.   4. Historic preservation—United States.
I. Title.   II. Series.
E159.H19   1998
363.6'9'0973—dc21   98-23921
CIP

Text and jacket design by Gary Gore.
Type set in Weiss by Tseng Information Systems, Inc.
Printed by McNaughton & Gunn.

9   8   7   6   5   4   3   2   1

Contents

Illustrations

Preface

In the United States, an ambitious attempt has been made over the last quarter of a century to achieve historic preservation on a scale far greater than would have been possible through the saving of structures one by one. Preservation is now sought and managed to a large extent through the designation of "historic districts." By 1991 more than eight thousand historic districts had been listed on the National Register of Historic Places, which was constituted in 1966 as a key provision of the National Historic Preservation Act. Many more districts have achieved "historic" designation at state and local levels.[1] As the number of historic districts has increased and they have assumed a conspicuous place in the urban landscape, they have received the attention of preservationists and planners. But there has not as yet been an analysis of their significance from an urban historian's point of view—even though most historic districts are parts of towns or cities and their existence is touted in publicity releases as an opportunity to "step back in time," to see what towns or neighborhoods were "really" like in the past. Historic districts are, and should be studied as, examples of applied urban history. As a result of the development and promotion of historic districts, ordinary citizens now find themselves provided with frequent reminders of the history of their communities: road signs point the way to the local "historic district"; plaques proclaim that one has entered a "historic district"; the blacktop turns into a red brick road. In many of these districts, controls are applied in the name of "history" to what people are allowed to do with their property. Indeed, in few areas of modern urban life is history being applied in such a direct way.

For a variety of reasons, notably the availability of tax credits for housing rehabilitation in National Register districts, the historic district phenomenon has developed a great deal further than many people associated with it in its early years expected. The process is still unfolding, and there are many new developments—described in the final chapter—whose significance is still unclear. For a long time the image of the historic district was very much that of Colonial Williamsburg, Beacon Hill, and Charleston—places of extraordinary architectural quality and appeal that have become major tourist meccas. The possibility that one's own neighborhood could also be a historic district has taken some time to sink in.

Most historic districts are parts of (or even, in the case of small villages and mining towns, the whole of) towns and cities, although there are also rural historic districts, which are certain to acquire increased significance as a means of conserving historic rural landscapes. This book, however, is confined to the nation's urban districts. It is intended as an exploration of connections between American urban history and historic preservation. It is not designed primarily as a history of historic preservation or of historic districts. The principal purpose is to place historic districts in the context of American urban history. That history is, however, not understood as being restricted to the era before a district was designated historic. Nor is it seen as confined to the history of which a district itself is claimed to be a legacy and embodiment. The emphasis is on the creation and functioning of districts as historic within the continuum of urban history.

While the academic subdiscipline of urban history has been growing rapidly, in the real world all sorts of representations of the past of America's towns and cities have been taking shape. One of the aims of this book is to draw the attention of urban historians to some of the implications of the development of historic districts. But it is intended too to have a broader appeal and to provide a historical context for those many Americans who in one way or another have become involved in the phenomenon—whether as residents of historic districts, members of preservation commissions, or tourists who visit the districts.

This is the first book devoted to an examination of the significance of historic districts from a historian's point of view. Historians have been slow to appreciate the significance of historic districts, for the concept, as it has been interpreted and implemented, has appeared to bear little resemblance to what historians perceive to have been the realities of the past. Common criticisms of historic districts have been that they convey sanitized versions of the past and are dominated by considerations such as real estate values, the urgent need for the rehabilitation of run-down inner-city areas, or the impulse to "gentrify" that have little to do with the history they purport to preserve. The needs of the present appear to account for their creation. The past that is remembered is a version of the past that suits modern needs. It is essentially the outcome of the workings of contemporary pressures rather than of a desire to see the past accurately depicted no matter what the historical record may reveal it to have been. The past is seen as having been filtered through all sorts of present-day pressures and preoccupations so that it reaches us in a highly distorted form in the shape of historic districts.

From the beginning, the use of the word *historic* to describe districts has been somewhat controversial. A phrase that I heard repeatedly when I explained to historians and preservationists the nature of the inquiry on which I have been engaged is, "But history has had very little to do with it!" Research into the processes that have led to historic district designation and into the motivations of those chiefly responsible for campaigns to secure this objective confirmed that there is much truth in this claim. And yet it has also seemed to me inescapable that there is a great deal of history *in* historic districts, whatever may have been the reasons they have been accorded that status. One of the principal aims of this book is to indicate what this history is.

Historic districts usually become historicized districts. They are often made over in the image of a particular interpretation of their past that it suits contemporary needs to establish. A variety of treatments are applied and controls established in order to develop and maintain the ambience deemed appropriate to a "historic" district. But this does not mean that they do not have a place in urban history. For historic districts are historic phenomena in their own right. They are an aspect of what will be studied as the urban history of the twentieth century, particularly the era since 1966. They also belong within longer-term trends and traditions in American urban history. For instance, many of them make a good deal more sense if seen as representing modern manifestations of American traditions of historicizing and beautifying villages and small towns. Historic districts themselves have a history, and one of the purposes of this book is to describe it. But they also have a place *in* American urban history. Viewing them from this perspective raises the issue of whether, while purporting to be a summation and representation of some of the features of American urban development, they are actually best understood as a continuation or ongoing manifestation of some of those characteristics, part of the history rather than detached from it.

Chapter 1 traces the development of the concept of the historic district down to 1966, and chapters 2, 3, and 4 analyze in greater depth the history of historic districts and survey some of the types of areas that have been designated "historic" and the aspects of history they represent. Although a survey of this kind cannot hope to do more than provide an introduction to some of the main kinds of districts, my principal aim has been to provide a basis for an assessment of which facets of American urban development are represented among historic districts and which are not.

Historic districts are a highly selective representation of America's history and America's districts. The National Register and other criteria state in very general terms what the principles of selection are, but on these criteria operate additional—and constantly changing—understandings as to what should be regarded as "significant" in the nation's history and worthy of commemoration and preservation. Historic districts are very carefully crafted and maintained creations. They are not as "history" would have left them. If that were the case, they would in many instances be a dreadful mess, and that, it seems, is not what people want to remember or keep as "historical." An object of this study has been to explore the concepts of the "historical" that have been used to fashion historic districts. Usually there has been a highly selective interpretation of the history of the "historic" district. In particular, evidence of decay and deterioration tends to be excluded as far as possible. Features of the past that do not fit the desired historical image are often airbrushed out of the scene. I argue that this is not a new development: a similar impulse can be traced back to earlier eras of beautification and "improvement," although there is now a good deal more emphasis on retaining the aesthetically pleasing aspects of the past rather than eradicating the legacies of the past in favor of future-oriented models of urban design.

Chapter 5 examines some of the connections between the development of historic districts and American traditions of urban boosting. This is the section of the book that has the most direct connection with my earlier work on urban history. In *New Towns in the New World*, my subject was images and perceptions of towns in "new countries" in the nineteenth century. The origins of the present book owe much to my experiences while researching that book in the United States. I kept coming upon images that had emerged in the nineteenth century and that are still in use today. I began to become aware of various reasons why they were being revived—or had never died. Not only was boosterism still alive and well, it seemed, but old booster slogans and images had survived and were being used in the present-day promotion of towns. In many instances, images and reputations from the past have been revived and put to contemporary uses. Had these, I wondered, been lying dormant in the community subconsciousness? I recalled how intensively and competitively towns had been boosted in order to attract people to them. Images given prominence then often turn out to have had a long, if at times subterranean, life. In particular, I found that historical imagery was being put to use in numerous towns, cities, and neighborhoods as a significant component of strategies to help communities cope with the challenges of the present and future. The theme that is often adopted in these strategies is the restoration of pride: the past is carefully and selectively interpreted as a source of this message. The prime and perhaps most influential example of this has been the restoration of the mill and canal complex at Lowell, Massachusetts. Historic imagery has also been valued highly by people restoring or "gentrifying" neighborhoods.

Historic districting has been used and valued as a mechanism for controlling, rather than representing and reflecting, change in urban environments. Modern "nonconforming intrusions," for instance, are not regarded with much favor. There are those who find this attitude to change profoundly unhistorical in terms of the realities of American urban development, where change has been the one abiding constant. But attempts to create historic districts that might be considered more representative of change and evolution are fraught with problems and go against some of the most basic objectives for which historic district designation has been desired. To render the past "usable" in this format, evidence of what has been perhaps the most significant feature of American urban development has had to be downplayed and even suppressed.

Chapter 6 moves on to the history of a historic district, after it has been so designated. Although they are frequently accused of freezing the past, we shall see that there are various ways in which historic districts, once established, can, like the American Constitution, have their meaning and significance reinterpreted to suit changing needs. An example is the alteration of boundaries. The advice often given to organizers of submissions for historic district designation is to proceed cautiously at first and avoid including areas and properties where there is resistance. The success of a district that has general acceptance from the start may pave the way for an easing of resistance in other areas not initially included in it.

The last two chapters describe some of the ways in which the history that has hitherto been neglected in the conceptualization and interpretation of historic districts is being restored. A great deal can be done through the interpretive regimes and strategies devised for districts. This aspect was not given much thought at the outset of historic district development, although educational programs were recommended in such studies as that of College Hill in Providence, Rhode Island.

There has been an increasing emphasis on a historic district as not just a collection of buildings but also a repository for and a means of reinvoking memories of ways in which people have inhabited and used buildings and the environment in which they are situated. These memories are said to form part of the "sense of place," and the historic dimensions of that sense are built into the cases on which many submissions for historic district designation are now based. History has lost some favor as an influence for community cohesion, particularly because of the divisive potential of controversy over whose history should be highlighted and what should be done about those episodes and aspects of history that have hitherto tended to be kept out of sight. The invention of meaning for historic districts is an ongoing process. Interpretation is a complex and sometimes hazardous matter, which no doubt is why it has so often been shied away from: it can open up a struggle to determine whose history should be dominant in descriptions of a district's past and in the uses to which that history is put. Recent developments are tending not to displace history but to submerge it in a variety of other ways of celebrating community. There is a tendency also to dilute historical controversy through an emphasis on history as fun and festival. Other terms are increasingly being used, such as "cultural." There has been a growing and powerful commercial emphasis on what Edward Relph has called "ambience," a vague concept signifying "environmental style and atmosphere," which is fostered in old or old-seeming places and is a key element in the postmodern urban landscape.[2]

New forms of district, larger in scope and purpose and the history that they are designed to represent, are coming into being and may eventually supersede historic districts as the principal focus of area preservation. In addition to historic districts there are and have been for some time historical parks, usually under the management of the National Park Service. Some of these, such as Lowell and Salem, are urban in character and may cover an area that is also a historic district or is part of one. Their development has conformed to a different model, the "park" model that emphasizes a landscaped, controlled environment for structures of major historical significance. Structures that do not belong to the era of chosen significance have often been regarded with less favor. There is a tendency toward a blurring of the distinction between historic districts and historical parks as there is a reaching out toward a more comprehensive inclusion of environmental and landscape characteristics in the definition of what a historic district should be.

⁂ During the course of my research for this book I endeavored to visit as many historic districts as possible, but inevitably those that I have seen for myself are a small proportion of the huge total, and I have had to rely on a wide range of sources for information concerning many others. Personal experience, however, has had a considerable influence on the making of this book, and any bias in my choice of examples relates to the fact that many of them are districts I have experienced at firsthand. If at any point this personal experience appears to obtrude, I make no apology. Many historic districts have been fashioned to be enjoyed. To the authors and compilers of innumerable walking tour guides, I owe thanks for many hours of well-informed urban explorations. Unless otherwise noted, all photographs in the book are by the author.

I am especially grateful to Zane Miller and Henry Shapiro, the editors of this series, for the patience and thoroughness with which they commented on several drafts. An anonymous reader also provided much helpful advice. For those defects that remain, I am, of course, solely responsible. For their hospitality and helpfulness on my visits to their institutions, I am grateful to Richard Candee at Boston University, Richard Longstreth at George Washington University, and Gene Lewis and Zane Miller in the Department of History at the University of Cincinnati. The staff at numerous libraries were generous with their assistance, but I would like to offer special thanks to the staff at the National Trust Library at the University of Maryland at College Park. Much of the research and writing for this book was carried out during a period of leave that I was granted by my university from June 1994 to June 1995. I am most grateful to the Leave Committee at Victoria University of Wellington for supporting this leave and to my colleagues in the History Department for their understanding of my lengthy absence after a long period of involvement in extradepartmental administrative duties. I owe a great debt of gratitude to the many people throughout the United States who answered my queries, sent me information, and helped me during my visits. They are too many to list by name, but I would like to give special thanks to Dee McIntire at Bloomington, Indiana, and to Eileen McGuckian of Peerless Rockville, Maryland. I was encouraged by their enthusiasm for the project and hope that this is the kind of book they felt needed writing. Among the people in Washington, D.C., who gave me help and advice I would like to make particular mention of William Murtagh and Nellie Longworth. A final and special word of thanks to my wife, Bea, who accompanied me on some of my travels and helped with her insightful comments on what we were observing.

One

Development of the Concept of the Historic District

PRIOR TO 1966 HISTORIC PRESERVATION IN THE United States dealt principally with the restoration of individual buildings. As Charles Hosmer has shown, area preservation was at best only on the fringes of the activities of the leading preservationists of the 1920s and 1930s such as William Sumner Appleton, founder of the Society for the Preservation of New England Antiquities.[1] Much of Appleton's energy had to be devoted to the rescuing and restoration of houses that were in imminent danger of destruction. According to Hosmer, these "brushfire crises ignited with such rapidity that Appleton could never indulge in campaigns for the preservation of whole sections of historic towns. He could focus on only one house at a time. It is unfair to say that the idea of saving a historic district had never entered his thinking, but he certainly did not spend much of his time pondering the subject."[2] A general area of historic significance was most likely to be noted by some sort of marker, a memorial to what had been, a substitute for what was no longer visible or in existence.[3] An enormous amount of effort and money was required to restore a house to the standard associated with museum status. It would have seemed quite impracticable to think of doing this for a large number of houses in a district. *That* was only possible if a commitment of wealth on the scale possessed by the Rockefellers and applied at Colonial Williamsburg was forthcoming.

The Early Historic Districts: Williamsburg and Charleston

One thread that in retrospect can be detected running through the history of the emergence of historic districts is the significance of precedents. There have been in effect, although not in intention, a series of models for development. There was no conscious strategy for developing historic districts in this incremental way. Nevertheless, at the outset a variety of options for the form they would take and the purposes they would serve began to emerge. The first of these models were set at Colonial Williamsburg and Charleston. Since the Colonial Williamsburg restoration was begun, perceptions of the potential for historic district development have been widened with each successful initiative.

Colonial Williamsburg has been influential in large part because of its success and has offered one model for exploiting the architectural heritage of "historic" towns. It has appealed in particular to cities with districts that contain that heritage in its original, concentrated, "walking city" form but to a large extent have been abandoned for other purposes. The Williamsburg model has proved to be more relevant to communities that sense that they possess, and that wish to exploit, a tourism potential in their heritage assets than to those where the priority is neighborhood rehabilitation. Subsequent initiatives have been more relevant to the latter objective, which was indeed eventually to assume a predominant place in historic district development. Williamsburg was a very small town which had decayed seriously since the period 1699-1779 when it was the capital of Virginia. Many of the buildings of that era had disappeared by the twentieth century. During the 1920s Dr. W. A. R. Goodwin, having supervised the restoration of Bruton Parish Church in Williamsburg, of which he was the rector, conceived the idea of restoring the entire town as it had been in the eighteenth century. His interest in this project was principally patriotic and commemorative: he saw Williamsburg as the "Cradle of the Republic" and "the birthplace of her liberty."[4] In 1926 he interested John D. Rockefeller, Jr., in the project, and Rockefeller gave it major financial support—some $79 million over the next decade. Although the original plan for Williamsburg was to restore individual buildings,[5] the focus gradually shifted to the whole town. More than seven hundred buildings that had been erected since 1790 were demolished and in many cases replaced by replicas of the structures that were originally on the sites. The replicas were as close to the originals as archaeological and historical research could ensure. The major reconstructions were completed in the early 1930s, and Duke of Gloucester Street was opened by President Franklin D. Roosevelt in October 1934. Attendance figures soared

Duke of Gloucester Street, Williamsburg, Virginia, ca. 1900–1910. This scene was to be transformed by the restoration of the 1920s and 1930s.

from a mere 4,047 in 1932 to 210,824 in 1941. The Capitol and the Governor's Palace are total reconstructions. The site occupies some 175 acres within which about ninety buildings have been restored. Many of these are open to the public who can see costumed guides and craftsmen interpreting the sites and the crafts being practiced therein.[6] Colonial Williamsburg is under the control of a foundation and is one portion of the modern city of Williamsburg, which, however, owes much of its employment and economic well-being to Colonial Williamsburg and the many theme parks and other types of entertainment catering to the needs of mass tourism that have developed in proximity to it.

The restoration of Colonial Williamsburg in the 1920s and 1930s was a major precedent for the creation of one sort of historic district—an original town site converted into a historic museum. The pattern that it set was one way for a town with a significant pre-1800 history to go and began to arouse great interest. Timothy Mullin, curator of museums for the Historical Society of Delaware, has recalled how in the 1930s "the people of New Castle wanted to do something very much like Williamsburg. . . . They wanted to buy up everything, tear down what didn't 'belong,' and reconstruct a 'colonial village.' " Kathleen Bratton, director of the New Castle

The selection of history to be remembered and preserved: the demolition of the old school at Williamsburg as the reconstructed Governor's Palace is erected behind, 1933.

Historical Society, is pleased that this did not happen. "New Castle is real," she says. "Williamsburg and Sturbridge were created, but here you can walk through town without a ticket."[7]

As it turned into a tourist attraction, Colonial Williamsburg cast its spell: towns with a substantial architectural heritage and an uncertain economic future in most other directions were tempted to dream of turning their historic areas into the "Williamsburg" of whatever region they were in.[8] Towns experimented with or at least thought of various ways in which their historic buildings could be developed into a local Williamsburg. When the old gold rush town of Columbia, California, was restored, it became known as "the Williamsburg of the West."[9] Many communities in the 1920s and 1930s, for example, St. Augustine, Florida, Portsmouth, New Hampshire, and Plymouth, Massachusetts, started to plan toward turning their own historic areas into "Williamsburgs." Hosmer rightly points out that "the more the local people wanted to imitate the Williamsburg restoration, the more they sought some benefactor who would drop out of the clouds and plan their work for them. The efforts to create northern and western Williamsburgs were all plagued by the inexperience and unrealistic viewpoint of the people who backed these projects."[10] The disruptions of World War II put an end to this dreaming. But there was continuity into the postwar era. The planning that had been done laid a foundation, in most of these communities, for more realistic and achievable strategies when urban renewal presented its challenges and opportunities in the 1950s and 1960s.

More significant in the longer term for the management of the kind of historic district we are accustomed to today was the approach taken to historic preservation in Charleston, South Carolina.[11] Charleston, a major port and urban center prior to the Civil War (it was the sixth-largest city in the country in 1820), stagnated for many years after the end of that conflict and became something of a backwater. Its isolation was one reason for the development of a highly distinctive local/regional culture with a heavy emphasis on nostalgia for the romantic antebellum past. All this appeared to be threatened after World War I as the car made the city more accessible and the outside world began to take an interest in its historic relics. Museum directors and antique collectors began to remove woodwork, ironwork, and so on, from houses. In 1920 Susan P. Frost, a real estate agent, formed the Society for the Preservation of Old Dwellings.[12] Frost and others in the society were concerned with the preservation of the entire historic neighborhood and were among the first preservationists to see attention to context as the appropriate strategy even for those whose primary concern was the preservation of individual structures. Between 1928 and 1931 community leaders and planners, following an adverse community reaction to the appearance of modern gas stations in the old sections of the city—and the prospect of more—worked to develop something for which there was no legal precedent: a zoning ordinance that would create what was the nation's first historic district. In 1929 the city council established a city planning and zoning commission, the main function of which was to be the granting or denial of approvals for new nonresidential uses anywhere in the city. When the Standard Oil Company proposed to erect another gas station, this time in the very heart of the historic district, the council took a further step in 1930 in the direction of control with a temporary zoning law that made it illegal to erect or institute any "service or filling stations, automobile repair shops, factories or other buildings or businesses which would serve to detract from the architectural and historical setting."[13]

The city council placed the eighty-acre Battery district—called the Old and Historic Charleston District—under a permanent zoning ordinance in 1931. This established a range of bureaucratic procedures of the kind that would later form the infrastructure for the management of historic districts across the nation.[14] What was done here represented a set of responses to a wide range of issues associated with controlling the environment of a district that was both "living" and "historic." Property owners who lived in it were henceforth restricted in what they might do with their property. The ordinance introduced a requirement that "applications for building permits and for Certificates of Occupancy . . . must be approved as to exterior architectural features which are subject to public view from a public street or highway." A board of architectural review was established to review plans for exterior alteration or new construction within the Old and Historic Charleston District. All exterior changes proposed for any pre-1860 structure had to conform with the architectural style of "historic" Charleston. The board was empowered to issue Certificates of Appropriateness and instructed to prevent incongruity in relation to "the old historic aspects of the surroundings." The features that were specified were "the general design, arrangement, texture, material and color of the building or structure in question." Over the years design controls for historic districts have adopted similar formats and become increasingly specific. They now commonly provide controls and guidelines for such architectural features as windows, doors, building heights, and roof lines. The initial Charleston policy was reactive: the community responded to changes to its "historic" buildings and threats to the city's "historic" character. In 1941 there was a major move toward a more proactive preservation strategy: a citywide architectural survey, undertaken by the Carolina Art Association with Carnegie Foundation funding, produced an inventory of 1,168 buildings (most of them not in the designated historic district). This was published in 1944.

But Charleston, while it did pioneer a wide range of strategies and procedures that were eventually to become commonplace in the management of historic districts, was also an exceptional place, with a legacy of outstanding architecture and streetscapes and a high degree of self-consciousness about its heritage. As Hosmer noted, the "successful Charleston approach has proved to be curiously unexportable in some ways." It *was* unique. "Charleston stands alone among America's historic cities because the sense of continuity has been so clearly reflected in the life of its people." And yet it did also turn out to have been the "laboratory that utilized nearly all of the most important urban preservation techniques: private restoration programs by real estate agents, historical zoning and a board of architectural review, a careful survey of architectural resources followed by extensive publication, and the creation of a foundation that could utilize a revolving fund to preserve and restore many old buildings."[15] Its particularity and uniqueness were probably influential in shaping perceptions of what a historic district is and should be. Later, we shall see that advocates of the "sense of place" approach to the interpretation of the history in historic districts draw attention to the strongly local and regional character of the inspiration behind the first historic district.[16] Although eventually, in 1966, the federal government was to enter the business of conferring historic district designations, the criteria avoided the imposition of rigorous *national* definitions and allowed abundance of scope for the recognition of local particularities.

New Orleans

What happened in the late 1930s to the Vieux Carré district in New Orleans was also significant.[17] The boundaries of this 260-acre district are those of the French colonial town that was platted in 1721. The plan was a grid but with many narrow streets—a fascinating mix of Old World mystery and New World order. Many features survived from the Spanish colonial period (ended by the Louisiana Purchase), including distinctive and romantic architecture. In the Victorian Era the city's central business district developed in a different part of the city, on the other side of Canal Street, and there was little demand for space for business activity in the Vieux Carré itself. However, after nearly two centuries of relatively little change, the early twentieth century saw the development of pressures, such as the creation of rail links with the waterfront and the establishment of industries along the river, that threatened to destroy the historic character of the district. It was during this era that the romanticization of the Vieux Carré set in as it began to attract artists and writers. To a considerable extent this tendency was actually stimulated by the evidences of decay that were appearing— and that may have had physical origins such as the lowering of the city's water table following the development of an electric pumping system.

In 1925 a commission was set up to advise on preservation in the Vieux Carré. In 1926 the city asked the consultant firm of Harland Bartholomew to conduct a study for a citywide zoning ordinance. The consultant's report recommended the creation of a Vieux Carré district with restrictions on height, use, and area "to preserve this unusual and historic section of predominant residential uses and small businesses." In 1936, by constitutional amendment, the Louisiana legislature increased the powers of the Vieux Carré Commission.[18] The City Council of New Orleans was permitted under this provision to confer on the commission powers to preserve buildings within a designated area and to exercise review over plans for new construction and alteration to existing properties within that area. But the Vieux Carré district was not subject to the controls of a zoning ordinance—as was the Old and Historic District in Charleston—and it was some time before the commission took the initiative in halting demolition of old buildings.[19]

The significance of the Vieux Carré for the development of historic districts came in the longer term as a consequence of the combined and interacting influences of, on the one hand, the imposition by the commission of the "New Orleans style" on new construction and, on the other, the growth of fascination with the district as a tourist destination. It has been described by one historian as becoming "the quintessential historic district and the prototypical nostalgic form from which all American cities would borrow." [20] The offerings of many modern historic districts—the "public" ones where tourism is actively encouraged—are a mixture of many of the ingredients that existed at the Vieux Carré and have been exploited over the years, such as a waterfront, warehouse districts, an old town plan, public markets, and local celebrations and carnivals. [21] One striking aspect of the early history of the development of historic districts was the prominence of southern locations. [22] There have been various explanations for this phenomenon, all related to a strong regional consciousness and the way this became focused in what seemed to be the expression of traditional, quintessential southern values to be found in the historic portions of cities that had been untouched by "progress" since the antebellum era. The South included an exceptionally large and conspicuous range of cities that had stagnated since that era. Southern nostalgia attached itself to these remnants of an increasingly romanticized past. As we shall see, other regions had districts that had also been "bypassed by progress," but in them historic preservationism was much slower to move from structure to district preservation.

Some towns that resembled Charleston and New Orleans in their retention of a largely intact historic area with great architectural and historic significance went through a much longer and more difficult process to obtain the same kind of protection. An example is Annapolis, the capital of Maryland since 1694, where the campaign spilled over into the post-1966 era. Its legacy of fine buildings reflected the great era of prosperity in the late eighteenth century and a long period of ensuing stagnation as wealth and commercial life shifted to Baltimore. Rockefeller had been interested in Annapolis before Williamsburg, but the chamber of commerce had opposed his plans because it feared restrictive zoning. Individual buildings were threatened for many years. An organization called Historic Annapolis was set up in 1952. In 1966 the downtown area was one of the first historic districts placed on the new National Register, and in 1969 the voters approved the adoption of a historic district ordinance. [23]

The Concept Expands

These districts stood out from most sections of most American cities for the quality and integrity of their architectural legacies and their associations with major episodes and significant people in American history. A development of historic districts along these lines would not have produced more than a few dozen at the most. However, Beacon Hill in Boston, given similar protection as a historic district in 1955, while another example of the exceptional district,[24] was significant both as a district in a large metropolis and as one of the first historic district developments outside the South. The Massachusetts legislature was indeed in the forefront of historic district development: by the end of the 1950s it had also authorized the creation of districts in Lexington and Concord, and another forty-one districts were authorized by enabling enactments between 1963 and 1973. It is important to note that this Massachusetts activity proceeded with broad support from the courts. In 1955 the state's Supreme Judicial Court delivered an advisory opinion to the effect that the creation of historic districts in Nantucket was a constitutional exercise of a state's general welfare power. The opinion contained a succinct statement of the purpose behind the "historic district" approach to historic preservation: "It is not difficult to imagine how the erection of a few wholly incongruous structures might destroy one of the principal assets of the town, and we assume that the boundaries of the district are so drawn so as to include only areas of special value to the public because of possession of those characteristics which it is the purpose of the act to preserve."[25]

Museum Villages and Parks: Alternative Models

One characteristic of the Williamsburg model is that the historic district is organized in such a way that the urban environment can be carefully controlled and maintained in a desired historic state. Noncompatible activities can be minimized. But few towns had retained a historic core with the density of historic buildings still available at Williamsburg, and few indeed had the resources or will to undertake clearance of nonhistoric structures on the scale practiced there. An option increasingly favored for achieving that kind of environment was to create a museum village.[26] This was to become one kind of historic district, the kind that is manufactured through the assemblage in one place of structures, usually authentic and imported from other locations, but sometimes replicas. The structures may then be arranged in a format that reproduces the type of settlement common to the region. Admission to some of the structures is usually charged. Sturbridge Village, Massachusetts (1946), is an example. The difference between it and Williamsburg is that it is not a reconstruction of a village as it originally was but a replica of a New England village with an arrangement around a green of eighteen historic structures, some authentic and imported from other locations (mostly in Connecticut) and others reconstructed.

Other possibilities for securing the protection and management of mul-

Independence Hall, Philadelphia, Pennsylvania, 1950. The photograph was taken look-ing north from the Penn Mutual Building, before the start of work on the creation of the Mall. (Photo courtesy of Independence National Historical Park Collection)

tiple historic structures began to be developed in the larger cities. Philadel-phia was responsible for two of these. In 1956 the Philadelphia Historical Commission became the first historical agency to have jurisdiction over all of a major American city; it was given control over all alterations proposed for any historic building throughout the city.[27] This was an alternative or complementary approach to that involved in the creation of historic dis-tricts in which every structure, irrespective of whether it has specifically been classified as "historic," is protected.

The second influential Philadelphia development was Independence Historical Park, created by an act of Congress in 1948. This project was to prove highly significant in the history of the conceptualization of the his-toric district, in part because the creation of the park went on for several decades, from the 1940s into the 1970s. Numerous people who were to con-tribute to historic district development, such as William J. Murtagh, the first keeper of the National Register, worked on it. The process incorporated, and to an extent synthesized, characteristics from several stages of the de-velopment of the historic district concept. On the one hand, Independence Historical Park resembled Williamsburg quite closely in a number of ways.

Independence Mall, 1964. The creation of the historical park entailed the removal of almost all evidence of the history intervening between the time that is now deemed significant and the present. (Photo courtesy of Independence National Historical Park Collection)

For example, there was wholesale demolition of buildings in the vicinity of the park that were considered incompatible with the desired historical focus. Much of the history of the area was simply obliterated. Until after World War II Independence Hall stood in an area dense with factories and warehouses. This was not considered a fit environment for the "shrine of American liberty." Today the park consists of seventeen city blocks focused on a three-block mall, and all trace of the nineteenth-century history of the area has gone. Independence Historical Park looked back to Williamsburg and forward to historical theme parks. But the form to be assumed by historic districts was to some extent also foreshadowed in the ideas of Charles E. Peterson, an architect advising the commission that oversaw the park's development. Although he was in favor of some reconstruction as at Williamsburg, he urged retention of the city's historic street patterns and the sense of enclosure provided by groupings of buildings. He also warned against overzealous demolition around the historic buildings: "If the pulling down is kept up long enough it will leave the historic buildings standing in large open spaces like country churches, a condition which their designers did not plan for." He preferred compatible new building as infill. Peterson "urged retention of at least fifteen houses a century or more old to reinforce the urban character of the area, while at the same time setting off the more monumental structures. Pointing out that it would be extremely destructive to 'freeze' the historic area as it was in any one period, he urged the preservation of important buildings constructed as late as 1850."[28] A long debate ensued as to whether some of these buildings, in particular the Jayne and Penn Mutual buildings, should be kept. Most were eventually demolished. In retrospect we can see that these were important debates about the nature of a historic district.

By contrast, a plan for the park produced by Edward Riley in 1952 called for restoration of the historic buildings that were significant in the period from 1774 to 1800 and the reconstruction of selected period buildings "to provide a stage setting as a proper ambience for the historic structures." The atmosphere would be further enhanced by landscaping, brick sidewalks, and period street lights, pumps, watch boxes, and other items of street furniture.[29] In this instance we can see definitions emerging of the appropriate furnishing and embellishments for a historic district.

The Impacts of Urban Renewal

Without a doubt, the crucial catalyst for transforming the agenda of historic preservation from concern for preserving individual buildings to concern for preserving or restoring districts and neighborhoods was the process that became known as urban renewal. The creation of historic districts was gradually propelled into an entirely new dimension outside the realm of the museum village and from the unique and special to the representative and typical. The negative and destructive aspects of urban renewal during this era are often stressed, and it has indeed acquired a bad reputation among historic preservationists. The two key measures were the Housing Act of 1949, under which federal funds could be used to purchase and clear deteriorated urban neighborhoods, and the Urban Renewal Act of 1954. The former launched a program of "urban development." It was in the latter that the term "urban renewal" made its first appearance. This change in terminology "was intended to indicate a new approach, that of restoring property in slum neighborhoods rather than simply leveling an entire area."[30]

In retrospect it seems that there was only one model of urban revitalization in vogue at this time: total demolition and reconstruction. Vast tracts of old buildings were destroyed.[31] Under the Housing Act the federal government provided finance to an LPA, or local public authority, for the purchase of slum properties. The idea was that the cleared land would then be sold at low prices to private developers for new construction. But these private developers often failed to appear, and vast wastelands were left.[32] Urban redevelopment and freeway construction made particularly dramatic impacts on the historic cores of older cities where so much deteriorated housing stock and urban blight existed. Here is a graphic description of what happened to the Pastures neighborhood in Albany, New York, which was selected for neighborhood preservation by the local urban renewal agency.

> The agency acquired every building and relocated every family and every business. Next, the agency demolished every "insignificant" structure [nearly half the buildings in the district], including every worker's house, every outbuilding and every commercial structure. Then the heat was turned off and the windows boarded up in the surviving buildings. There they sit now in desolation while the agency tries desperately to sign up a single developer who will "do" the Pastures neighborhood. This example of "neighborhood preservation" is as much an example of neighborhood destruction as any land clearance project ever was. That neighborhood ceased to exist on the day its last resident was trundled off to a distant housing project. The best that can be hoped for now is the survival of a few shells of historic buildings dotted around in a landscape of parking lots and infill housing. The Pastures is a failure of enormous proportions.[33]

By 1962, 588 communities had urban renewal projects. It was predicted that by 1964, 750 cities would be engaged in more than 1,500 projects. For a time, there was much enthusiasm for urban renewal.[34] It fitted in well with the postwar mood of making a new start and ridding cities of the burdensome legacy of the past—which for most people was primarily identified with the grim depression years. There was mounting evidence of the beneficial consequences for Europe's cities of the compulsory urban renewal effected by the ravages of World War II. The buildings associated with urban redevelopment—such as housing projects—were designed in the modernistic style "stripped of all past symbolism." In the new urban landscape the past was not only ignored, it was destroyed.[35] It has to be kept in mind that concern to retain the past in city planning is a relatively recent development. It did not feature in the City Beautiful movement, for instance. In the American city planning tradition, negative attitudes toward the past were not an aberration.

A large section of the nation's urban heritage seemed to be fast disappearing. Since the oldest districts were naturally often the most deteriorated, it looked as if urban renewal and historic preservation would be hard to reconcile.[36] Furthermore, such districts usually did not correspond to what was emerging as the stereotype of the historic district as exemplified by Charleston and Beacon Hill. Many of the districts being targeted for urban renewal were regarded as slums, not the type of area that preservationists had had much experience or interest in conserving. Preservationists have been criticized for not acting soon or fast enough to counter the damaging effects of urban renewal on the nation's legacy of historic neighborhoods. But urban renewal was well under way before an awareness of its likely impact on older neighborhoods developed. When urban renewal began, the historic preservation movement was still small-scale and traditional. It was not organized to combat a policy that had such widespread support and funding and that appeared to be the answer to some of the nation's most pressing urban and social problems.

But urban renewal itself proved to be a crucial catalyst for the emergence of a constituency for action on historic preservation. This was not just because it was a challenge for historic preservationists. It was also an opportunity, and preservationists were frequently able to use the financial resources made available via a host of urban renewal programs to promote preservation—at the same time as they mobilized indignation at the more negative aspects of what was happening to secure support for major legislative advances.[37] "Urban renewal" was a complex phenomenon whose mix of strategies included concern and assistance for the retention, protection, and restoration of existing housing and neighborhoods. Much depended on the extent to which preservationists were able to get involved at the local level, where the plans to implement, for example, authority under the Urban Renewal Program of 1954 to use funds for the rehabilitation of older buildings were formed and put into effect.[38] Under the provisions of the Department of Housing and Urban Development's (HUD's) 701 program, authorized by the Housing Act of 1954, eligible preservation activities included preparation of historic district legislation and the development of a historic preservation program for local government.[39] It was under the latter provision that historical surveys of major significance were carried out at Savannah and Natchez. Planning studies produced reports that underscored the historic or residential values of the areas in question and led the way to conservation efforts.[40]

An urban renewal-funded demonstration project at Providence, Rhode Island, was particularly important for the development of historic districts. In the late 1950s the Urban Renewal Administration granted $50,000 for a joint City Planning Commission–Providence Preservation Society study of a 380-acre area. After an investigation that took almost three years, the report was published in 1959. The study involved an extensive inventory of College Hill and the preparation of a preservation plan. In these respects, it was to be a model and prototype for many more historic districts.[41] It recommended what it called "historic area zoning" for a substantial portion of the study area. Down to this point little published advice was available concerning how a historic area might be renewed or how a large number of historic houses might be preserved. The study developed a historic area zoning ordinance, a system for rating historic architecture, and a technique for integrating areas of historic architecture into proposed redevelopment plans.[42] The methodology for discovering a historic district was now in place. The Rhode Island legislature accepted the case for a historic district and passed the legislation that enabled the city in 1961 to create the College Hill District.

Urban renewal projects brought progress in historic preservation at the area and district level in several other communities.[43] For instance, a great deal was accomplished in urban renewal programs in Savannah, a celebrated area of historic district pioneering. It was the inventory of the National Historic Landmark completed and published in 1968 that provided the basis for the 1973 city legislation protecting Savannah's historic core with a historic zoning district designation.[44] A trend-setting urban renewal project in which a redevelopment authority and preservationists were allies was Society Hill in Philadelphia. The plan included selective demolition and public and private rehabilitation of historic townhouses. While this was just a small part of urban renewal in Philadelphia, and did not represent the prevailing model, it has been acclaimed as "a brilliant testimony to a new approach to preservation and planning."[45]

However, the reaction against urban renewal was largely in favor of historic preservation and against the hostile attitude to the legacy of the urban past that was assumed to be at the core of urban renewal. Baltimore's mayor, William Donald Schaefer, said, "Urban renewal was a total concept, a concept of removing everything. We didn't care about history even though we were a very young country. . . . I think we're in a new era now where preservation is paramount, and you only build something when you can't save the old."[46] In local histories and surveys of architecture published subsequently, the impact of urban renewal has almost always been judged very unfavorably. A typical statement reads, "The destruction of historic architecture causes dislocation, disorientation, and an overall loss of physical and historical place."[47]

The Historic District as Fragment: A Legacy of Urban Renewal

One abiding legacy of urban renewal is the district that is a fragment. Fragments are all that remain of many districts that were intact before urban renewal. Indeed, they were then often much less clearly discernible and identifiable as distinct districts. Now they are preserved explicitly as fragments and made to fulfill a symbolic function as representative of all else that has been removed. Areas that were spared from urban renewal, or fragments and enclaves surviving from that experience, feature prominently among historic districts.[48] Hyde Park–Kenwood in Chicago (NR 1979/1984/1986), for instance, became an island surrounded by the wasteland of the South Side that resulted from urban renewal. This made its character as a "district" more pronounced: indeed, it returned Hyde Park–Kenwood to something more like the exclusive enclave vision of its founder, Paul Cornell.[49] Beale Street in Memphis (NR 1966) is one of the most notorious examples of a fragment left by urban renewal. By the early 1970s all but the two-block historic area in a 115-acre project had been cleared.[50] Its present condition has been described as "one of the saddest examples of what Urban Renewal did to American cities. It stands isolated in a green desert of grass that grows where once a thriving, or at least throbbing, black community lived and gave sustenance to one of the greatest centers of black culture in the United States." The area to its south, Vance-Pontotoc, was placed on the National Register but had to be removed "because of its continuing collapse."[51] The Rondout–West Strand Historic District in Kingston, New York (NR 1979), is virtually all that remains after urban renewal devastated the center of this historic river port. The Corktown Historic District in Detroit (NR 1978) is the last remnant of a once very extensive Irish neighborhood largely destroyed by clearance for a freeway and by urban renewal.[52] Denver's Auraria 9th Street Historic District (NR 1973) is a fragment consisting of a block of Victorian houses preserved in a parklike setting within what was being redeveloped as a college campus.[53]

The story of Lacledes Landing in St. Louis is typical. This district consists of a few blocks of nineteenth-century commercial and industrial buildings and warehouses which are all that remain of a vast riverside area on the site of the original eighteenth-century trading post. Most of it was cleared away in the 1930s to make way for the creation of the Jefferson National Expansion Memorial. The centerpiece of this landscaped park is Eero Saarinen's Gateway Arch, completed in 1965. By 1968 the real had been almost completely replaced by the symbolic. It was reported that "St. Louis awaits a decision on the future of its small but important section where still survives the last tangible record of a period celebrated symbolically in the Gateway Arch."[54] Approval of a plan for its retention was described as having "opened the way to a new era in urban historic preservation."[55] Even so, in 1979 a geographer could comment, "St. Louis now faces the problem of having to build a downtown and central city to go with its symbolic arch."[56] This situation is comparable to the way in which museum villages, representing idealized places, developed in New England at the very same time as the "real villages" were succumbing to "deterioration and misuse."[57]

What has emerged more generally as a "fragment" approach to historic preservation has been seen as an outcome of urban renewal. Indeed, Roberta Brandes Gratz has referred to a "Remnant Complex" in historic preservation. "Meager pieces of urban fabric," she writes, "are being rescued, restored and celebrated as if the city itself had been rewoven back to full strength." Cities "cling to bits and pieces, rejoice in their salvage—pitifully few pieces that there are—and then let megastructure blight and parking lots dwarf those remnants."[58] M. Christine Boyer has recently analyzed the process whereby in preservationism "a special vocabulary developed in the 1960s and 1970s which spoke of districts, ensembles and fragments." In this way, she argues, an accommodation was reached between preservation and new developments. There were parts of cities that for a variety of reasons planners overlooked or were not interested in. These were placed behind regulatory boundaries, and "their architectural patrimony [was] entrusted to protection societies and their aesthetic appearances constantly rehabilitated and revitalized."[59]

The "fragment" approach having begun in the reactions to the aftermaths of urban renewal, many districts that are fragments from earlier episodes in urban history are now also being displayed and publicized as such. For example, Jackson Square in San Francisco (NR 1971) is a small collection of commercial buildings that survived the 1906 earthquake and fire. Publicity for these remnants also often claims that the reason they have been preserved is to show what the whole once looked like. The value that is placed on many historic districts is that they are examples of once-widespread urban phenomena that have almost disappeared. Thus Liberty Street in San Francisco (NR 1983) is publicized as of interest because it is one of the few remaining San Francisco streets with more or less intact blocks of single-family Victorian homes.[60] One of America's most famous and often-visited and admired urban fragments is Elfreth's Alley in Philadelphia (NR 1966). The oldest continuously inhabited street in the country, it has retained its present appearance for two hundred years.[61] In the South districts that survived destruction in the Civil War are now used as rare examples of architecture dating from the antebellum era.[62] Some of these are the "towns that Sherman thought too lovely to destroy," although what the basis is for this claim is not always clear.[63] Some fragmentary districts, such as Twickenham in Huntsville, Alabama (NR 1973), may have benefited from being occupied by Federal troops from an early stage in the war. The houses and public buildings were needed by the army and were therefore spared destruction. Others such as Franklin, Louisiana (NR 1982), escaped destruction because of the strong Union sympathies of the townsfolk (the early settlers having come from the Northeast).

The Creation of the National Register

In 1965 came a landmark publication in the history of historic preservation *With Heritage So Rich,* produced by the Special Committee on Historic Preservation set up under the auspices of the United States Conference of Mayors in association with the National Trust for Historic Preservation. It declared that the preservation movement must go beyond saving individual historic buildings and called for concern for the "total heritage." This reflected both the reactions to the devastating impacts of urban improvement and freeway construction and a shift in preservationist thinking that was changing the emphasis from individual buildings to entire districts. The report's recommendation that a national register be created which would include not only buildings, sites, and structures but also districts was implemented in the National Historic Preservation Act of 1966, which created the National Register of Historic Places. Prior federal law, for example, the Historic Sites and Buildings Act of 1935 and the Act of 1949, which chartered the National Trust, had defined historic resources only in terms of "sites, buildings, and objects." By adding districts, the 1966 act set the scene for a dramatic shifting of the emphasis of historic preservation.

A great deal of systematic action to foster historic districts had been taken at the state level well before passage of the 1966 act. Congress was responding to, and reflecting, a growing tide of support for, and knowledge about, this type of historic preservation. The subsequent entrusting of responsibilities under the act to state-appointed officers reflected an already existing emphasis on state initiative. Rhode Island had passed its Historic District Statute as early as 1959. Texas already allowed zoning regulation in historic areas. In 1960 Massachusetts enacted a statewide statute that created mechanisms for controlling external changes to buildings in historic districts. By 1966 eight other states had passed historic district enabling laws. This process went on after 1966. By 1980 most states had legislation that enabled the creation of historic preservation commissions.

The distinctive contribution of the 1966 act to the process was as a federal initiative, creating a national register, providing means and principles for the directing of federal funds to historic preservation, and ensuring some measure of protection for local historic areas from the intrusive and damaging impacts of federal activity such as public works construction. The implementation of the act was soon decentralized and entrusted to state agencies—with major implications for the development of the new historic preservation structure. The secretary of the interior wrote to all state and territorial governors asking them to appoint someone to be responsible for implementing at that level the functions that Congress had assigned to him in the act. These persons, the state historic preservation officers, have subsequently played a major role in the development of historic preservation programs at the state level.[64]

From this perspective, the 1966 act appears not as a critical catalyst and transforming event but as the point when the federal government took account of its own responsibilities in the fast unfolding program of historic preservation. However, there is one area in which the federal government did subsequently take a major initiative that tilted the balance substantially in its direction. There is widespread agreement that the single most important cause of the rapid surge in nominations of both individual buildings and districts to the National Register was the existence of attractive tax incentives as provided in particular by the Tax Reform Act of 1976. Depreciation expenses were recoverable on income-producing structures certified to be important to a historic district. The result was that many developers and business people supported historic district designations and the creation of historic districts was given an enormous impetus. Some developers even initiated the process.[65]

The Criteria

The 1966 act authorized the secretary of the interior to establish criteria by which "significance" was to be determined. The National Register criteria begin by stating that significance may be in history, architecture, archaeology, engineering, and culture. The addition of culture and architecture as sources of value considerably widened the scope for definition of historic districts. The criteria go on to specify that buildings, structures, objects, and districts must "possess integrity of location, design, setting, materials, workmanship, feeling, and association." In addition, they must satisfy at least one of the following criteria:

- association "with events that have made a significant contribution to the broad patterns of our history";
- association "with the lives of persons significant in our past";
- embodiment of "the distinctive characteristics of a type, period, or method of construction, or that represent the work of a mas-

ter, or that possess high artistic values, or that represent a significant and distinguishable entity whose components may lack
individual distinction";
- having yielded, or being likely to yield, "information important
in prehistory or history."

Although the register was to be a *national* one, significance did not have to
be at the national level. It could also be at state and local levels. It has been
estimated that 90 percent of the listings now have a primarily or exclusively
state or local significance.[66]

States have adopted definitions and criteria for their own historic districts that are usually very similar to those used for nominations to the
National Register. For example, in 1979 North Carolina defined them as
"areas which are deemed to be of special significance in terms of their history, architecture and/or culture, and to possess integrity of design, setting,
materials, feeling, and association."[67] A common practice has been to link a
definition to the National Register criteria.[68]

The National Register is maintained by the National Park Service.
Every few years a volume containing the list of properties and districts that
have been accepted onto the register is published by the American Association for State and Local History, the National Park Service, and the
National Conference of State Historic Preservation Officers. By 1991 the
list contained nearly 58,000 buildings, structures, sites, objects, and districts. If the individual buildings within districts are taken into account, it
is estimated that approximately 800,000 properties are included. In other
words, 86 percent of the properties are in historic districts. Properties get
onto the register by a process of nomination, mostly by state agencies (93
percent).[69] Usually there will have been a local or state survey, and then the
local historical commission will initiate a nomination. This will be reviewed
by a state agency, which will forward the nomination to the keeper of the
National Register, who has the final say.

A National Register historic district is any area of a community that
has been deemed to be of historic significance in accordance with the criteria established by the U.S. Department of the Interior.[70] There are some
important distinctions to be made between National Register and locally
designated historic districts. National Register designation per se does not
impose any restrictions on private property owners. Its main significance
has been in imposing certain obligations on federal agencies to consider the
impact of their activities on historic sites before proceeding with projects
that have been federally funded or licensed. Preservation incentives such as
historic rehabilitation tax credits are also available to qualifying buildings

in National Register historic districts. The major function of a National Register historic district, however, is simply to recognize the historical significance of the resources within it and to use this information as a planning tool. If federal funds are not involved, National Register designation provides *no* protection.

Locally designated historic districts go much further in establishing regimes of control over properties, involving the creation of a regulatory process and method to protect their "historic" character.[71] It is at the local level that historic district commissions and design review processes operate.[72] Local historic districts are essentially a form of local zoning ordinance and one aspect of the movement in the twentieth century toward zoning as a key feature of urban planning and management of land use within towns and cities. While zoning ordinances in general were validated by the Supreme Court in 1926, it was not until 1954 that the Court ruled—in a case involving slum clearance for urban renewal—that such ordinances could properly be used for aesthetic purposes. At the state level courts were also finding the sorts of controls associated with historic districts acceptable from the early 1950s. Indeed, as early as 1941 the Supreme Court of Louisiana had upheld the legal propriety of the Vieux Carré ordinance. While states had been passing enabling laws for particular communities since the 1930s,[73] from the late 1950s they began to pass general enabling legislation authorizing all cities, and sometimes counties, to establish historic district and landmark programs. Rhode Island was the first to do so, in 1959. By 1963 perhaps a dozen states had passed historic district or landmark legislation in one form or another.[74] Now almost all have such legislation.[75] In 1966 there were probably fewer than two dozen historic district ordinances in effect. By the early 1970s, 120 historic district commissions had been created. By 1971 New York City's Landmarks Preservation Commission had designated eighteen historic districts, containing more than 6,000 properties.[76] By 1986 almost 2,000 historic districts had been designated by local governments.[77] An ordinance usually provides for the creation of a historic district (or landmarks or historic preservation) commission. It is the responsibility of these commissions to review applications for alterations, additions, new construction, or demolition.[78] Ordinances regulate all properties within locally designated districts, whether or not the properties are individually significant.[79]

Let us take a state example of how local historic districts come into being and operate. In Massachusetts local commissions are established by votes of the town or city government under authority granted by the legislature.[80] The role of the commissions is to ensure that preservation concerns are considered in community planning and development decisions. When it is decided that an area might be appropriately established as a local historic district, a district study committee is set up to conduct a survey. On the basis of its final report the local authority will pass an ordinance or bylaw creating a local historic district. A local historic district commission is then set up to review applications for exterior changes to properties within the district.[81]

﹏ I have outlined in necessarily summary form the history of the emergence both of the concept of the historic district and of provision for historic districts within the National Register of Historic Places. But what was a historic district supposed to be? When the National Register was introduced, no committee sat down and drew up a list of the districts that should be on it. It is not a register of *the* historic places of the United States as predetermined by some authority. In inspiration and development it is a very "democratic" creation, very American. The National Register has been compiled, and continues to take shape, through a multitude of initiatives at state, city, and local levels. The emergence of the concept of historic districts has been essentially incremental in character. Legislation that has been passed to enable historic districts to be created has seldom provided guidelines of any great substance. The National Register and other criteria for acceptance as designated historic districts have, deliberately, been made very general.[82] This elasticity has permitted a great expansion in their numbers, but there has been little clear definition of what a historic district actually *is* or should be.

In the following chapters I look back from the vantage point of thirty years of evolution and adopt a history-based mode of analysis. It is the thesis of this book that there are four stages of history that are represented in and by historic districts. The sequence is a chronological one. The first stage is the history that a district has been assessed, and is now being interpreted, as embodying in accordance with established criteria. This is the "original" history that is now being made the justification for the district's preservation as a historic district. "Original" is not necessarily the same as "initial." It may be some event or sequence of events that occurred in the district at some point subsequent to its initial establishment and settlement.

The second stage is the history of what happened to a district between the point at which the events or impacts that are now being regarded as historically significant occurred and the present day when the judgment as to that significance is being made. This is the history of survival and of continued use of the buildings in the district, perhaps for quite different purposes. The third is the history of historic preservation itself as it has been brought to bear on these places and has led to their being classified as "historic." The fourth is the subsequent history of the district as a historic district. The argument is that the preserved state of a district—as of a historic structure—may be interpreted as embodying a combination of contributions from these four stages or layers of history.

The historian's approach that I am adopting in this study looks at this entire sequence as a continuum and at the process by which ingredients from each stage in it have fused ultimately to create the phenomenon of a preserved district. The historian's conclusion is that what has emerged and exists today, although it is interpreted and justified as "historical," is very different from anything that actually existed at any previous given point in the history of most districts. A historic district is a unique artifact, deserving of study in and for itself quite apart from the history that its official interpretation usually claims it represents. It transcends that history. The aim is to arrive at an understanding of how certain features from each of the first three phases—original history, the era of survival, and the era of modern historic preservationism—have combined to fashion this modern phenomenon, the historic district. My argument is that the key to understanding the continuities very often will be found to reside in the second or intermediate phase, which is the one least noticed and understood—or, if noticed, regarded in a predominantly negative light. This is the period during which the history now thought worth commemorating was left behind because there were as yet no influences and agencies at work aiming at preserving as "historic" the legacies of the "historic" era.

The book follows the history from the "original" significance and the stage of survival to the application of criteria for designation as a historic district. The questions that I shall be asking include the following: What is the history that is remembered in historic districts? What kinds of representation of the urban past of the United States have emerged out of the interpretation and implementation of the criteria that have been instituted for the designation of districts as "historic"? What kinds of history are most likely to be represented as a result of the strategies and priorities associated with modern historic preservationism? The next three chapters will seek some answers to these questions.

We will then look at the various kinds of history that have failed to achieve recognition via this process and embodiment in the format of the historic district. What urban history is *not* included, and why? What emerges from this is that there have been influences on selection that have produced outcomes very different from those that would have followed a once-and-for-all determination by a team of historians of what districts were worthiest of selection on purely historical grounds. Consideration of what these influences have been will lead us into the third stage, the one in which the creation of historic districts is affected both by a wide range of contemporary pressures and interests and by modes and formats of historic preservation that happen to be predominant and in favor at the time.[83]

Two

The Urban History in Historic Districts

ISTORIC DISTRICTS ARE A CULMINATION AND summation of history. Each of them possesses an individual history that has been assessed as complete and coherent enough to be remembered in this form. In addition, through the application of the criteria, they are identified as significant in relation to broader themes of American history. Underlying their creation are assumptions as to the character and course of American urban development, even if these may not have been consciously articulated. What are they? What stories are being told in the creation and interpretation of historic districts?

The basic narrative framework within which the American historic district has been conceptualized is one of evolution. This concept establishes the path from past to present that has led through the stage of survival to the historic district of today. For example, in a work describing the development of Old City, Sacramento, that district is considered as a reference point in time. Its significance is that it will place in historical perspective and thus proclaim the ultimate importance of the city. Preservation of this evidence of Sacramento's early history "will be most worthwhile in its progress into the space age of the future."[1] The justification for having historic districts in the modern city environment is often that it is essential to have a past against which to measure the present.[2]

However, there is a complication. The classic interpretation of the process by which towns and cities emerged in the United States was that it was evolutionary: towns developed from villages on the frontier and then "grew" and "matured."[3] While this traditional theme influences the emphasis on the past that is involved in the creation of historic districts, its application is affected by the fact that the context now is often one of decay and retrogression. There is still a linear model, but the line has been running backward or downhill for some time. The evolutionary model once fed into and sustained urban boosterism through holding out the prospect of a glorious future that lay beyond the particular stage that a town's evolution had reached at a given time. At first sight historic districts, because they look to the past for inspiration and for a model for urban living, appear to mark an end to that particular tradition of American urban boosterism with its anticipation of great urban *futures*. The appeal of historic districts suggests a decline in optimism about the future, a turning away from the linear model of faith in perpetual progress to a nostalgic invocation of the past.

However, the aim of historic preservation is often defined as preventing change from overwhelming historical continuity, not stopping or giving up on it.[4] It is a matter of proportion among the various components of the evolutionary vision. The future remains important, but it is vital to preserve a sense of direction, and that means establishing patterns of continuity out of the past. This is the mission of historic preservation and a major justification for the presence of historic districts in a modern, forward-looking city environment.

There is nothing particularly new in this use of the past. Urban boosters of the nineteenth century, for instance, certainly did not overlook the past of their towns in their promotional efforts—although there was a good deal less of it. There was considerable reference to "history" in early booster publications, quite a few of which even took the form of histories.[5] They too displayed buildings and sites associated with the early settlement of the district. They contrasted these, of course, with the much more advanced state of development that their town had now reached. "History" was used to trace and celebrate the evolutionary process that boosters claimed was leading inexorably to a great destiny for their town.[6] Historic districts today are similarly frequently interpreted in relation to an evolutionary process—through being justified as representing stages in a town's development. Within a total city context, historic districts can preserve a sense of the architectural and historical continuum of the life of that city, even if one district viewed in isolation may appear to be confined artificially to just one era. Old City, Sacramento, has been criticized severely for being that kind of district.[7] But it can be argued that in the Old City historic preservation was in fact inspired by a wish to *preserve* a sense of evolution and change. In other words, the old city has been preserved in this way to ensure that in Sacramento as a whole *something* remained from a significant period.[8] This fits in with the growing tendency to plan a structure of historic districts for a city so as to ensure that each major phase in its history receives a clear representation in at least one of them.

A variant on the linear pattern is the idea that historic districts function as visions, ideals, and models of urban and cultural order, with the emphasis on the restoration of an order that once existed but has been corrupted, obscured, or overlaid. The origins of the belief that they can and should perform this function may be found in the ideological intent and subsequent mythologizing of Colonial Williamsburg. The narrative here embodied has been summarized by Mitchell Schwarzer in his claim that the American preservation movement "has generally represented the history of its architecture and cities as a series of dramatic discontinuities: the mythologization of an original golden age followed by a long period of neglect and destruction, culminating in rediscovery and renewal."[9]

What we see here is an updated version of the cyclical view of history that held sway in the eighteenth and early nineteenth century. Cities had a central role in that theory. Civilizations and empires were seen as typically progressing to the stage of having great and luxurious cities and then falling into decline and eventual collapse because of the vices and corruption associated with "overcivilization." This was one reason why Thomas Jefferson was so anxious that large European-style cities should not develop in the New World. At first sight, the terrible deterioration that has been experienced by so many American cities would appear to lend renewed and powerful credibility to the cyclical model of urban history. Preservationists believe that, through preservationist strategies, there is still hope that the rise-and-fall may be followed by a new rise. Their mission is to ensure that it does. James Biddle summed it up thus in 1974: "One New Orleans urban pioneer has referred to 'the swing of a great historic pendulum that affects all cities. This swing dictates the passing of the long night of urban crises and the dawn of a new era in America.'"[10] Historic preservationism recognizes that there has been a cycle of rise and fall: the Mansion Rows and Silk Stocking districts that are so common are testimony to the glory that once was and then vanished. But historic districts also tell a story of fall and *rise*. The cycle is one of decay *and* revival. Furthermore, the story that preservationists tell, more often than not, is a moral one—of redemption through the practice of such moral qualities as endurance in adversity and the hard work exemplified in "urban pioneering." In the literature of historic preservation, the moral qualities, the courage, enterprise, and commitment, of those who have restored decayed districts and the houses within them are constantly extolled. The immorality of their foes, those who are seen as having been responsible for the decay and corruption of city life—the absentee landlords, the drug pushers—is constantly emphasized. There is also constant reference to the immensity of the trials that preservationists have heroically endured and overcome—whether urban renewal or hurricanes such as Agnes and Hugo.

The Phenomenon of Survival

The story of historic preservation that is told in historic districts is especially a drama of survival. It is a story that is accommodated well in both the evolutionary and the rise-and-fall models of urban development. On the one hand, the districts are testimony to faith and endurance during the long night of decay and deterioration. If an evolutionary model is preferred, they might appear to be irrelevant, mere accidental fragments left over by the inexorable march of urban progress. But there too they have a purpose, which is to demonstrate where we have come from, to keep alive hope and faith that there is an evolutionary process at work.

The historic districts and buildings that are now listed on the National Register are what remain after great tides have repeatedly and frequently swept over America's towns and cities. These are the tides of fashion, of transportation revolutions, of movements of population, industry, and trade. Each has been devastating in its impact and has superimposed a new layer of urban living and land use that has left little room for the relics of earlier layers to survive. But some have, and so the history of historic districts is in substantial part the history of these survivals. In that sense they are thoroughly *unrepresentative*, for the history of American urbanization has overwhelmingly been the history of change and destruction of impeding features of outmoded forms of urban life. Historic districts are representative of features of urban development that have allowed for, or have protected, survival and continuity. As the great majority of districts in American towns and cities testify, those features are not at all characteristic of the overall process of urban development.

There are certain processes of urban change that have allowed the survival of some districts in a form we accept as "historic." Historic districts reflect these processes. As a result they are a selective guide to some of the significant features of the history of American urban development. What they also reflect is the advent of historic preservation as an intervention in processes of change. In other words, what these districts have succeeded in surviving into is what I am defining as the fourth stage of their history, the era of historic preservation, during which there has been management and preservation of a selection of resources classified as "historic" through a range of incentives and controls. Some kinds of urban districts have remained sufficiently intact, or at least capable enough of restoration, to now be considered worthy of receiving the status of historic districts. But many others, indeed the vast majority, lack the characteristics that, according to the criteria, would entitle them to be deemed historic. Their survival as districts with distinguishing characteristics derived from their pasts is now, as we shall see, actually being further jeopardized by the selection of other districts as alone entitled to protection on grounds of historical merit.

The survival of the districts that are now being treated as "historic" has seldom been planned. Accident is a significant element in explaining the range and location of today's historic districts.[11] Many are fragments that remain from urban renewal and other programs of managed urban change such as those referred to in the previous chapter. Seldom was it intended that they should be left as reminders of what had been cleared away. Their survival more often than not simply reflects the ebbing or cessation of the activity that led to the destruction of tracts surrounding or adjacent to what is now visible as a fragment, perhaps because of a change in city policy, the advent of a new administration at city hall, the bankruptcy of a developer, or the upsurge and success of a campaign opposed to the destruction of buildings in the area. Survival is also often attributable to a decline in a town's economic vitality.[12] Many historic districts have been created in areas in which pressure for utilization of the space currently occupied by historic structures is at least temporarily absent. Many are located in inner-city areas that have "deteriorated" but where a stock of nineteenth-century structures is still largely intact, for example, large warehouse districts.[13] There has been a low level of demand for the space on which warehouses are located, and their sheer bulk has given them a relative invulnerability. However, the development of a desire in a community for historic district status may reflect an awareness that developers are becoming interested in the area.[14]

The survival of a building or a district is also usually dependent on adaptability to contemporary needs. If buildings have not survived, this is often because they cannot be adapted for some use in our own time, or their adaptation would have been too expensive, or other uses for the site on which they were located have been considered more important or potentially lucrative. Historic preservation emerges from various processes of determining usefulness in present-day society. Districts are no different from buildings in this respect. Their survival too usually depends on the degree of present-day usefulness and adaptability they are perceived as having and which will justify the expenditure of public or private monies on their restoration and protection. The price to be paid for being thus saved and rehabilitated may be loss of the sort of historic "integrity" that is referred to

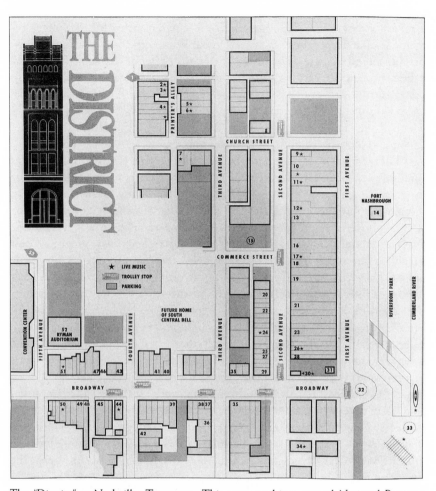

The "District" at Nashville, Tennessee. This area combines several National Register Historic Districts. The Broadway Historic District (a) is an area that was once devoted to the furniture and hardware trades. In the Second Avenue Historic District (b and c) most of the buildings front also on First Avenue where, during the days of heavy river traffic, they figured in the warehousing and merchandising of goods shipped by river. The District also includes the old printing and publishing district of Printers Alley. "Tying The District together are the red and gold trolleys of the Metropolitan Transit Authority," described as "charming reproductions of mid-nineteenth-century horse drawn street cars." The District today contains cafés and restaurants, art galleries, shops, antique shops, warehouses converted for loft apartments, and nightclubs. This combination of historic preservation and economic development was modeled on the National Trust's Main Street program. (Information derived from brochures issued by the Historic Riverfront Association, Nashville)

a.

in National Register and other criteria. As with buildings, the uses to which districts are put may be very different from their original use. In many warehouse districts, for example, numerous buildings have been adapted for use as restaurants, offices, and shops.[15] Districts for which an identity and purpose as a whole can be established help buildings to survive which might not otherwise have survived on their own merits. A "critical mass" of adaptable warehouse structures, for instance, may create a "district" that can be given a commercially exploitable image and reputation. An example is the vast "District" in Nashville which was created as a concept for the area of Victorian warehouses on Second Avenue and Broadway and now features restaurants, stores, antique shops, and nightclubs.[16]

The Original History

Returning to the concept of an "original" history, we need to look closely at one of the most important and influential of the established criteria, that there should have been a period of principal historic significance, an era the historical legacies of which are now to be identified, emphasized, and

b.

protected from incompatible change. This approach permeates several of the National Register criteria

(A) in its reference to "events that have made a significant contribution to the broad patterns of our history."

(B) in its reference to association "with the lives of persons significant in our past."

(C) in its reference to embodying "the distinctive characteristics of *a type, period, or method of construction*" (my emphasis).

This sort of approach to defining what history is to be remembered in the medium of historic preservation has been particularly controversial, indeed a principal target of critiques of the entire historic district phenomenon. For instance, the statement in Criterion A raises the question of what is to be done about the rest of the history of a district that has been selected be-

c.

cause *some* of its history made contributions of these kinds. The definition in Criterion B has similar implications: what about the buildings, and so on, that relate to the lives of persons in the district who were part of its history but were *not* "significant" in the nation's past? Critics have been concerned that as a result of the application of these criteria what we get in historic districts is a highly selective interpretation and presentation of the past.[17] The most common criticism has been that the recent history of a district and indeed all other phases of it are ignored and it is taken back as far as possible to a pristine moment in time with all traces of intervening occupation removed.[18] Districts are, it is alleged, restored to a past that is more or less mythical and then frozen in time. Whole eras in a district's past can be expunged, as if they never existed. Some preservationists, concerned about the distorted interpretation of the past to which the emphasis on a period of significance gives rise, have advocated eliminating this requirement. Such a view is likely to be held in particular by the growing number who are concerned about the preservation of the recent past, especially that of the previous fifty years, which is only allowed for in the criteria in exceptional cases and as ancillary to significance primarily gained via the history of earlier periods.[19]

In the early phases of historic district development the focus on one period was certainly deliberate. It was done physically through alterations to the built-up elements of the district and also through the interpretations

of the history of the district that were allowed to predominate. In this regard the example of Colonial Williamsburg proved contagious. Gratz has
attacked "prettified" restoration projects such as La Villita in San Antonio
(NR 1972) in which, she argues, the accumulated effects of time are stripped
away to achieve the historic accuracy of an earlier moment. In her view
such districts become "gussied-up artifacts that have no relationship to the
complex functioning of a city except as a curio, a museum piece, a useful
tourist attraction." Because "fake" old reflects the fashion of one moment, it
quickly fades and appears dated. "Setting for a goal a historical theme or a
singular time period cuts off the organic development of a community and
substitutes a stage set."[20]

New Orleans has been another target of those who have accused historic districts of "freezing" history at a favored point in time. There was
much criticism of the attempts by the Vieux Carré Commission to enforce
and prescribe the dominance of one architectural style in that district.
Another controversial example of trying to restore a place to its "original"
state has been Old Sacramento. In the November 1977 issue of *Preservation
News*, there was a discussion about the absence of "history"—in the sense
of continuity and change—from Old Town reconstructions such as Old
Sacramento. Layers of history, it was pointed out, had been omitted there
as everything was taken back to the initial pioneering period. Thomas L.
Frye, curator of history at the Oakland Museum, said, "My history is what
I remember, and nothing of what I remember has been preserved. . . . Old
Town's 20th-century history has been eradicated as systematically as possible. The successive layers of the buildings have been peeled back and
thrown away, leaving no evidence of their varied use as rooming houses,
bars, wholesalers, pawnshops and labor headquarters. These middle years
are not represented in the restoration. Not even a few examples, with their
plastered-on additions, are being kept for future interpretation by the urban
historian."[21] In the official explanation of Old Sacramento, the twentieth
century is referred to largely as a time when old buildings disappeared.[22]
It has been pointed out that in Sacramento preservationists from early on
assumed that "only the period from about 1839 to 1880 would be commemorated, and that vestiges of the more recent past would be removed. There
was never any mention of retaining parts of the townscape added between
1880 and 1950; it was assumed that what was important to preserve and display was Sacramento's contribution to the Gold Rush and early settlement
history of California."[23] So the district that became known as Old Sacramento was radically changed.

The Priority Accorded Harmony and Consistency

In assessments of both the original history and what has emerged from the era of survival, perhaps the single most influential criterion has been that the structure or district possess "integrity." Usually this has been interpreted as meaning that there should be a high degree of harmony and consistency among the component elements of a district. A perhaps somewhat extreme but by no means untypical definition of this concept of a historic district is the following statement in the 1967 *Guidebook for the Old and Historic Districts of Nantucket and Siasconset:* "The beauty of an area derives from the order and harmony of the components. . . . Many older cities in the East contain hundreds and even thousands of historic and beautiful structures yet the whole environment remains so ugly and discordant that it repels the visitor. Beauty is balance, order, and harmony; ugliness is disproportion, confusion, and discord. The ugliness of so many communities that have succumbed to 'progress' lies in the disorder and lack of harmony created by the hot dog stand next to the cemetery, the gas station alongside the home, the used car lot abutting the park, and the development houses scattered without design among the traditional."[24] Definitions of this type would rule out most urban districts in the United States and render such districts as were accepted highly unrepresentative of urban development.

Subsequent documents and practice have, on the whole, reinforced this interpretation of "integrity." For example, the 1977 *Criteria of National Significance* issued by the U.S. Department of the Interior stated, "To possess national significance, a historic . . . district . . . must possess integrity. . . . For a historic district, integrity is a composite quality derived from original workmanship, original location, and intangible elements of feeling and association inherent in an ensemble of historic buildings having visual architectural unity."[25] Murtagh, former keeper of the National Register, has written that he approved the Miami Beach Art Deco Historic District because of "the sense of locality that any neighborhood gives to a city and the sense of homogeneity, cohesiveness and lack of nonconforming intrusions, such as buildings of different scale, color, texture, materials, proportions."[26]

A crucial issue has been the extent to which "homogeneity" and "integrity" should be interpreted as synonymous.[27] In 1991 a National Register bulletin entitled *How to Apply the National Register Criteria for Evaluation* attempted a fuller definition of a district with the aim of providing a more flexible interpretation of integrity.

> A district possesses a significant concentration, linkage, or conti-
> nuity of sites, buildings, structures, or objects united historically
> or aesthetically by plan or physical development. . . . A district

derives its importance from being a unified entity, even though it is often composed of a wide variety of resources. The identity of a district results from the inter-relationship of its resources, which can convey a visual sense of the overall historic environment or be an arrangement of historically or functionally related properties. . . . [T]he majority of the components that add to the district's historic character, even if they are individually undistinguished, must possess integrity, as must the district as a whole.[28]

The starting point remains the "period of significance." As for the survival stage, the "relationships among the district's components" must, according to the bulletin, have remained "substantially unchanged since the period of significance."[29]

The emphasis on homogeneity produces a bias in favor of certain types of district. There are, of course, various reasons why a district may be naturally homogeneous—as distinct from the sort of homogeneity forced into existence by Williamsburg-style restoration and removal of nonconforming structures. A particular example is the district in which large-scale rebuilding has had to be carried out following a calamity such as a fire. In such circumstances the architectural designs tend to represent the style then in vogue in a particularly concentrated form. An example is South Jefferson Avenue in Saginaw, Michigan (NR 1982). "While the fire [of 1893] was a major catastrophe for the community, the reconstruction of South Jefferson transformed the avenue into a unique chronicle of the architectural styles that prevailed as Saginaw left its lumber era and adjusted to a new economic order."[30] The rebuilding of Upper Main Street in Bisbee, Arizona, after the fire of 1908 produced a new streetscape with "a kind of architectural homogeneity."[31] The rebuilding of a portion of Bangor, Maine, after the fire of 1911 "in the most avant-garde styles" has led to the naming of a historic district as the Great Fire District (NR 1984) and the use of the experience and its lasting architectural legacy for modern-day boosting purposes.[32] Another town whose historic districts show the effects of having to rebuild after a fire (1916) is Paris, Texas (NR 1988).[33] At Medina, Ohio (NR 1975), the "consistent Victorian design" that resulted from the merchants having to rebuild after serious fires in 1848 and 1870 is credited with giving the business district "a natural renovation theme." The chairman of the Community Design Committee in 1982 explained that "without the consistent design, it would have been more difficult to formulate a successful plan, and harder to persuade owners to renovate without the experience of seeing other restorations of the same style of architecture as their own."[34]

Support for the Focus on One Period of Significance

Why did the criteria relating to a period of significance become so established and influential? One major reason is that they reflect public opinion receptive to and supportive of preservation in this form. Americans have been described as liking to isolate historic places from their newer surroundings and as preferring "simplified historical landscapes"—hence districts that are almost entirely of one historical style.[35] Thus there has been public endorsement for the requirement that a historic district represent a specific period of significance, even though this may mean that the subsequent history of the district is overlooked or eradicated from commemoration.

The emphasis on the marking of eras of significant events and achievements has provided an opportunity for boosters to hark back to an era when their town was prosperous. A strategy that responds to this opportunity and has frequently been followed by towns seeking some sort of salvation, or at least easing of their contemporary woes, through the resurrection of usable historical images has been to define an "apex" period—a concept developed by the preservationist T. Allan Comp. He believes that many towns have an "apex," or key area or zone, that has set the tone for a town's development and should be made the theme of its historic district. It "may be a business district or an industrial district, but it is always there. It is an area that, once built, sets the direction and viability of that town's historical development for a great many years." An example he gives is the commercial core of Pocatello, Idaho, which he describes as "an apex of remarkable integrity. It is in its building form and architecture eloquent testimony to aspirations and successes, to the architectural and civic pride of the people who built it."[36] A visitor with a view of history as change and continuum may initially be uncomfortable with such an obsession with one episode or epoch. So much else obviously has happened in a town, yet nobody seems to be interested in remembering and describing it. In Gettysburg, Pennsylvania, a downtown walking tour brochure issued by the visitors' bureau focuses entirely on locations linked to the Civil War battle and its aftermath. At Johnstown, Pennsylvania, the interpretation of the downtown area is dominated by the events of the great flood of 1889. Tourism is one motivation, yet this preoccupation with one dramatic and traumatic episode often also speaks to how townspeople have perceived the place of their town and themselves in history. A particular episode may, for a variety of reasons, have become the central drama of their history, and much that has happened thereafter has been filtered through the memories of that experience and tested against it.

The criteria relating to the predominance of one episode or period have also become widely accepted and applied because of the influence of popular perceptions of the "historic." A long history of development of ideas as to what is and what is not historic is now reflected in the nation's inventory of historic districts. The concept of setting aside certain places as special and historic did not emerge fresh and newly minted from the modern historic preservation movement. The historic district concept has a history. It would not have taken hold if it did not have deep roots in American perceptions of the historical. There are various ways in which this sort of continuity and the transmission of such perceptions can be detected. Some historic districts, for instance, are in places where antiquarian traditions have long been strong. This is one type of historic district—the place where there is a long-standing tradition of perceiving the community as historic, where a substantial antiquarian infrastructure has developed (historical societies, museums, etc.) and perhaps some exploitation of "heritage" has become important for the local economy (tourism). A good example of this is Bethel, Maine (NR 1970/1990), described as "a town that delighted in historical pageants and 'antiquarian suppers' as early as the 1850s."[37] Such places, of course, had a head start when it came to collecting materials for historic district nominations and are therefore well represented in the early lists of districts accepted onto the National Register.

History Represented in Historic Districts

The Boomtown Historic Districts

In examining some of the predominant types of historic district, one discovers a common pattern, a combination of "significant" original history, a transitional era in which various preservative influences have assisted survival, a range of characteristics that have attracted preservationist concern in modern times, and a variety of attributes that satisfy the criteria for designation.

One of these types is the boomtown. This is a town (now perhaps just one portion of a larger community) that for some reason, such as a gold rush, the arrival of a railroad from which great prosperity was expected, or the anticipation of some dramatic improvement in its fortunes, suddenly started to grow very rapidly. Episodes of this kind usually lasted only a short time. The towns then either declined or at least did not progress beyond the initial point. Those that are now historic districts have retained a legacy of "boomtown" or "bonanza" architecture.[38] The sudden cutting short of a boom era could leave a district suspended in time, its development frozen. Integrity of the setting and the buildings that make up such districts is usually assured both by the homogeneity of the architecture, which mostly belongs to the one, intense period of development, and by the subsequent

The James & Hastings Building, Water and Tyler streets, Port Townsend, Washington. Built in 1889 during a brief boom period that has left Port Townsend a legacy of ornate buildings. Some had not been completed when the boom ended.

lack of pressure for new uses of the space on which the buildings stand. The best-known examples of such places are the towns that mushroomed during gold rushes and in their architecture reflected the frenzied speculation and sudden access of great wealth that marked such episodes. More often than not these towns were in remote, inhospitable areas where otherwise no one would have dreamed of starting a town. Once the rush had subsided, the site had little appeal for other uses and the buildings continued to stand forlorn in increasingly incongruous splendor.

Boomtowns developed in many circumstances other than gold rushes. Calvert, Texas (NR 1978), for instance, was a boomtown from 1870 to 1900 because of a thriving cotton economy and the advent of the railroad. It now exploits this former glory as "the antique capital of Texas." The architecture of Port Townsend, Washington (NR 1976), reflects a sudden and dramatic boom period in the late 1880s that ended abruptly in 1890 when the Oregon Improvement Company, a subsidiary of the Union Pacific, went into receivership after having promised in 1889 to construct a rail line that would link Port Townsend to Portland and turn it into one of the major ports on Puget Sound. In a few years four of the town's six banks closed and the population shrank from 7,000 to 2,000. Today one can still peer behind the impressive facades to see that some of the buildings remained unfinished when the bubble burst.[39] There were numerous other towns that had spurts of ambition associated with the advent—actual, promised, or rumored—of railroads. One such was Ellensburg, Washington (NR 1977), which, platted in the early 1870s, "indulged in a frenzy of expansion and optimism" when it came on to the transcontinental route to Puget Sound in 1886. The town's boosters were extravagant in their hopes for its future. Even after a great fire in 1889, the rebuilding of the town reflected continuing optimism. Another boom came in 1907 when an additional railroad connection was secured. The town's architecture today reflects this series of booms.[40]

Numerous towns show the consequences of many other kinds of booms that were anticipated but never actually arrived. In these towns legacies of fine buildings now represent the thwarted dreams. An example is Delaware City, Delaware (NR 1983), where a boom was expected when the Chesapeake and Delaware Canal opened in 1829. But the railroads superseded the canal, and Delaware City did not flourish. A boom era may have been brought to an abrupt halt by some kind of catastrophe. The Albany Heritage Historic District in Decatur, Alabama (NR 1983), is a Victorian neighborhood that enjoyed a boom period at a time when Decatur was becoming known as the "Chicago of the South." This boom was curtailed by a yellow fever epidemic in 1888. The population of Chappell Hill, Texas (NR 1985), a major transportation center in the mid-nineteenth century, was decimated by a yellow fever epidemic in 1867, and the town never recovered.

If these districts have survived down to modern times with their historic architectural legacies substantially intact, there are several reasons why they have been of interest for historic preservation. These legacies have been ripe for revival in an age of renewed interest in the more flamboyant architectural styles of the Victorian boom eras. The exploitation of this "heritage" has become for many small towns, such as Calvert, a lifeline to a new prosperity. It certainly seems that one way to tell a town with a historic district is the number of antique shops lining its streets.[41] That is not to say that all towns with this kind of legacy have turned readily to the past for succor in the present. Port Townsend's legacy of splendid late Victorian commercial buildings has been a perpetual reminder of dashed hopes. For the next eighty years its citizens are described as having "seized on anything new as a possible solution to their economic woes. What was old (and that surely included the old homes and buildings) was more often thought of as a retardant to economic growth."[42] In this case, there appears to have been a negative attitude to the symbols of the town's onetime glory. This was a town that had suffered from a boom-and-bust cycle and did not want to be reminded of it. It is only relatively recently that Port

Townsend has begun to come to terms with its past as an asset that can be exploited for the town's economic benefit in a way that was only briefly possible when the past was the present.

Areas Affected by Changes in Transportation and Communications

Another major category of historic districts is the historic cores of towns that were once significant in relation to now-outmoded forms of transportation. Survival has occurred if there has not been major subsequent pressure on the location and the buildings and facilities associated with the original activity have remained in situ in a good state of integrity. First came the sea- and river ports. Along America's seacoasts and innumerable rivers are the remains of many ports that have now lost their function but preserve sufficient relics of their heydays to warrant historic district designation. Historic districts line the banks of all America's major midwestern rivers, notably the Ohio and the Mississippi. Survival has not been easy: such places are particularly vulnerable to the twin forces of neglect and flood. The Mississippi floods in 1993 did immense damage to the low-lying historic areas of numerous river towns, the most publicized of which was Ste. Genevieve, Missouri (NR 1966).[43] In many places little now remains of the river-transport era. For example, while Elsah, Illinois (NR 1973), preserves much of the atmosphere of a river port, "mills, warehouses, river shipping, two railroads, numerous local businesses, and throngs of farmers during the wheat shipping season all have disappeared."[44] Just about all that remains today of the once-busy port and riverboat community of Canemah on the Willamette River near Oregon City, Oregon (NR 1978), are some of the homes of the riverboat captains.

Many river towns such as Madison, Indiana (NR 1973), preserve the Water Street–Front Street–Main Street pattern, although flooding may have removed Water Street altogether, as has happened at Carrollton, Kentucky (NR 1982). Rail tracks often congested these areas adjacent to rivers and left them in poor condition for rehabilitation.[45] But riverside towns often have a dual historical inheritance and therefore a split personality. Most of them, having developed because of their river location, later turned their backs on their rivers in favor of Main Street, especially after the arrival of the railroad. Now some are attempting to rediscover and landscape their riverfronts. Restored riverfronts can be found in many places, for example, Van Buren, Arkansas (NR 1976). Such restoration is sometimes only partially successful because the commercial buildings still present their unappealing rear facades to the river, and Main Street rehabilitation programs dictate a continued emphasis on the Main Street side of their profiles.[46]

There are also districts that contains the remains of canal installations and warehouses and other commercial buildings associated with canal traf-fic.[47] Many towns on canals developed industries,[48] and their buildings re-flect the prosperity that the canal traffic generated. Other towns grew and prospered at junction points between canals and rivers, for example, Kingston, New York, mentioned earlier. Many towns whose high point came during the canal era have stagnated since.[49] Attica, Indiana, is an example of a town with significance in relation to several early forms of transportation. It was laid out in 1825 by the operator of a ferry, which was the only means of crossing the Wabash River until a bridge was erected in 1861. But the town's most prosperous era—represented today in the fine Greek revival mansions lining streets in the Brady Street Historic District (NR 1990)—was the decade following the opening to Attica of the Wabash and Erie Canal in 1847.[50]

Towns that prospered in the canal era and then managed to achieve a railroad connection usually maintained at least some of their former afflu-ence. Brookville, Indiana (NR 1975), became the county seat early on, in 1811, and was then the location of a federal land office at a time of intense interest in land acquisition by immigrants and speculators. A setback that occurred in 1825, when the office was moved to Indianapolis, was short-lived because construction of the Whitewater Canal began at Brookville in 1836. Canal traffic collapsed in the 1850s, but the railroad replaced it. Popu-lation grew steadily but not spectacularly.[51] Cambridge City, Indiana (NR 1991), followed a similar course: it was first on the National Road and then the Whitewater Canal, and then the railroad arrived in the 1850s.[52]

Railroads made and broke towns in the nineteenth century. If a line went elsewhere, a town would stagnate or, more often, decline or even disappear. Numerous historic districts bear testimony to hopes of urban greatness that were dashed for this reason. A town may have been of sig-nificance as a coaching stop, as a crossroads, or as a point of enforced delay on a journey, only to be ruined when the railroad went to a town nearby.[53] New Castle (NR 1967/1984), an important trade center, was on a major stagecoach route. It prospered and developed a remarkable en-semble of fine Georgian and Federal architecture. The War of 1812 and a disastrous fire were major setbacks, but it survived the transition to the railroad when the New Castle-Frenchtown Railroad arrived in 1832 and took the same route as the stagecoach. However, the rerouting of the rail lines through Wilmington at midcentury took New Castle definitively off the map of modern transportation—to the great benefit of lovers of architecture today.[54] Nearby Odessa (NR 1971/1984) was a major grain-shipping port but declined once bypassed by the railroad. Its historic core is close to being a museum town today with four mansions maintained by the Winterthur Museum.

Towns on the National Road across the north-central United States also declined if they were not along the rail line. An example is Centerville, Indiana (NR 1971), which lost out to Richmond twice, first as a railroad center (1853) and then as county seat (1873). "Its architecture remained practically untouched. . . . Today, Centerville is essentially a tourist mecca with an outstanding ensemble of historically and architecturally significant buildings and more than a dozen antique shops."[55] Newburgh, Indiana (NR 1983), overshadowed by Evansville, followed a similar trajectory.[56] Mantorville, Minnesota (NR 1974), has the architectural legacy of a very brief time in the sun and is also best described as being "close to being a historic museum village." It was platted in 1856 and bypassed by the Southern Minnesota Railroad in the late 1860s. The majority of the people promptly moved to Kasson, a town that was on the rail line.[57]

More modern variants on the bypassed town have resulted from such developments as the closing of railroads and the construction of highways and freeways. An example is Albany, Oregon (downtown, NR 1982; two residential districts, NR 1980 and 1982). New industry moved to its outskirts, the main highway bypassed the downtown, and post–World War II housing developed outside the original core of the city. The old downtown and residential neighborhoods were left almost intact. Such a development frequently stirs efforts to restore the threatened downtown, which happened in this case.[58]

Railroads often profoundly altered the structure of towns and cities that had been established in the prerailroad era. There are numerous historic districts that reflect this facet of the history of the towns in which they are located. There are, for instance, towns such as Las Vegas, New Mexico, where historic districts show the change from an original town site to a new one preferred by the railroad for the location of its depot. In Las Vegas there is a remarkable contrast between the Spanish adobe style of the Old Town (NR 1983) and the boomtown Victorian architecture of the railroad-inspired New Town of the 1880s (NR 1983).[59] Some historic districts reveal the sudden prosperity that ensued when a town became a railroad center.[60] Distinctive features of railroad towns are the hotel and warehouse districts adjacent to the depots. Only vestiges of these remain. The Billings, Montana, Historic District (NR 1979) is the original business district that grew up around the depot.[61] The Hotel Row in Atlanta is a tiny historic district (NR 1989) consisting of a few of the once-vast number of hotels that lined the main thoroughfares leading from the downtown railroad station. Then

Hotel Row, Atlanta. A historic district on Mitchell Street. It contains a few survivors of the many hotels built to accommodate travelers who had arrived at the nearby railroad station.

there are the districts, sometimes whole towns, of railroad workers' homes.[62] The East Side Residential District in Livingston, Montana (NR 1979), consists largely of homes built for railroad workers in the early 1900s.[63]

Towns that Lost Political Status

Some historic districts represent a period in which a town became, or at least hoped to become, a county seat or even the capital of a territory or state. This ambition could fuel great hopes of development and lead to a boom in building in the most up-to-date architectural styles as befitted such dreams.[64] Henderson, Minnesota (NR 1988),[65] and Aaronsburg, Pennsylvania (NR 1980),[66] are examples of towns that failed to become or to remain the capital or county seat but whose architectural legacy reflects that ambition. Colorado City (NR 1982), near Colorado Springs, boomed briefly first as territorial capital and then as county seat but lost the latter status in 1873. Its former glory helped its revival in the 1970s when it was extensively restored and given appropriate "historic" outfitting (red brick sidewalks, period streetlights, etc.) to commemorate the Colorado centennial. Brownville, Nebraska (NR 1970), founded in 1854, quickly became a booming port on the Missouri River. There were high hopes that it would be selected as the site for the capital of the new state. Not only were those hopes dashed, but it was also bypassed by the railroad and replaced as the county seat by Auburn. Today it is a tiny settlement (population 200) with a wonderful legacy of nineteenth-century residential architecture. A Far West example is Cimmaron, New Mexico (NR 1973), which was a major location on the Santa Fe Trail but languished when it lost its position as county seat. The railroad came in 1905 but to a site across the river. The old town that is now the historic district is "little more than a ghost."[67] Port Tobacco, Maryland (NR 1989), is no more than a few restored and reconstructed houses today, and the population is a mere 177, but in the seventeenth century it was a thriving river port. During the nineteenth century it lost both a railroad connection and its site as county seat to La Plata and never recovered.

In these once-prosperous towns that, to use an often-employed phrase, progress has now passed by, the architecture of the era of prosperity has often survived reasonably intact because there has been no need for new buildings to accommodate new and increased population and business. John W. Reps comments on Monterey, California (Old Town, NR 1970), "When San Jose became the capital city in 1850, much of the potential for Monterey's expansion was lost. One happy outcome was that many of the older buildings from the Mexican period managed to survive until programs of preservation and conservation in the modern era could guarantee their continued existence."[68] An article in *Historic Preservation* on New Castle declares, "Being passed by is both New Castle's curse and its blessing. If the economic and political world hadn't overlooked the town years ago, it would surely be just another reeking smokestack in another megalopolis."[69]

Many historic districts are located in towns whose economies were based on extractive industries that subsequently went into serious decline. The historic districts of these communities, especially their commercial areas, are likely to exhibit marked boom characteristics in their architecture. In the West are many gold, silver, and copper towns whose heritage is now one of their principal sources of wealth. Isolation and the lack of any major economic activity since the days of the "rush" have left some of these towns such as Ouray, Colorado (NR 1983), with a fine array of Victorian architecture. These towns are facing their past in a variety of ways. One of the most written about is Bisbee, whose copper mines closed in the mid-1970s. Bisbee then commenced an aggressive campaign to market its history for tourist consumption. The old booster slogan "Queen of the Copper Camps" was revived.[70] With some, most famously Tombstone, Arizona (NR 1966), the emphasis is on a largely synthetic reconstruction of the West of myth.[71] Others such as Central City, Colorado (NR 1966), are allowing their heritage to become the backdrop to the development of gambling—which draws heavily on stereotypes of the West. One defender of this development in Cripple Creek, Colorado (NR 1966), said that he "thinks gambling halls are more in keeping with the spirit of the town's past than the 'cutesy shops' that now line the street."[72] The better-preserved mining towns today, such as Nevada City, California (NR 1985), have an appearance that rather belies the stereotype of the rough-and-tumble western town. The towns that were and remained rough-and-tumble, like Bodie, have mostly disappeared. The towns that remain are mostly the larger ones where the architecture was strongly influenced by the desire to be and to appear as urban and mature as possible.[73]

Boomtowns connected to the extractive industries occurred all over America. Their architecture reflects their temporary association with the exploitation of some resource and the expectations of wealth that flowed from this discovery which was not always realized. There were innumerable causes of "booms." Oil was discovered in Casper, Wyoming in 1890, and a boom had developed by 1916. The prosperity of the town at that time is reflected in the architecture of the South Wolcott Street Historic District (NR 1988).[74] Then there are the gas boomtowns of the Midwest such as Anderson, Indiana. The discovery of natural gas in 1887 transformed Anderson into the "Queen City of the Gas Belt," to use the term favored by the local boosters.

If the extractive industry has been the mining of coal or some other resource the removal of which has taken place over a considerable period and with substantial investment of resources, one is likely to find the remains of the housing provided for the workforce. Numerous old coal mining settlements are now historic districts, for example, Roslyn, Washington (NR 1978),[75] and Bramwell, West Virginia (NR 1983).[76] In some a considerable effort is made to maintain the traditional layout and appearance. One of the most notable is Eckley, Pennsylvania (NR 1971), which is now open to the public as "a living history museum of the daily and seasonal life of the anthracite miner and his family."[77] It was one of hundreds of company mining towns, or patches, in the anthracite region, but few have survived in such good condition. Some miners or their widows still live in the village. The director of the museum, Mary Ann Landis, described it as "a rare find" when it was discovered in the 1960s. Some controversy has surrounded the village because of the retention of certain structures such as a huge wooden "breaker" built and used as props when the film *The Molly Maguires* was shot at Eckley in 1968.[78] Some districts are the locations of homes of the middle class of the mining communities, distinct because they were established at a distance from the dirt and noise of the mining areas, whereas the miners had to live close to their place of work. East Hancock Neighborhood in

Hancock, Michigan (NR 1980), for example, was the residential area of the Quincy Mining Company's agents and the local merchants and professionals.[79]

Another major extractive industry was timber milling. In such states as Washington, Michigan, and Wisconsin there are many towns with an architectural legacy that reflects the enormous prosperity of the lumber era.[80] In the First Street Historic District of Menominee, Michigan (NR 1974), for instance, one can see in the commercial and civic buildings testimony to the wealth of the 1890s. Then Menominee was the largest pine lumber shipping port in the world.[81]

The Legacies of the Industrial Revolution

Many towns with railroad connections developed a range of local industries that flourished but later collapsed. Here too the architecture in the historic districts remains as a reminder of that era of prosperity and growth but appears somewhat incongruous and inexplicable in its modern setting. Often there is substantial evidence of nineteenth-century prosperity but not much sign of anything comparable having happened since. Devoid of their original industrial context, the fine houses and public buildings are something of a puzzle. The circumstances that accounted for the flourishing of industry have long since disappeared. Typical of such towns is Hudson, New York (three NR Historic Districts, 1970/1985), which had knitting and cotton mills, brick yards, and the Allen Paper Car Wheel Works. By the end of the century the economy was already in decline. Yet this decline "enabled the city to retain its architectural heritage."[82] The arrival of the railroad at Huntingdon, Pennsylvania, made a dramatic impact: its population grew from under 1,500 in 1850 to 3,034 in 1870 to more than 6,000 by the end of the century. All sorts of industries developed, and a board of trade was set up to secure more. "In the half century between 1865 and 1915 more than fifty large commercial buildings—an average of one a year—went up in downtown Huntingdon. Nothing remotely approaching such a boom has occurred in the same area since then."[83] This legacy forms the substance of the town's remarkable historic district (NR 1986). Hollidaysburg, Pennsylvania, a major industrial center during the Civil War which produced arms and ammunition, has a superb legacy of nineteenth-century architecture in its historic district (NR 1985). The Civil War's immense stimulus to industrial growth can be appreciated by studying the history of many northern historic districts.[84]

Towns that developed industries were those that had resources such as timber, coal, iron, or sandstone close at hand. Water power was also important. As the concentration of industry proceeded, such local assets lost their value.[85] Marietta, Pennsylvania (NR 1978/1984), prospered when the Pennsylvania Canal was built in the 1820s. It acquired planing mills, lumberyards, and carpentry shops. By midcentury, there were six iron smelters as well as rolling mills. Marietta is now on the National Register as a "well-preserved example of a mid-nineteenth century industrial town."[86] The buildings of Bridgeton, New Jersey (NR 1982), reflect the prosperity of the nineteenth century, when it was not only the county seat but also had a woolen mill, a nail factory, and an ironworks. Studying the number and spread of these towns gives one a good idea of the geographic diversity and impact of the American industrial revolution.

There are many mill towns that have historic districts, especially in New England. Derelict mill buildings are an all too common sight in this landscape, and strenuous efforts are being made to turn the history of these places into a new form of economic asset. Embedded in cities are some vestiges of old industrial villages, usually located by rivers.[87] A few detached communities devoted to a particular industry may still preserve something of the atmosphere of the times when that industry flourished.[88]

Among industrial towns of more recent vintage that now stand bereft of their mills and factories is the great steel community of Homestead, Pennsylvania (NR 1990). The visitor can obtain a map and guide prepared by the Steel Industry Heritage Corporation with support from the National Park Service. "Today," we are informed, "the communities are forming strategies to rebuild following the decline of 'Big Steel'. An important part of the rebuilding strategy is the appropriate commemoration of the industrial, labor and cultural heritage of the area. The history continues." Another town with a celebrated and controversial labor history is Pullman, Illinois (NR 1969), built by the company that manufactured Pullman railroad cars. The architectural, labor, and town planning aspects of its past still compete uncertainly for predominance in its interpretation.[89]

The company town such as Pullman was a significant feature of American industrial development, well suited to representation in historic districts. The "integrity" sought in the National Register criteria is usually present, particularly because of the homogeneity of the company towns and their distinctive architecture, settings, plans, and layout. As a highly specialized form of community, developed specifically for the workforce of one adjacent industry, they have tended to survive in much their original form because the site has not been adapted for new purposes, which would have involved overlaying or replacing the original architecture with new buildings. They are also extensive and therefore not easily destroyed. For example, at Natrona Heights, Pennsylvania, the Pennsalt Historic District (NR 1985) contains sixty brick or frame houses, built between 1850 and

1900, which survive from the town built by the Pennsylvania Salt Manufacturing Company.[90] Of particular interest are the model company towns of the "New South" such as Anniston, Alabama (NR 1985/1991/1993), where eastern architects were engaged to design the buildings. Much later came Chicopee, Gainesville, Georgia (NR 1985), designed by Earle S. Draper in 1927, which "fully embraced contour planning and low-density detached housing."[91] Large northern steel companies also developed company towns. Dundalk, Maryland (NR 1983), was a company town for Bethlehem Steel's Sparrows Point steel plant.[92] There are several mill towns in New England where companies provided housing and planned environments. The Cheney Brothers Historic District in Manchester, Connecticut (NR 1978), preserves the history of a company that, according to the historian of these towns, created the first company town to place equal emphasis on producing a good environment and manufacturing a good product.[93]

There are also towns that were built by lumber and mining companies for their employees, often in remote places where other housing was not available. Companies were anxious to anchor the workforce by providing homes for families. Potlatch, Idaho, was built by the Potlatch Lumber Company, beginning in 1906. The architect, C. Ferris White of Spokane, was engaged to design houses for the workers and their families. A number of services were also provided by the company for the town. Today there are three districts on the National Register (all 1986). These reflect the tripartite arrangement of the town: the Commercial Historic District, Nob Hill, and the Workers' Neighborhood.[94] Selleck, Washington, is another lumber town that is now on the National Register (1989). It was owned by the Pacific States Lumber Company and was established in 1909. Today one can see the bungalows in the family section of the town—a three-street grid built close to the mill "yet discretely apart from housing for the 'rougher element.'"[95] A company town founded in West Virginia to house timber workers is the basis of the Cass Historic District (NR 1980). It includes what was said at its time of construction to be the largest company store in the country.[96]

At Central, Michigan, the Central Mine Historic District (NR 1974) is what is left of a town built for Cornish miners by the Central Mining Company, which operated a copper mine there from 1856 to 1898.[97] Some of these towns were primitive places. By the twentieth century some of the planned towns associated with the extractive and processing industries were very elaborate. An outstanding example of town planning by a lumber company is Longview, Washington, established by the Long-Bell Lumber Company in the 1920s. The Civic Center in Longview was placed on the National Register in 1985.[98]

The history in some historic districts is of communities that originated in the planned provision of housing for workers. The Fairview District in Camden, New Jersey (NR 1974), was built in 1917 to house workers and their families and has an overall design that reflects the planning concepts of Clarence Perry.[99] In East Chicago, Indiana, Marktown (NR 1975) was a 190-acre town constructed in 1917 by Clayton Mark to provide housing for workers at the Mark Manufacturing Company. A distinguished Chicago architect, Howard Van Doren Shaw, designed the community, and it was completely self-contained. The town was only partially completed, and the houses have been privately owned since 1942. Nevertheless, a distinctive character remains.[100] The Mechanics Block Historic District in Lawrence, Massachusetts (NR 1973/1978), marks a very early effort to provide company housing: the Essex Company built this block of "handsome red brick homes with stone lintels" in 1847.[101] Civic Park in Flint, Michigan (NR 1979), was a planned neighborhood of automobile workers' houses built by the Modern Housing Corporation, a subsidiary of the General Motors Company. It has a most distinctive plan.[102] Workers' housing makes a distinctive contribution to the historic districts in Cohoes, New York. The Olmstead Street Historic District (NR 1973) includes row houses adjacent to the huge Ogden Mill and overlooking a now filled-in arm of the Erie Canal. "The district still retains the sense of a cohesive community, detached from the city which surrounds it, as the rows of tenements and massive mill look inward toward each other across the remains of the canal which is now a park." Nearby is the Harmony Mills Historic District (NR 1978). It, too, contains numerous blocks of factory housing—plus, on the bluff overlooking the mills, the mansion built for the mill manager.[103]

Some districts are based on planned government developments of housing for workers. The Pembroke Village Historic District in Bethlehem, Pennsylvania (NR 1988), embodies a village that was planned and partially built by the United States Housing Corporation in 1918. This was one of the early entries of the federal government into the provision of housing, in this case, for workers engaged in the defense industry. Hardly had construction started when the war ended. The properties were sold to private individuals, and the full planned community was not finished. The plan was a significant forerunner of New Deal communities such as Greenbelt. The district today still reveals some of the distinctive and attractive features of the development.[104] A similar World War I development can now be found in the Harriman Historic District in Bristol, Pennsylvania (NR 1987). The multifamily workers' homes here (likewise using Tudor and Colonial Revival styles) were financed by the U.S. Shipping Board's Emergency Fleet Corporation (EFC) to provide housing for 11,000 workers employed at the EFC shipyard, owned by W. Averill Harriman. After the shipyard closed in 1921, the homes were sold to private owners.[105] Another EFC town is commemorated in the Dundalk Historic District in Maryland. It reflects "'Garden City' community planning concepts, with curvilinear streets [and] community center."[106] There are a few municipal housing projects, some of quite recent vintage, such as Sunnyside Gardens in New York City (NR 1984), built by the City Housing Authority in Queens between 1924 and 1935.[107]

Some historic districts contain examples of model housing for workers. A notable example is the City and Suburban Homes Company's First Avenue Estate Historic District in New York City (NR 1986). This was "a limited-dividend corporation dedicated to the construction of decent affordable housing for the working poor." Its projects were experimental, and the model tenements in the historic district—thirteen brick apartment buildings—represent the oldest extant project built by the company (1898–1915).[108]

Places that Once Were or Aspired to Be Independent Towns

Finally, there are communities that might be described as buried rather than bypassed. These are towns that were originally independent of or at least peripheral to other towns that eventually grew to dominant positions within their region. They may once have been rivals of those cities, perhaps even of approximately equal size and ambition. Some of them aspired to the metropolitan status that the rival was ultimately to achieve and took on many planning features and institutional attributes associated with such aspirations.[109] But once the rivalry had been decided, they found themselves too much in the shadow of the metropolis and ultimately became overwhelmed by its development. A historic district established in such a place revives and draws renewed attention to features of that earlier history which have lain buried, dormant, and neglected—but not entirely destroyed—ever since. Using the information assembled to contribute to the case for the creation of a historic district, one can peel away the layers of subsequent metropolitan encroachment and discover the remnants of the once-separate town. A telltale sign of such a district is the combination of a set of imposing institutional buildings, such as churches, town halls, and fire stations, often converted to other uses, and a withered and perhaps barely functioning commercial section.[110] An example is Columbia City in Seattle (NR 1980). Land speculation commenced here as soon as the rail line from Seattle arrived in 1891. The district then prospered through exploitation of the timber in the surrounding forests, and a "city" was incorporated in 1893. However, Seattle gradually caught up: in 1907 Columbia City was annexed. Today, in the historic district, one can find the old business blocks, the former Columbia Hotel (a sure sign of significant rail business out from a major city), and the park with its 1914 Carnegie Library, which has been described as "small but important-looking."[111]

Some places of this kind have been using historic district designation to assist them to recover or retain and strengthen a distinctive identity in the face of continuing metropolitan encroachment. At Monroe, Michigan, booster slogans of the past have been reinvoked: "Some predict that Monroe will be swallowed up in the megalopolis that will link Detroit and Toledo. The rapid commercial growth of the 1980s is moving the county in that direction. With this prospect, the architectural heritage of the city and county assumes greater importance as a means of asserting Monroe's uniqueness of place. Restoration is under way in the old business district of Monroe, where merchants view their historic buildings as assets. With this element to help distinguish themselves in the region, perhaps the city and county can again lay claim to what was called in its heyday in the 1830s, 'the independent state of Monroe.'"[112] Rockville, Maryland (NR 1976/1985), has been all but overwhelmed by the enormous spread of the Washington, D.C., metropolitan area. But the local nonprofit historic preservation organization has adopted as its name the title of a booster publication of the 1890s called *Peerless Rockville*, which depicted Rockville as an independent community.

Zane Miller has provided another example in his account of what happened in the Cincinnati suburb of Clifton when the local neighborhood organization requested assistance with the preparation of a history of Clifton's historic houses and chose mansions from the mid-nineteenth century when it incorporated as a village. The historians who undertook this task came to appreciate that for Cliftonites those mansions "symbolized the supposed autonomy in Clifton's past" before it became a Cincinnati suburb. Its subsequent history of absorption into the life of the city was simply being blotted out. In 1975 the Cliftonites produced a "community plan" that "asserted Clifton's uniqueness and right to self-determination." It "projected an image of Clifton as an independent and isolated mid-nineteenth-century village, its present continuous with its past." The truncated account of its history left out the eighty years since annexation to the city and, on this basis, "projected an optimistic view of Clifton's future without reference to the city or the metropolis, the history, current status, and future prospects of which it blithely ignored."[113]

Other towns have succumbed to absorption into metropolitan regions and have found that their historic ambience, if restored and protected, can have appeal to their commuter residents and to the realtors whose job it is to entice them. Or they offer a pleasant weekend jaunt or getaway for city people. This, of course, changes their character. The accent is placed on their residential districts, and the downtown area is left in something approaching limbo—unless it can be filled with restaurants, antique shops, and bed-and-breakfasts that appeal to the weekend visitor. Marietta, Georgia, has four attractive residential historic districts (NR 1975/1985/1989) with a good representation of the ever-popular antebellum homes. As for its downtown, one commentator has written, "Unless one has a traffic ticket to pay or has been called for jury duty, there is little need to go downtown. A resident could live for years in Cobb County without ever seeing the square, but the visitor should not make this mistake."[114]

Three

Places Apart

*A*NOTHER BROAD CATEGORY OF HISTORIC DIS-
tricts consists of those whose predominating characteristic deriving from their history is separateness and exclusiveness. In this respect,
at least, historic districts may be regarded as representative of American
urban development. The original history of these historic districts represents the evolution of areas predominantly inhabited, whether voluntarily
or not, by people belonging to one ethnic, racial, or class group. The separation of populations along these lines, a persisting feature of American
urban society, is prominently represented among the nation's historic districts. The fourth phase of their history, the era in which they are being
"historically" preserved, has further entrenched the characteristics of separateness and exclusiveness, in particular through the design controls that
have accompanied local historic district status.

Exclusivity as a Planned Feature of Urban Life

While the separateness of some districts has developed out of the characteristics of the terrain and is therefore attributable, if not to "nature," at least
to an exploitation of the opportunities that features of the terrain have afforded, many historic districts bear the stamp of traditions of planning for
exclusivity within the city environment. Many districts that are now enclaves were originally designed as such.

A significant category of historic districts consists of nineteenth-century suburbs that were developed for affluent residents.[1] In the era of Andrew Jackson Downing and Calvert Vaux well-to-do middle-class people sought rural-seeming retreats from the growing congestion and pollution of the industrial city. These were the suburbs for which picturesque Gothic cottage styles were favored. The appeal of these suburbs as historic districts today owes much to the reflection in their designs and architecture of the romantic ideals that influenced suburban development from the mid-nineteenth century.[2] An important influence at this time was the great landscaped cemeteries that had been developed close to many of the nation's major cities. The suburbs were often laid out on estates subdivided from farms, and their names and ambience were designed to retain some of this antiurban flavor. Cottage Farm, Brookline, Massachusetts (NR 1978), for example, was a development of the 1850s on the site of a farm. It was "laid out as a picturesque residential suburb in which the landscape's design and the domestic architecture complemented each other."[3]

The growth of suburbs in the late nineteenth century was intimately connected with the building of railroads, especially commuter lines.[4] The following description of Waban near Boston can speak for the character of many of these suburbs: "Daily commuter trains linking the village to downtown Boston soon brought a steady influx of businessmen, professionals and tradesmen who built houses ranging from simple wood frame structures to large, elaborate residences, many of which were designed by architects and set on spacious lots."[5] Railroad and land companies and other developers laid out a number of attractive subdivisions to entice wealthy commuters. A celebrated example is Chestnut Hill, Philadelphia (NR 1985). The symbol of these districts was the picturesque railroad station, a few examples of which remain today. Henry Hobson Richardson was commissioned to design the stations on the Highland Branch of the Boston and Albany Railroad, and in Philadelphia the main architect was Frank Furness. Only Furness's station at Gravers Lane, Chestnut Hill, still exists. These stations and their modern replacements functioned as important anchors for and gateways into these romantic suburban commuter neighborhoods. Their rapid development in the style or styles that were fashionable at the time and were expressed by the foremost architects of the day made them particularly homogeneous neighborhoods possessing the sort of "integrity" that subsequently made them obvious candidates for historic district status.[6]

Inman Park (NR 1986), Ansley Park, and Druid Hills in Atlanta (NR 1979) represent different phases of the evolution of the planned suburb. Inman Park was developed in the 1880s by the operator of a streetcar line, Joel Hurt. For two decades, before fashion favored the new developments at Ansley Park and Druid Hills, it was a highly fashionable and prestigious neighborhood. Inman Park is old enough to have gone through the whole cycle of decline, subdivision of large lots, conversion of larger houses into apartments, and then rediscovery and renewal in the 1960s. Its winding streets, parks, and trees testify to the planning ideals of its era. A major difference between it and the other two suburbs is that it was an affluent streetcar suburb whereas they were geared to the automobile. A telltale sign for the modern visitor is the difficulty experienced in trying to explore these suburbs on foot.

The influence of land companies on the original pattern of settlement conferred a durably distinctive character on numerous districts. For instance, the Brookline Land Company had a major impact on the character of the Pill Hill district of Brookline. The company was formed in 1860 and purchased eighty acres between Brookline Village and Jamaica Pond west of Boston. By 1876 it had sold thirty acres and laid out two miles of streets and avenues. The company worked with Frederick Law Olmsted to ensure that its plans harmonized with those for the Muddy River Improvements — which would greatly increase the value of the land still remaining in their possession. The name "Pill Hill" was given to the district because of the large number of wealthy doctors who were living in it by the early twentieth century.[7]

Cleveland Park, Washington, D.C. (NR 1987), was developed by the Cleveland Land Company beginning in 1892. The architecture was of a high order: leading Washington architects were engaged, and many of the houses were designed by the president of the company and his wife. The company tried to give the district as much distinction and distinctiveness as possible: a lodge at its entrance, a stable, and a fire station.[8] In the West there are numerous towns laid out by land companies. For example, Glendive in Dawson County, Montana, was platted in 1880 for the Yellowstone Land and Colonization Company. The Merrill Avenue Historic District (NR 1988) is the main business street, which was laid out with business lots facing the railroad.[9] The historic district in Twin Falls, Idaho, is named the City Park Historic District (NR 1978). The park was planned by the Twin Falls Land and Water Company "as a centerpiece for churches, a high school, and the county courthouse."[10]

Many historic districts within cities are areas ranging from large blocks to tiny one-street enclaves that bear the indelible stamp of a particular architect or developer.[11] In these planned residential developments survive some distinctive layouts. An example is Highland Park, Denver (NR 1985), promoted by a company organized in London in 1875. It was advertised as "the most complete and beautiful villa residence park in the United States."

Its 288 acres were laid out on "a most marvelously bewildering plat of curving streets, avenues, places, crescents, roads, and drives, all with Scottish names."[12] It takes a great deal to destroy the character of a district of this kind.

Ashland Place, Mobile (NR 1987), consists of thirteen houses designed by C. L. Hutchison in the early twentieth century and is significant as "Mobile's first early 20th century suburban development geared toward the upper class property owner." The developers used an irregular grid plan and entrance gates.[13] Another small district is Alvarado Terrace, Los Angeles (NR 1984), a collection of about a dozen houses and a landscaped park established at the turn of the century. Ten of the houses were built by Pomeroy Powers, who constructed them one at a time and often lived in each house until he sold it.[14] The houses built by Samuel and Edward Philbrick add greatly to the character of the Pill Hill Historic District in Brookline. LeDroit Park in Washington, D.C. (NR 1974), still has about two-thirds of the houses designed and built by James McGill. "All were set in a picturesque parklike setting with continuous lawns within a fenced enclave with its own street pattern that deliberately did not coincide with the city's."[15]

Alta Vista Terrace, Chicago (NR 1972), is a small enclave of terraced houses developed by S. E. Gross between 1900 and 1904 and designed to resemble London townhouses. It is now appreciated because its "distinctly human scale creates a unity and harmony rarely found elsewhere in the city." This description from its 1971 Chicago landmark citation shows the appeal such districts have today as a contrast with the predominant highrise styles of city buildings—which surround Alta Vista Terrace itself and enhance and emphasize its enclave character.[16]

A New York example is Prospect Park South in Brooklyn (NR 1983), Dean Alvord's ambitious attempt after 1899 to "create a rural park within the limitations of the conventional city block and city street." The entrances to most of its streets are still guarded by pairs of brick piers containing cast-iron plaques with the letters PPS in a monogram. Alvord planned lawns and malls and hired an architectural staff to design the houses.[17] Another example is Schenley Farms, Pittsburgh (NR 1983), a small area adjacent to the University of Pittsburgh which contains a fine array of houses in various eclectic styles. It was established around 1905 by the real estate developer Frank F. Nicola who designed it as "a model suburban upper middle class development." Like all such developments, it shows a great deal of attention to landscaping.[18] This is one reason these places survive so well as *districts:* they were not just collections of fine buildings but were planned within a landscape. Longwood in New York City (NR 1983) had a single developer and a single architect of distinction, Warren C. Dickerson, for most of its houses.[19] Albermarle-Kenmore Terraces in New York City (NR 1983) are two cul-de-sacs lined with houses designed by a local firm.[20] Carroll Gardens, also in New York City (NR 1983), has been praised as "an outstanding testimonial to the intelligence, cooperativeness and civic imagination of an early group of real-estate developers. . . . [A] rare sense of community consciousness [was displayed] by using for each house a design that would be in harmony with its neighbors."[21] Henderson Place, New York (NR 1974), has twenty-four Queen Anne houses surviving from an enclave of thirty-two houses built in 1881 by a developer. It was intended for "persons of moderate means" but became a fashionable enclave.[22]

Often the enclave character was planned to provide maximum isolation and privacy. Among New York City's historic districts are numerous examples of such developments. The Tudor City complex (NR 1986) developed in the late 1920s has been described thus: "Everything faced in toward the private open space and away from the surrounding tenements, slaughterhouses, and generating plants. As a result, almost windowless walls now face the United Nations."[23] Such enclaves are a marked feature of the historic districts of large cities. They have been refuges from the pressures of big-city life for people able to afford the protected lifestyle they have offered. They may have fulfilled this function once in their historical origins, and do so again today in their newly protected status as historic districts. They illustrate two of the major "historical preservatives" and guarantees of survival defined by Grady Clay: plutocracy and privacy. Clay describes "islands of plutocratic power with strength to keep all others away, or . . . places so deliberately or accidentally removed from the thrust of development, so protected from the Iron Law of Progress, that they remain beautiful and well preserved."[24]

The Effects of Planning Features

Planning features, especially those that have firm and durable boundaries, have often provided an enclosed arena within which the exclusive occupation of a district by people belonging to one particular social group has occurred. Many plans have had a durable and revivable influence, providing both an enduring context for the development of a district and the means whereby an identity for it can be reaffirmed. Some of these features may be capable of restoration and renewed emphasis in such a way as to render the districts in which they appear particularly well suited to categorization as a historic district. One of these is the focal point or anchoring feature such as a park or public gardens.[25] Parks have served to pull localities together and give them identities and character as *districts*.[26] A district may have decayed since, but if the park is still there, it can probably be relatively easily revived and put to use again as a neighborhood-defining feature. An example is the way in which Irvine Park has been revived as the centerpiece of the district in St. Paul, Minnesota, which bears its name. The Irvine Park neighborhood was once one of St. Paul's most fashionable. A period of decay that began in the early twentieth century has been reversed with the nomination of the district to the National Register in 1973 and its establishment as a St. Paul Heritage Preservation District in 1981. The park was deeded to the tiny village of St. Paul in 1849. For some time after houses began to be built in the vicinity, it was little more than a common grazing ground. But residents put pressure on the city to improve the square, and in 1871 it was graded and given the name Irvine Park in honor of John Irvine, its donor. Among the improvements then put in were an iron fence, a drive around the park, gas lamps, wrought-iron benches, a fountain, walks, flower beds, and a pavilion. During the twentieth century these features gradually disappeared, and by 1970 the park had become "the local depository for retired playground equipment and a regular stopping point for vagrants." A key feature of the rehabilitation of the district has been the restoration of the fountain and the redesigning of the park by a landscape architect. The park is again what it was intended to be in the district's nineteenth-century heyday, the focal point of a stylish residential area.[27]

Many founders of towns created parks as focal points. The Rittenhouse Historic District in Philadelphia (NR 1983) owes much of its character to being focused on the most successful of the four squares set aside in William Penn's plan for that city. One of the historic districts of Florence, Alabama (NR 1976), preserves the name of Ferdinand Sannoner, the Italian engineer who designed the town (and named it after his birthplace). The town's parks and plazas are the fulfillment of Sannoner's plan. The park after which the Bronson Park Historic District in Kalamazoo, Michigan (NR 1983), is named is on land donated by Titus Bronson, the town's founder, for this purpose. It is likely that an even older focal point already existing here, an Indian mound, was a reason for his selection of this site. As with Irvine Park, the potential of Bronson Park was not realized until improvements, including a fountain, were effected in the 1870s.[28] The park in the DeWitt Park Historic District in Ithaca (NR 1971) has been that city's focal point ever since Simeon DeWitt put it into his plan in 1806. In 1826 he confined new construction to its northern part and ordered that the southern section be "at all times kept as a public walk and promenade, . . . that no houses or other buildings, except ornamental improvements, be erected . . . thereon." This initial care paid off, and today, with its fine churches and institutional buildings, it has been deemed worthy of historic district status.[29]

The aim of parks in new residential developments within cities was to provide both a focus and a selling point. Wooster Square in New Haven (NR 1971) was created in 1825 by promoters who hoped that a real estate boom would follow the opening of the Farmington Canal. Enough of an historic ambience has remained to enable Wooster Square to be the focus of a major early rehabilitation effort.[30] Landscape designers created such features to have exactly this kind of relationship to a neighborhood. For instance, the St. James Square Historic District in San Jose (NR 1979) preserves the focus that that park has provided since it was laid out by Frederick Law Olmsted in 1868.[31]

Of course, what gives a square- or park-focused district much of its character today is what has been placed either within or surrounding the square or park. Bronson Park in Kalamazoo is now surrounded by civic and institutional buildings, as, it seems, Bronson himself had intended. Many courthouses—or old state capitols, as at Corydon, Indiana (NR 1973/1989) —are located in squares and provide the defining feature of the numerous courthouse square historic districts.[32]

Anchoring features of this type seem to be so rare that only a small minority of districts are able to qualify as historic districts according to such criteria. Why is this? One major influence has been the predominance of the grid, which means that most town plans are little more than patterns of straight right-angled street lines. Sam Bass Warner has some suggestive comments in *Streetcar Suburbs* as to what happened in large cities. The physical arrangement of late-nineteenth-century suburbs, he argues, "failed to provide local centers where all the residents of a given area might, through frequent contact, come to know each other and thereby be encouraged to share in community-wide activities." This meant that "aside from class segregation there was nothing in the process of late nineteenth century suburban construction that built communities or neighborhoods: it built streets." The result was not integrated communities arranged about common centers but "a historical and accidental traffic pattern." According to Warner, this "centerless tendency" is particularly noticeable in the placing of schools. "An amorphous and weak neighborhood structure was the consequence of compounding communities with a mix of side-street grids, commercial strips, and small historic centers." Warner comments on one exceptional district, John Eliot Square, and it is significant that it *has* become a historic district: "In West Roxbury . . . the [Boston School De-

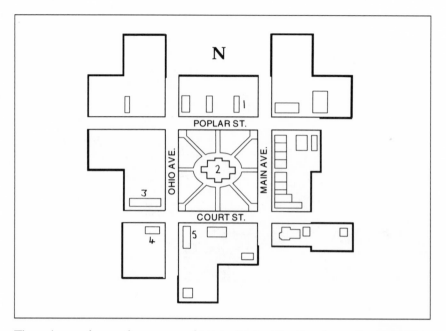

The make-up of a courthouse square historic district. The Courthouse Square Historic District at Sidney, Ohio, was placed on the National Register in 1980. A remarkably cohesive townscape with only four of the eighty-one buildings being "nonconforming intrusions." (a) Commercial premises on the public square (see #1 on map). The central building was one of four constructed following a fire in 1914. It has housed a jewelry firm throughout its history. Glazed architectural terra cotta was touted as a "fireproof" building material. (b) Shelby County Courthouse in the public square, 1881 (#2 on map). The land for the town site was donated to the Board of Commissioners of the newly formed Shelby County in 1819 by Charles Sidney Starrett, and his grant specified that one acre be reserved for a public square. The surveyor placed the square in a central location. (c) Monumental Building, Ohio Avenue at Court Street, 1876 (#3 on map). This Victorian Gothic structure was built from proceeds of a lottery originally designed to raise funds for a marble shaft to memorialize the Civil War dead. Town and township offices and municipal court were lodged here, as were the fire department, waterworks office, and post office. An opera house was on the third floor. (d) The Spot Restaurant. Originally a 1913 frame structure, this building was remodeled in 1941. "The Spot to Eat" was a different kind of community landmark and meeting place (#4 on map). (e) The People's Federal Savings and Loan Association building, 101 E. Court Street, 1917 (#5 on the map). Designed by Louis H. Sullivan, this building attracts nationwide attention as a landmark of American architecture. (Information from "Their Buildings Now," a booklet published by the Sidney/Shelby County Chamber of Commerce, Sidney, Ohio)

a.

b.

c.

d.

e.

partment's] school building policy maintained the historic center at Eliot Square [unlike at other places]."[33]

One finds represented among historic districts subdivisions and developments whose plans represented a deliberate reaction against the monotony and featurelessness of the grid. Many historic districts are non-gridded enclaves adjacent to, and sometimes even within, the huge grids that characterize so many American cities. Grids characteristically offer minimal protection against the forces that erode the boundaries and the integrity of districts, as well as the ability of people to perceive them as distinct. A contoured area, often a subdivision deliberately laid out in an alternative style to look romantic and noncitylike, offers more protection. The winding streets in such a district can be a deterrent to traffic, especially if there are straight alternative thoroughfares available nearby.[34] Careful traffic management can further enhance the sheltered quality of the environment of this kind of historic district.

Some of these districts are "additions" whose developers conferred on them plans that would distinguish them from the older, originally platted parts of the town to which they were "added." At Lafayette, Indiana, the Perrin Historic District (NR 1979) is based on Perrin's Addition, created in 1873 on land purchased by a wealthy Lafayette banker, James J. Perrin. "Laid out as a residential neighborhood, the streets follow the contours of the hilly terrain, in contrast to the rest of the city's grid pattern."[35] We find districts from the late nineteenth and early twentieth century that embody attempts at realization of City Beautiful and Garden City ideals of planning.[36] There is a superb example of Garden City development in the Oak Hill Historic District at Hagerstown, Maryland (NR 1987): "large lots, curving streets, deep setbacks, and tree-lined boulevards."[37] The Garden Homes Historic District in Milwaukee, Wisconsin (NR 1990), which was begun in 1920 (and marks the first American cooperative housing built under an agreement between a municipality and its residents), was inspired in part by the ideas of Ebenezer Howard.[38] A historic district can also be distinctive in situations in which there is a grid but it has been laid out on terrain for which it is not suited. In Bellefonte, Pennsylvania, for example, the grid contributes to the town's picturesque appearance, "pitting streets and buildings against the rise and fall of the land and providing 'much the aspect of a European village.'"[39]

Boundaries

A planning feature that deserves special consideration, because it has been so crucial for the definition of a historic district, is the boundary. It is through their boundaries that many historic districts acquire an enclave quality. Of course, the sharply defined character of a district in relation to surrounding and adjacent districts may owe much to nature and terrain. Many historic districts are in locations that have been kept isolated and distinct by topography. An example is the North Side district in Peoria, Illinois (NR 1983), whose growth was limited by a bluff and so was complete by the end of the nineteenth century.[40] Topography has had much to do with conferring an enclave quality on Point Richmond in Contra Costa County, California (NR 1979). This district not only preserves to a striking degree the atmosphere of a late Victorian Era industrial town but also stands out conspicuously as a historic district because of its hillside location between the vast industrial and commercial flats of Richmond on the one side and San Francisco Bay on the other. However, while boundaries existing in nature, in the terrain and topography and set by rivers, lakefronts, and hills, were extremely important in creating and limiting areas of early occupation, transportation, earth-moving machinery, and bridges eventually enabled most such natural boundaries to be overcome as limits on the spread of settlement. Boundaries that derive from nature are seldom impermeable and usually have had to be protected or fortified through planning decisions and regimes of control over land use. Nevertheless, they have continued to have a lingering imprint on patterns of living and use of the land, and are likely also to have a continuing visual impact. As Fred Schroeder argues, "natural" divides usually become social divides as well. The only question is which has come first. "Natural barriers and natural attractions establish orientations that are rarely free of class differences. The riverfront will be shantytown or king's row, the mountainside will be hillbilly haven or doctor's demesne; any sign to the contrary is most likely not democracy but incomplete transition."[41]

A strong sense of distinctiveness has often survived in districts that have continued to be topographically enclosed or limited. Topography has provided a degree of protection against traffic, the noise, pollution, and congestion associated with which can be so detrimental to sense of place. Recent studies have shown that gentrification is most likely to become established in neighborhoods that carry relatively little through-traffic, either because there are barriers to such movement or because they are not directly located between the central business district and more outlying and modern suburbs.[42] There are other districts that have acquired a distinctiveness through the development of prominent demarcation features between them and adjacent districts. The construction of roads may create this kind of isolating barrier. For example, Hunters Point in New York City (NR 1973) is an enclave of row houses left stranded by road and subway construction that drew the traffic away but also left the area relatively unaffected by the often fatal impacts of such developments.[43] Finally one can add to all this the ways in which people have used such sites and the opportunities they present. In enclaves formed by nature the topography may have been valued and exploited to create, entrench, and protect a *social* terrain characterized by exclusivity or separateness. It has been argued that historic districts are most defensible and accepted where clearly demarcated neighborhoods are associated with topography. This argument has been applied to Cincinnati, for example. Steve Bloomfield, former director of the city's Department of Neighborhood Housing and Conservation, has said, "I think part of it comes from the contours of the land. Different ethnic groups settled in different pockets. Over the last 200 years they grew into a city but never quite gave up their neighborhood identities. Even today you hear people say, not 'I'm from Cincinnati,' but 'I'm from Mt. Auburn — or Mt. Lookout or Westwood.' . . . Each enclave has a distinct look and feel." "People like to keep that separate identity," Mary Ann Brown, executive director of the Miami Purchase Association, the regional preservation group, is quoted as saying. "That's why preservation is so successful in Cincinnati."[44]

Planned Communities

One type of planning that is well represented among historic districts is that which reflects and seeks to fulfill the purposes of entire communities.[45] Nineteenth-century communitarian enterprises are an example. There are several sites associated with the Harmonists. At Economy, Pennsylvania (NR 1985), many of the Harmonist structures remain and are now preserved as a museum to which admission is charged. Harmony, Pennsylvania (NR 1973), preserves the remains of a Harmonist (later Moravian) community, and New Harmony, Indiana (NR 1966), is famous for its Owenite as well as Harmonist history. J. W. Reps has described the historic district at Zoar, Ohio (NR 1969/1975), which was laid out by the Separatists in the early nineteenth century, as "a reminder of what utopian America was like a century or so ago."[46] Several Shaker communities are represented in historic districts.[47] There are also planned communities of considerably more recent vintage, notably those of the New Deal era, distinguished by such features as greenbelts, curvilinear streets, and styles of the houses and apartment blocks.[48]

Elite Districts

The discussion so far has suggested a close connection between planned separateness and social exclusivity. Areas once—and often still—lived in by a town's or city's elite are prominent among historic districts. Such districts were often built on hills or other geographically detached areas where they were intended to be conspicuous and admired from a distance but where exclusivity was also easily maintained.[49] The Fountain Hill Historic District in Bethlehem, Pennsylvania, for example, was where the wealthy industrialists and businessmen built their mansions high above and well removed from the steel factories. These characteristics of detachment and conspicuousness contribute to the survival of such districts today. Distinguished architects were often employed and the latest, most fashionable architectural styles commissioned. Each town had at least one such district,[50] and big cities had many.[51]

The "precincts of privilege" have always had a fascination for Americans.[52] Their newfound status as historic districts can be traced to their long-standing significance in the boosting of towns. Displaying them prominently is not a new phenomenon. They were publicized by boosters to demonstrate that their town was a place where people grew wealthy and gained their just reward—social ascent. The houses were conspicuously sited by their owners and given the most extravagant and attention-grabbing designs.

One important contributor to the survival of elite districts has been the status they have acquired as landmarks in the lives of townspeople. This has been in part because of the prominent yet detached sites on which they have developed. Local people have been able to see these houses yet have not been permitted to enter them except as servants or tradespeople. The combination of visibility and exclusiveness has invested them with an aura of mystery and glamour. Today the appeal of these districts is kept strongly alive by the opening of selected houses within them for tours. At these times the veil is temporarily cast aside and the interior mysteries disclosed. The house museum, usually based in a locality's grandest, best-preserved mansion, plays an important role as anchor in many historic districts. While many districts have house tours, these may be held only once or twice a year and a visitor may happen on one only by chance, whereas house museums usually have regular hours for visitors. House museum docents are frequently the most accessible and knowledgeable people available to provide information on the history of a historic district, which otherwise can be well hidden, and so that history tends to be conveyed from the perspective of the district's most prominent and wealthy family. However, this may not be false to the significance that a landmark mansion has had in a neighborhood.

The status of elite districts and of their mansions as community landmarks has been analyzed by several writers. W. Lloyd Warner, for instance, discussed the significance of "Hill Streets" in the life and traditions of a town in his book, *The Living and the Dead.*[53] He described Hill Street as "the most important public symbol of the upper classes of Yankee City [Newburyport, Mass.]. . . . The beauty of the tree-lined street and the common sentiment of its residents for the venerable elms unify the homes of Hill Street in the minds of its people, the fine old trees providing an outward symbol of that superior region's self-regard." S. Frederick Starr's *Southern Comfort* looks in detail at the history of the Garden District of New Orleans. Starr examines how all sorts of sentimentalized myths about that district developed and describes it as having been "a metaphor that embraced notions of high economic status, political and social identity, a gracious style of life, and architectural opulence."[54]

Particularly distinctive are elite districts that were developed by and for families and friends. An example is the North Washington Historic District in Bloomington, Indiana (NR 1991). In the 1890s the Showers brothers whose furniture factory was Bloomington's major industry developed a two-block area adjacent to their own homes on Walnut Street as a residential district for their families and friends. At least eleven of the homes were built and owned by the Showers family. The Queen Anne homes of the Showers brothers and the colonial revival houses built by their children now constitute a most appealing streetscape.[55] Another notable example is the Cottage Farm Historic District in Brookline with houses built by Amos and William Lawrence in the mid-nineteenth century. The National Register nomination cites the fact that "many of the early structures were financed and built by one family" as one reason why "the diversity of the district is a composite harmony." Nearby is the Longwood Historic District, which was developed in the 1860s by David Sears as an exclusive suburb for himself and his family and friends.[56] In a similar category are districts developed by companies for their professional employees, such as Wawaset Park in Wilmington, Delaware (NR 1986) (the DuPont Company)[57] or the G. E. Realty Plot Historic District in Schenectady, which was planned by the General Electric Company's principal directors at the turn of the century for its managers and officers.[58] Such districts as prestige places tended to have houses built in the currently fashionable architectural styles.

The Grand Avenues and Fashionable Streets

The most famous elite districts were probably those located along "grand avenues." Interest in their history has been rekindled by a recent book and exhibition that surveyed the place of the grand avenues in the histories of a number of cities, pointing out that many "became 'the best address' of the city's leading churches, synagogues, museums, libraries, shops, and businesses." Charles Mulford Robinson described them as "the open-air salons of the city, adorned to stamp it with majesty."[59]

Main Street in Hartford, Connecticut (NR 1984), was such a street. "Its width and the setback of its buildings vary, but the scale of its buildings is consistently grand. Most of the early side streets have survived and are an important factor in shaping the character of the street."[60] The equivalent in New Haven was Hillhouse Avenue, which Charles Dickens is said to have called America's most beautiful street. It was "an avenue of majestic width, with houses set back 50 feet from the right of way, the intervening strip planted with trees and called 'the Grove.'" Yale University moved increasingly into this district, and it deteriorated rapidly to the point where it can be described as "a sad place."[61] It is a historic district today (NR 1985), largely in recognition of former glories.

A few districts of this kind survive today only in remnant or fragment form, for example, the Prairie Avenue District in Chicago (NR 1972).[62] In the 1860s and 1870s a number of wealthy manufacturers and brewers made their home on Dayton Street in Cincinnati (NR 1973). It became Cin-

Houses in Dayton Street, Cincinnati, ca. 1860–68. "Distinctive for their narrow lots, high-stooped entrances, and elaborate Italianate ornament, these freestanding mansions are midwestern cousins of New York City's brownstone rows" (Rifkind, *Field Guide*, 70). This once highly fashionable district was left stranded and detached by freeway construction and the clearance of deteriorated housing all around it in the 1950s and 1960s. It was designated a National Register Historic District in 1973.

cinnati's version of New York's Fifth Avenue and in the 1870s and 1880s compared in elegance to Chicago's Prairie Avenue. Most of the grand residences remain, although usually converted into apartments, and in recent years there has been "a quiet renaissance."[63]

Some grand avenues developed as landscaped boulevards, perhaps as part of a city's boulevard system, and then became the focus of prestigious residential districts. An example is seen in the Logan Square Boulevards Historic District in Chicago (NR 1985). This system was developed to link Humboldt Park with Logan Square and attracted people to build fine homes, many of which are now being restored.[64] A New York City equivalent is seen in the Grand Concourse Historic District (NR 1987): this grand boulevard was designed in 1892 to provide access from Manhattan to the Bronx.[65] The visitor can now see the "milelong concentration of apartment houses and institutional buildings" that developed along it.[66] Sometimes a street that had already developed was reconstituted as a parkway, for example, Highland Boulevard in Milwaukee (NR 1985). In several cities "patrons after 1870 sponsored massive park-and-boulevard projects, conceived with their avenue at the heart of the system: they hoped to ward off the spillage of unruly urban growth and enhance the elegance of the city's streets."[67] Subdivisions, especially at the turn of the century, reflected the popularity—influenced by City Beautiful ideals of urban planning— of planned tree-lined boulevards or "parkways." Ditmas Park in New York City (NR 1983) is still adorned by the great trees that Lewis H. Pounds, the original developer, planted in 1902.[68] Such boulevards are one kind of distinctive feature created by developers that can now be restored. An example is Harrison Boulevard in Boise, Idaho (NR 1980), which was turned into a tree-lined avenue by W. E. Pierce as part of his North End real estate promotion.[69] Hyde Park in Kansas City, Missouri (NR 1980), is an area that was beautified in the 1890s by the landscape engineer George E. Kessler. "Between 36th and 39th Streets on Gillham Road he converted a rocky ravine covered with a tangle of brush into a tasteful parkway lined on both sides by the mansions of rich owners who no longer needed to fear the growth of a pest spot in the middle of their neighborhood."[70] Its renaissance began in the mid-1970s when individuals discovered that "once fine old houses could be acquired fairly cheaply, thus enabling new owners to invest in their rehabilitation, often returning interiors to single-family occupancy."[71]

Boundaries of Privilege

Some residential districts had their exclusivity marked by distinctive boundary markers. Those that survive today demarcate the historic district in which they are located. At Beaver Hills in New Haven (NR 1986), laid out as a development in about 1910, "gateposts with beavers may still be seen at the head of Norton, Ellsworth, and Winthrop Avenues," and there is a gate cottage.[72] The Stoneleigh Park Historic District (NR 1988) in Westfield, New Jersey, was an upper-middle-class planned residential neighborhood of the early 1900s consisting of thirty large single-family houses set in approximately twenty acres of parklike land. The park entrance is marked by paired, massive brick posts.[73] Swiss Avenue in Dallas (NR 1974), the district in which the city's elite built their homes between 1900 and 1925, has "imposing stone gates" at its entry.[74] Gate posts and other markers also appear in Atlanta at Atkins Park (1910; NR 1982) and as one approaches Avondale Estates (1920s; NR 1986).[75] Some fences and barriers became targets of protest. For example, when LeDroit Park in Washington, D.C. (NR 1974), was established in the 1880s, the intention was that it should be an exclusively white community, and a fence was built around the neighborhood, with guards to restrict access. Black protesters tore it down, but it was promptly rebuilt.[76]

Arch marking the entrance to Avondale Estates, a small town near Atlanta, developed between 1924 and 1941. It was a "new town" promoted in the 1920s by George F. Willis, a patent medicine manufacturer. The arch is typical of the boundary markers found on the edges of many exclusive privately developed suburban estates and subdivisions.

Some developments occurred around London-style residential squares that contained private residents' parks. The first of these was Louisburg Square in Boston within the Beacon Hill Historic District (NR 1966). The central oval park was to be, and still is, owned by the property owners in the square who were taxed for its maintenance. A fence was built around the park after statues had been vandalized, and proprietors were given keys to the gate.[77] Gramercy Park in New York City (NR 1980) still owes something of its special character to Samuel B. Ruggle's original 1831 plan of a prime residential neighborhood, with a small private park open only to the owners of the adjacent lots. This park too was enclosed with a tall iron fence.[78] Washington Park in Troy, New York (NR 1973), is another private residential square on the European model which attracted the wealthy elite of its city and became a prestigious place to live. The Washington Park Association still assesses the surrounding property owners for park maintenance.[79]

Do Historic Districts Entrench Exclusivity?

Upper-middle-class residential neighborhoods, especially if still inhabited by well-to-do people or undergoing gentrification, have received a good

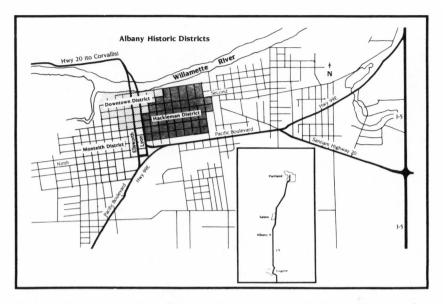

The historic districts in Albany, Oregon. The Monteith and Hackelman districts reflect the establishment of separate town sites. Walter and Thomas Monteith laid out theirs in 1848 and called it Albany after their hometown in New York State. Abram Hackleman laid out 70 acres to the east in 1850. A focal point of the Monteith District is the Monteiths' frame house, built in 1849 and still standing and open as a museum. The river was then the focus of economic activity (milling) and transport (steamboats). The railroad arrived in 1870: businessmen subscribed $50,000 to make sure it passed through the town instead of bypassing it. But highways constructed after World War II, notably I-5, did bypass the town. The two districts had sharply differentiated histories. There is a long tradition of rivalry between the two parts of the town and the two families. Monteith residents were mainly Republican merchants and professionals who supported the Union, whereas Hackleman residents were mainly working-class people who sided with the Confederacy. At one time a hedge was planted to separate the two communities (near Baker Street). The Monteith Historic District was placed on the National Register in 1980; the Hackleman, in 1982. There is an original Hackleman house to match the Monteiths'. (Information, including map, derived from "Historic Albany: Seems Like Old Times: A Guide to Historic Albany Oregon," Historic District Signage and Publications Committee, Albany, Oregon, n.d.)

deal of attention in the historic district process. Other areas that may be more significant as a historic resource for a town may not receive so much attention, perhaps because they are less prestigious in terms of a town's overall desired image or because they do not have residents with the same levels of education and wealth to fight for them. According to Starr, elite districts helped to create the standard two-part American city—slums and suburbs, despair and affluence.[80] It has been argued that historic districts revive and accentuate this historic divide. Thomas W. Sweeney commented in January 1993, "Although every major city claims exclusive historic residential enclaves, the contrast between these enclaves and historic areas inhabited by the poor has never seemed more marked or divisive."[81] Often it is these districts that, because of the initiative of their residents, are the first to become locally designated historic districts. The ensuing operation of design and other controls serves further to differentiate them from other less protected localities.

Survival and Revival

The survival rate of onetime elite residential districts has been variable. The intermediate or second phase in the history of many of them has been a sad one in which their distinctive features have been subjected to corrosive pressures that in numerous instances have been totally destructive. The fate of many shows the impact of tides of fashion with dramatic clarity. The rejection and desertion of such districts by the wealthy have often been sudden and brutal, and they have needed—and sometimes received— a good deal of rescuing and rehabilitation in our time. Examples of such movements include the shift of the well-to-do from De Tonti Square and Church Street East to the Oakleigh Garden District in Mobile, Alabama, in the early 1900s (all three districts are now on the National Register). Whitney Avenue (NR 1989), once one of New Haven's most fashionable streets, indeed "the patrician showplace of the city," lost ground to other districts after World War I and a long decline set in.[82] There have been innumerable shifts in fashion in Washington, D.C., for example, the change from Lafayette Square to Massachusetts Avenue in the early twentieth century or from Logan Circle to Dupont Circle in the 1880s.[83]

The reasons for the changes have been many and various. Sometimes the "pull" factor has predominated. There are districts that reflect the relocation of the wealthy to more extensive suburban space as it became available and prestigious. The environs of the great parks that were developed, often under Olmsted's inspiration, became the locations of mansions. For example, the Allentown district that is close to downtown Buffalo gave way to the areas around Delaware Park (NR 1986) at the turn of the century.[84] In other places one finds a combination of "push" and "pull." The flooding and disease often associated with riverside districts influenced wealthy people who initially located there to shift to higher ground when it became available. An example is the decline of the Ohio riverside area in Covington, Kentucky, as the fashionable district in that city in the 1850s. This area had long been troubled by flooding. The more elevated ground of the Seminary Square district (NR 1980) became available when the closure of the

Western Baptist Theological Seminary over the slavery issue resulted in the subdivision of its land.[85] Other districts have experienced lengthy erosion of status for a variety of reasons. In the 1850s fine homes rose around Lafayette Square, the first public park in St. Louis (NR 1972/1986). But in 1896 a tornado caused great damage in the area and initiated a long decline. Most of the original families moved to the West End. New mansions were built, but the area could not regain its lost status and in 1918 was zoned for business. Just enough of its former glory remained to excite interest in rehabilitation in the 1960s and 1970s.[86]

Why, in these circumstances, has survival occurred as often as it has? One reason is that in numerous once-elite districts whose well-to-do residents have long since left and been succeeded by much poorer people, frequently African-Americans, many of the larger houses remain. Their very size has helped them to survive in these circumstances through making them attractive for intensive subdivision for multifamily rented accommodation. In addition images associated with the once-elite status of these areas often continue to be available and can be exploited long after the elites themselves have gone. The aura of elite districts tends to linger, even when the people living in them are no longer from an elite stratum of society. An example is Mount Auburn in Cincinnati (NR 1973), which had been an elite and fashionable suburb in the nineteenth century. It remained "a bastion of gentility" well into the twentieth century but changed fundamentally in character after World War II when blacks dispossessed from Cincinnati's West End by highway construction and various forms of urban renewal came to live in the city's hill suburbs. By the 1960s the district was inhabited predominantly by African Americans. It became wracked by crime and drug-dealing. The area's history was then used consciously as "a strategy to regenerate pride" and attract residents. Carl Westmoreland, a black activist who took a leading role in the district's rehabilitation, said, "We didn't originally make it a great big issue because it smacks of something that has traditionally been something that the white upper class has been involved in. Our idea was to provide good sound housing. The way we brought the historical thing in was . . . in saying the finest people in Cincinnati have lived here."[87] Austin (NR 1985), an exclusive residential Chicago suburb of the 1880s, underwent repeated social change in the twentieth century, experiencing first, after 1920, an influx of blue-collar workers and clerks and then, after 1960, large-scale movement into it of blacks. Throughout all this it retained the original image of an affluent suburb, largely owing to the continued presence of its fine homes. This image and the homes that had sustained it were available to provide a focus for the restoration of the neighborhood.[88]

In some former and now-restored elite districts, neighborhood associations are torn between the essential task of fostering pride among homeowners in the fine architectural legacy represented by their houses and the need to play down their aristocratic origins. At Elmira, New York, a walking tour brochure of the Near Westside (NR 1983), produced by the Near Westside Neighborhood Association, emphasizes that "despite its aristocratic heritage, the Near Westside from its earliest days has been home to people of all social backgrounds, races and economic levels."

The Survival of Affluent Suburbs

Decay has certainly been the common fate of numerous nineteenth-century districts that were once affluent suburbs but were located close to the inner city and vulnerable to its expansion and to commercial and industrial encroachments. But many suburbs, especially those that developed farther from the central city core as commuter districts, have retained not just an aura of affluence and exclusiveness but the substance of these characteristics through a continuity of occupation by people from higher income groups. They have remained, as Elizabeth K. Burns has described them, "residential islands within the regional mosaic." Their main characteristics are typical of many features that are most likely to ensure the survival of "integrity" in districts—and qualify them for Historic District nomination. Burns refers, for instance, to the "abrupt visual transitions" that mark their boundaries and the deliberate limiting of traffic by prohibiting through-routes. Districts of this kind have continued to attract wealthy, high-status residents, and their population and residential densities have increased slowly enough not to put unmanageable pressure on their environments. Burns shows how public and private decisions have controlled change within these communities and diverted incompatible development outside town boundaries. Critical in all this have been the ways in which an elite orientation that was established at the outset has been reinforced over time. "Typically, early decisions constrain future community change and ensure the stability of affluent suburbs. . . . Internal policies consistently prevent any land development that would deviate from the long-term trend of exclusive residential use."[89]

In a recent article Mary Corbin Sies has studied the persistence of selected exclusive, planned communities. Her conclusions have considerable relevance for the study of the significance of local historic districts. She places particular emphasis on local control measures. Her tests of the circumstances in which persistence is most likely to have occurred in an exclusive suburb include "the creation of a defensive framework of property restrictions, local ordinances, and a variety of formal and informal boundary-marking strategies." She shows how the original developers of the suburbs she studied looked for the existence of or potential for contriving distinctive boundaries. "Strong, clearly demarcated borders helped to protect planned, exclusive suburbs from development that might threaten their quality of amenities or their identity as a place apart." Some were natural ones already there. But others were contrived, such as buffer land purchased in the vicinity or a different street pattern. Since their foundation, the maintenance of exclusivity has depended very much on the development of a defensive strategy. These might be traffic patterns that discouraged through-traffic and thereby promoted a sense of neighborhood protection and privacy. But they also included the boundary-marking strategies already alluded to, policies limiting access to nonresidents, and deed restrictions, and finally the development of zoning and other ordinances.[90] This is clearly where historic districting comes in. It builds on a tradition in such districts, reinforcing, reviving, and cementing in place characteristics that were inherent in the original planning and in the ways in which, prior to the availability of such a mechanism, the exclusivity was protected. The reference to "history" distinguishes it from other forms of zoning. It is a reference to a highly significant part of the history of such districts, the history of protection of the planned environment of exclusivity.

Covenants and other controls and restrictions on subsequent sale and changes in use of land and properties have helped to preserve the original characteristics of some suburbs. These relate to historic district development because of the continuity involved: local historic district designation provides for regimes of control that are similar to and build on the foundations of controls already established and built into the fabric of the community by restrictive covenants—a feature of the creation of many exclusive suburbs. An example is Fisher Hill, Brookline (NR 1985), which Jacob Pierce, the leading subdivider, was determined to maintain as a "high-class" residential area. He sold lots to people of wealth who he believed would maintain it in this fashion. In 1914, alarmed by a development nearby which involved the erection of "wooden triple decker apartment houses," 165 property owners entered into a covenant aimed at protecting their holdings against "deterioration through the construction of apartment houses, two family houses, public garages, stores, and hospitals. . . . The covenant was designed to be valid through 1940; since that time, zoning laws have, in many respects, accomplished much of the intent of the covenant. In addition, the Fisher Hill Neighborhood Association remains an active and influential group; a 'watchdog' against undesirable development."[91] In the Pill Hill/High Street Hill area of Brookline (NR 1977) the Brookline Land Company had deed restrictions attached to the sale of its land. These prevented "any occupation or erection of any building which could work injury or annoyance to residents."[92]

Tight covenant restrictions imposed by developers at Swiss Avenue, Dallas (NR 1974), have had an effect that continues today. The district experienced serious deterioration, but a very distinctive landscape awaited resuscitation. According to the restrictions imposed by the developers, houses had to be individually designed by an architect, each house had to be two full stories, uniform setbacks were required, and water, sewage, and telephone lines were installed in the alleys.[93] Roland Park, Baltimore, has retained its character in large part because Edward H. Bouton, the resident manager of the Roland Park Company, had land use restrictions inserted into every property deed. These provided for uniform thirty-foot setbacks and forebade subdivision. A house had to cost at least $3,000, and the architectural plans had to be approved by the company.[94]

Thus it can be seen that the enclave character of many middle-class suburbs was deliberately planned. Robert Fishman goes further. Because of the lifestyles of the people who lived in these places, he describes the landscape of such suburbs as a communal creation.[95] They were genuine *districts,* just waiting, one might say, for classification as historic districts.

The ultimate expression of the suburb as self-contained rural retreat are the communities that were developed in connection with the creation of country clubs. Several of these have become historic districts. At Brookhaven (NR 1986), Atlanta, the country club opened in 1911, and a planned residential development to complement it was created subsequently. It remains a highly distinctive and attractive district today. By 1930 the Country Club Historic District in Edina, Minnesota (NR 1982), had emerged as "one of *the* places to live" in the Minneapolis region after three golf courses, including a country club, had been developed.[96]

Working-Class Districts

Districts that exemplify characteristics of working-class history also survive. Districts of workers' housing close to their place of employment are particularly common. The Haughville Historic District in Indianapolis (NR 1992) marks the ethnic settlements that developed there when immigrants were attracted to work at Benjamin F. Haugh's iron-casting factory, established in 1875.[97] Alkali Flat in Sacramento, where there are three National Register historic districts (1984), was on the eastern edge of the railyards and was a convenient location for railroad employees to live. Row houses built for workers in nearby factories can be seen in such historic districts as East Brandywine, Wilmington (NR 1985). The Hackleman Historic District in Albany, Oregon (NR 1982), contains the homes of people who worked at the nearby mills, factories, and railroads. A tiny but fascinating example of this type of district is to be found in the Baxter Street Historic District in Quincy, Massachusetts (NR 1989), which consists of exactly four houses. They were built here in the 1880s by John E. Drake who operated a huge shoe and boot factory in Quincy at this time (250 men were employed in the early 1880s). Drake and others put up houses such as these and then rented them out to workers in the nearby factories. The houses are of a highly distinctive vernacular design known as the "Quincy cottage."[98]

Relationships between Classes

Because of the emphasis on homogeneity and consistency as desired characteristics, what historic districts represent less well is the history of interactions among classes and, indeed, also among diverse ethnic groups. There is a likelihood, in other words, that if one used only the existing range of historic districts as evidence of the predominant characteristics of American urban development, one would end up exaggerating to a considerable degree the extent of segregation and exclusiveness. An alternative or at least earlier history of relationships between classes is perhaps best represented in the structure of some of the older districts in eastern and southern cities. Here one can trace the lineaments of the "all-together" community in the preserved central cores of towns that were established in the colonial and federal eras. Many historic districts are what survives of the historic core, which largely constituted the walking city, whose limits were fixed to a substantial degree by the walking distances between people's homes and the locations of places of work (if not, as they frequently were, in their own homes), schools, stores, and churches. The creation of a historic district has often involved an attempt to preserve or draw attention to what are perceived as the essential features of towns at that stage of development. Indeed, they are among the best-known, most often experienced historic districts because their outlines can be reconstituted through walking tours.

By contrast, the residential-commercial divide that evolved as towns grew is revealed in the basic format of historic districts in so many towns and smaller cities: Main Street and assorted prestigious residential areas, the commercial and the residential districts. In a number of towns an effort has been made to develop a pairing that will illustrate these two facets of their history.[99] In particular there is the distinction between the "downtown" area—another name used for many historic districts—and the suburbs. This division may exaggerate and entrench a distinction when in fact the interrelationships were significant and an organic connection existed.

In some towns an attempt has been made to create and maintain extensive historic districts that preserve the historic integration of downtown life and the immediately adjacent residential districts. A good example of this approach is the Salisbury Historic District in Salisbury, North Carolina (NR 1975), which covers parts of twelve blocks and includes approximately 240 buildings. It encompasses both the central business district and a substantial adjacent residential area that developed after the advent of the railroad in 1855 adversely affected the appeal of other areas where residence had hitherto been concentrated. Another is the North Union Street Neighborhood in Concord, North Carolina (NR 1986), one of the few remaining examples of the "fine residential areas" that grew around the central business districts of the industrial towns of the North Carolina piedmont in the late nineteenth century "so that industrialists, merchants, and professionals could live within walking distance of their places of work and the downtown commercial establishments they patronized."[100]

Historic districts can be structured to represent and re-create the dimensions of various types and models of urban community. In the "walking town" people of diverse sections of society were obliged to live close to one another. Here there were subtle, intricate patterns of social separation often typified by the small cottages in alleys adjacent to the mansions of the rich. In areas where the well-to-do resided, servants had to live close by their employers. This pattern is preserved, for example, in Old Dauphin Way in Mobile, Alabama (NR 1984), where one can find both the grand houses of the merchants and the "shotgun" cottages of the servants who worked in those houses. Where such neighborhoods have undergone gentrification, they tend to be socially more homogeneous today than they were originally. Nevertheless, much of the mythology surrounding them does emphasize "village"-style togetherness. In contrast, there are neighborhoods established at later periods where community was unabashedly, and from the start, based on homogeneity of ethnic origin, religion, or class. These communities appeal because of the stability a highlighting of their allegedly natural and historic homogeneity can appear to offer. The imagery and publicity associated with some historic districts suggest a nostalgic reaching back to eras in which cities were seen as made up of neighborhoods that were inhabited by people predominantly from the same ethnic or social background.[101]

Historic Districts and African-American Segregation

The particular aptness of the historic district format for representing the history of separateness is being revealed by attempts to constitute historic districts that will reflect the history of African-Americans. While there are several historic districts outside the main cities that are associated with black history, the best known of which, perhaps, are the "black towns" of the West, such as Allensworth, California (NR 1972), and Nicodemus, Kansas (NR 1976), most are in inner-city areas. Many are now in an advanced state of decay, having been devastated by urban renewal and other processes that gave little thought to the histories of the people whose lives were being disrupted and environments destroyed.[102] Historic districts with significance in African-American history reflect a number of characteristics of historic districts in general. The stronger the impact of segregation, the more certain it was that there would be neighborhoods with a heavy concentration of African-American population. That was what segregation was meant to achieve. In such neighborhoods, a community life would have developed which now enables the district to satisfy to a high degree the requirement for homogeneity in a historic district. A result of segregation was the extreme difficulty black people had in gaining access to services that, for white people, tended to be dispersed over ever-widening areas. There was, therefore, a high degree of concentration of these services and amenities *within* the black communities, and thus an intensive community life. There were black real estate businesses, mutual benefit societies, insurance companies. Virtually everything that was needed for a viable community had to be created within the confines of the segregated neighborhood.[103] "By limiting or denying the access of African Americans to existing facilities, the white community spurred the creation of a separate set of institutions created specifically to serve the black community."[104] There were even black resorts, the best known of which is Idlewild in Michigan (NR 1979). It was affected by the opening up of resorts and clubs elsewhere to African-Americans and became known as Michigan's "only all-black ghost town." It is now being restored as a retirement and vacation community.[105]

But survival of these districts in the form enforced by segregation has been affected by recent history. A scrutiny of the entries for historic districts in the National Register publication on African-American historic places reveals the disintegrating effects of desegregation on many of these neighborhoods. Take, for example, the Fourth Avenue Historic District in Birmingham, Alabama. Its buildings are described as reflecting "the black community's attempt to fulfill its social and cultural needs within the confines of racial segregation and discrimination." But when the segregation laws were dismantled in the 1960s "the district's black customers dispersed into other parts of the city and were never replaced."[106] The same comments are made about the most celebrated of all black business districts, Sweet Auburn in Atlanta (NR 1976).[107] Another example is Indiana Avenue in Indianapolis (NR 1987). The history of this district has been described as showing what has tended to happen to black communities as restrictions on living and acquiring homes elsewhere have eased. "Restrictive housing practices forced a cohesive Black community until the 1950's. As the housing market expanded, the avenue suffered a major decline in population and wealth. As the shops and services lost their middle-class clientel, the buildings were closed, vacated, abandoned, vandalized and demolished. . . . Little of the vitality of thirty years ago remains on the avenue."[108]

In many cases a historic district is at one and the same time both a reminder of a shameful era in American history when segregation was enforced by law and an opportunity for commemoration of achievement in community building by African Americans. In the history of the structuring of districts within cities, there are many distinctive features among black community districts. For instance, we are told that a town as small as Anniston in Alabama (population 9,695 in 1900) would not normally have had a secondary business district. But Anniston did, at West Fifteenth Street (NR 1991). It developed as a shopping and social center for the black population at a time when "tougher segregation was being imposed."[109] Black neighborhoods that supplied servants for wealthy white people are frequently found cheek-by-jowl with prestigious white upper-class areas that have been made historic districts.[110] Indeed, in some of the historic districts whose image is dominated by huge antebellum mansions, such as Madison, Georgia (NR 1990), domestic servant houses can be found behind many of the mansions, and are an integral part of the story of how the district functioned.[111]

Myths about the Old South that appeal to southern nostalgia and to tourists have influenced the alteration and manipulation of space in historic districts in such a way as to obscure these original features. For instance, W. W. Law, the famous Savannah civil rights and black preservation leader, has described how the historic nineteenth-century character of the old downtown has been misrepresented. Before the turn of the century, when blacks were removed from what is now regarded as the historic area, working-class blacks and whites often lived side by side. "The houses in which blacks had lived were torn down throughout the downtown historic district, and in their place appeared gardens attendant to the large residences that were being restored. One result is that the downtown is far less congested than it was in its heyday."[112]

A feature of the evolution of neighborhoods in most parts of America by the turn of the century was the separation of people along class lines. In the larger cities districts evolved which were occupied predominantly by black middle-class people. The names of the Strivers' Section Historic District in Washington, D.C. (NR 1985), and of Strivers' Row within the St.

Nicholas Historic District in New York City (NR 1975) reflect this characteristic.[113] But the history of districts in smaller cities, such as Smithfield, Birmingham (NR 1985), Pleasant Street, Gainesville (NR 1989), and Pleasant Street, Macon (NR 1986), shows that one consequence of segregation on *racial* lines was that many black neighborhoods included people from *all* social classes.[114] Desegregation has meant a loss of this particular feature, as upper- and middle-class blacks have dispersed to other areas.[115]

A comparison may be made between women's history and African-American history. A recent survey of historic preservation associated with women's history scarcely mentions *districts*.[116] There are many sites associated with women's history,[117] and more are being identified and added to the National Register. But there are also districts whose history is being interpreted in new ways as the contributions of women are being researched and given new prominence. An example is the work of women architects. The work of Joel Roberts Hinde (1874–1916) is now a, perhaps *the*, major feature in the presentation of the architectural heritage of the South Wayne Historic District in Fort Wayne, Indiana. She had no formal architectural training, but the design that she did for a house for herself and her husband was noted and became popular. Eventually she became the designer in a construction firm founded by her husband and was responsible for the design and construction of more than three hundred houses, mostly in the colonial revival and Craftsman styles.[118] The emphasis on her work as giving a distinctive identity to a historic district can be compared to the new emphasis being placed on the work of black architects such as Wallace A. Rayfield (ca. 1870–1941) in the Smithfield Historic District of Birmingham.[119]

But by and large, women's activity has not been of the concentrated kind that focuses historic preservation into the district format. The Women's Rights Historical Park at Seneca Falls in New York State essentially consists of only one site plus a museum, and interpretation is greatly complicated by the overlapping existence in this small town of three "district" developments. On the one hand, there is the park that is under the jurisdiction of the National Park Service. On the other hand, there are both a historic district and an urban cultural park developed under the New York State scheme, and both of these, while incorporating features associated with women's rights, focus primarily on the history of the town, which has multiple pasts of which the women's rights campaign is but one.

Four

The History that Is and Is Not Represented in Historic Districts

*E*VERY DISTRICT, EVERY PLACE, HAS A HISTORY of some sort. But most districts in the nation's towns and cities are not Historic Districts. *Their* history is not being remembered in this way. Clearly there are distinctions between "historic" and "non-historic" districts that are different from those that might exist between districts that have a history and those that might not. In this chapter I shall describe some of the reasons for this distinction.

The History that Is Represented in Historic Districts

The Significance of "Significance"

The historic district is intended to represent in physical form, via buildings, townscapes, and streetscapes, "significance" in history with particular reference, as the criteria require, to certain episodes, periods, and famous persons. This criterion is interpreted in various ways. Some places owe their status as historic districts and the preservation of the buildings therein in large part to their associations with a famous person, usually literary or political. For example, Lockerbie Square, Indianapolis (NR 1973/1987), is associated with the poet James Whitcomb Riley.[1] Independence, Missouri, has its Harry S. Truman Historic District (NR 1971) whose basic walking tour traces the route of the former president's favorite walk around his neighborhood. The aim has been to preserve this district to the greatest possible extent as it was when Truman was a resident at 219 N. Delaware. Associations with famous people control the publicity surrounding numerous other districts. An example is the dominance of the Adams family heritage (involving not just one but two former presidents) in Quincy, Massachusetts, even though that city has had an enormous amount of post-Adams history. A walking tour brochure enables the visitor to see some of the non-Adams sites, such as the Crane Memorial Library, designed by Henry Hobson Richardson, but in terms of a cohesive impact and community identity one is tugged back toward the Adams connection. This anchors the district with major landmarks at the ends and in the middle. These landmarks attract most of the many visitors, have the National Park Service's resources at their disposal for interpretation, and are linked by a regular trolley service.[2] The Central Springfield Historic District, Illinois (NR 1978/1986), is dominated by associations with Abraham Lincoln, especially after the old courthouse was restored to its appearance as the statehouse of Lincoln's time. The need to attract tourists to these and other places with strong associations with famous people or events contributes powerfully to reinforcing the dominance of certain epochs or incidents in the way the history of the community is presented.

Understandings of significance have also been reflected in a preoccupation with particular phases or periods. The colonial and Revolutionary War eras and the Civil War, the antebellum era in the South, and the pioneering and Old West phases of midwestern and western history have exerted a powerful tug in deciding what history should be remembered in historic districts. Other aspects of a town's heritage may be given much less emphasis. In a 1977 report on the creation of a historical park at Lowell, a Massachusetts industrial city with substantial remains from its nineteenth-century mill history, reference was made to "a missing time and place link in a series of historical cities along the eastern seaboard." A stereotyped image of the "historic" developed in New England and became deeply entrenched in the popular imagination and the strategies of admen and commercial developers through the endless repetition of a stock historicizing vocabulary, for example, the insertion, restoration, or retention of such traditionally "historic" features as cobblestones, brickwork paving, and gaslamps. In 1978 Jane Holtz Kay and Stanley Taraila seemed to be fighting against the tide when they urged that not everything be stripped back to the colonial in New England. They could see that there was an urgent need to develop a sense of how towns grow. Salem, for instance, had "matured slowly in time, building by building, each worthwhile."[3]

The state of affairs in New England was analyzed in a 1988 report on historic preservation in Connecticut, which included comments on what happened when an effort was made to have Wooster Square, New Haven, designated a historic district. Both the study committee and the New Haven Preservation Trust had to work hard to overcome "the popular myth that only 'colonial' or 'quaint' buildings belonged to an historic district." It was clear that if further historic districts were to be created in Connecticut, a major educational strategy would be required. The Connecticut Historical Commission, according to the report,

> estimated that there may be as many as a thousand potential historic districts in the state, yet Connecticut's historic districts are located disproportionately in residential village-green settings. In many of these localities, decades of work by historical societies, village improvement societies, antiquarians, and others have conditioned residents to think of their areas as historic. This education has been absent or is only beginning to be carried out in industrial villages, urban downtowns and neighborhoods, rural hamlets, and farming areas. Efforts to establish historic districts in these areas, which are no less historic in nature than traditional village centers, have proved far more difficult.[4]

The report advocated easing Connecticut's tough voting requirements to make historic district designation easier. Somehow the barrier to acceptance of other forms of history worthy of historic district designation had to be breached.

Certain New England towns were centers of industry in the nineteenth century—and in some cases well into the twentieth. But now that industry is gone and they are faced with an urgent need to rely on "heritage" as a substitute source of economic sustenance. This has led to a downplaying of those aspects of the past that do not fit in with a historic image defined in traditional New England terms. The visitor to Marblehead, Massachusetts, today finds it hard to appreciate that it has a considerable industrial past, notably shoemaking, although it must be acknowledged that two disastrous fires not only ruined the industry but largely obliterated its physical presence. Today the large Georgian mansions that delight visitors are largely relics of maritime and related activities that were important at one time but are not the whole story of Marblehead's past. The Victorian homes that were built by people associated with industrial development are often in the nonhistoric part of such a town—and sometimes have to be drawn to the visitor's attention by separate guidebooks sold rather than given free.[5] Salem, Massachusetts, also had a substantial industrial past. Fire and urban renewal have taken away most of that part of the town's historical legacy.

Salem has multiple historical inheritances, but a furious simplifying process is constantly at work under the intense pressures associated with catering to mass tourism. Unfortunately, the witch trial episode appears at present to be gaining the upper hand.[6] At New Bedford, Massachusetts, the emphasis is on the city's whaling past. The whaling industry went on well into the twentieth century and has recently collapsed, leaving the city in the economic doldrums. The industrial past was substantial but not one happily remembered or capable yet, it seems, of being placed in historical perspective.

America's Symbolic Landscapes

Historic districts are an embodiment of *perceptions* of significance in buildings and landscapes. Not surprisingly, therefore, there are close relationships between the images of history purveyed by historic districts and America's symbolic landscapes, stereotypes of communities that D. W. Meinig has called "part of the iconography of nationhood, part of the shared set of ideas and memories and feelings which bind a people together."[7] Historic districts are representative, or have been chosen because they have been deemed to be representative, not just of architectural styles or district forms but also, to an extent that is seldom fully acknowledged, of America's major symbolic landscapes, which appear to invoke and embody in a particularly coherent and powerful way distinctive and admired American values. It is not surprising that this has not been recognized, for it has only been quite recently that cultural geographers such as Meinig and John A. Jakle have defined what a symbolic landscape is and how it influences our perceptions of our environment. In historic preservation the most dramatic and sustained resurrection of a symbolic landscape has been in the Main Street movement.

Increasingly historic districts, in becoming representations of America's symbolic landscapes, have developed a generic and stereotypical character. After beginning as very special places, one of a kind, they have evolved into a format and concept that by the 1990s had the potential for mass production. Historic districts would not have multiplied so rapidly if these stereotypes had not been available to facilitate their ready acceptance as features inherent in and waiting to be drawn out of the urban landscape.

Two of the three principal archetypal landscapes that Meinig has identified are the New England village and Main Street. Both are heavily represented among historic districts. The third, the Californian suburb, is too recent to be represented in large numbers, although, as we have seen, many suburbs of an older vintage are historic districts. There is little place in this gallery of symbolic landscapes for the city and the modern metropolitan landscape.[8] There is a strong tendency for historic districts in cities to be accorded either a "village" or a "Main Street" interpretation and treatment to conform to these two basic stereotypes.

The manufacture and protection of the symbolic landscape of the New England village has a long history. In New England there are numerous towns in which a consensus had emerged well before historic districts were heard of that the "colonial" era, loosely defined, was the one of greatest significance in the community's history. This consensus became reflected both in architecture and in the attention given to historic preservation and commemoration. As Joseph S. Wood has pointed out, towns that failed in the nineteenth century to become cities "were romantically refigured as symbols of an idealized past."[9] They became what are most accurately termed "colonial revival" historic districts in that what they represent today is essentially the outcome of decisions made in the late nineteenth and early twentieth century as to the style in which their environment should be stabilized and protected. A well-known example is Old Bennington, Vermont (NR 1984). Even more famous is Litchfield, Connecticut. A 1988 report on Connecticut's historic districts commented that Litchfield's history is "a study in the persistence of a myth, namely the image invented at the turn of the century that Litchfield was America's best-preserved 'colonial' town." In fact, the streetscapes are "a combination of surviving elements of its colonial past and post-Revolutionary 'Golden Age' and later additions." These elements were "merged at the turn of the century into one of the nation's best and most influential examples of a Colonial Revival streetscape."[10] There are now vested interests in maintaining the myth of the "colonial" community, although many Connecticut "villages" are now New York commuter suburbs and their centers are no longer the center of anything in particular and largely drained of their original historical meaning. "The term *village center*," the report commented, "suggests the classic image of the New England historic district: an old residential village of clapboard houses surrounding a green, its centerpiece the tall spire of a white clapboard church. From legislative testimony concerning the first districts proposed in Connecticut, it is clear that this setting is what the framers and early advocates of the historic district enabling act had in mind when they passed the law." But, it went on, "the reality of Connecticut's village centers challenges this idyllic vision." The problem is that the "history," the image, has become important for these towns. "In each of these communities the historic character of the town center, not to say the historic district, is a factor in the local economy." Many gift shops, boutiques, and antique shops now trade on the myths.[11] We see here the combination of an original history widely

Pulaski Village, upstate New York (NR 1983). A typical "Main Street" in a historic district.

agreed to be "significant," a high rate of survival of features of that history through efforts to preserve and commemorate them, and the correspondence of those features today both to the priorities set by the criteria and to community priorities as to what should be preserved.

Another major symbolic landscape that is represented in many historic districts is the one identified by Meinig as "Main Street." Although the term "Main Street" may primarily suggest a commercial district, characterized by one long street lined with impressive late-nineteenth and early-twentieth-century facades, there are really two stereotypes involved here which overlap and sometimes combine into one historic district and sometimes are separated out. The broader use of the term to describe an entire community has a long history, reaching back at least to Sinclair Lewis's *Main Street.* By contrast, Main Street as a commercial district has been the focus of Main Street programs. Meinig uses the term in the larger sense. His analysis of the "archetypal" structure of a "Main Street" community bears a striking resemblance to the structure of a set of historic districts within a medium-sized town. Close to the churches is "the academy and perhaps a small denominational college. The residential area begins with big Italianate and Victorian houses on spacious tree-shaded lots and grades out to lesser but still comfortable homes."[12] As he points out, certain parts of town and certain social groups are excluded from this landscape. It is a selective vision of an idealized community.

The overlap occurs because Main Street itself, the town's original and central commercial district, is celebrated for more than just its commercial ethos. It is the core of the larger community, the arena in which its values are celebrated. The publicity associated with Main Street historic districts reveals the powerful impact of nostalgia for the ideal of community embodied in the broader concept of "Main Street." The sentiments represented in this concept are well exemplified in one of the leading books on the subject, Carole Rifkind's *Main Street*. In her introduction Rifkind celebrates Main Street as "uniquely American, a powerful symbol of shared experience, of common memory, of the challenge and the struggle of building a civilization." "A vital force in the nation's history, Main Street," she says, has "provided tangible proof of progress over three centuries. It is our own generation that seems powerless to sustain the health of our urban environment. . . . Only in the very recent past—though perhaps too late—have we come to realize that the health of our urban centers depends on the strength that we draw from our past. And Main Street is the historical root of urban America. . . . Main Street was the face of a town, the expression of its identity, . . . a magnet for human activity."[13]

"Main Street has deep roots in American memory," Rifkind writes.[14] That memory is drawn on in the later sections of her book where she recalls the pride with which Americans regarded Main Street, especially in the first thirty years of the twentieth century. Memories of life and activity in this era are stirred with illustrations of parades and other activities that were focused on Main Street.[15] With books such as Rifkind's and a significant predecessor, Lewis Atherton's *Main Street on the Middle Border*, as well as sentimental depictions of Main Street in movies and as the focal point of Disneyland, Main Street left behind the era of Sinclair Lewis in which it had become identified with small-town bigotry and philistinism. It became fashionable again.[16] There was renewed interest in the architecture of Main Streets, and guidebooks were published to assist appreciation of it.[17] A wave of nostalgia for Main Streets was stimulated by the success of historic preservation programs in restoring them to what is in many cases something more than their original charm. This nostalgia is captured in Pat Ross's 1994 book, *Remembering Main Street*, which simply could not have been written twenty years earlier. The Main Streets visited by Ross were very much the creation of the historic preservation movement. Again we see influences in the present day that have ensured high priority for the preservation of a particular type of district.

As for survival, again the Main Street phenomenon needs to be placed in historical perspective. Here too manufacturing of the "historic" landscape set in well before the era of historic districts. Many of the Main Streets that are so admired today, and that are the target of improvement strategies, are themselves the product of similar campaigns a century or so ago. Main Street programs are a tradition. They are not a radically new departure for small towns. The challenge to many small towns in the late nineteenth and early twentieth century has been well described in Atherton's book. The growth of larger cities and their dominance of regional business through railroads and mail-order trading threatened many of the vast number of small towns founded in the early phases of settlement. The response was often to form civic improvement associations that did much to create today's admired streetscapes. "Fancy iron fences, statues, bandstands, new town halls and theaters were built. Often trees and gardens were planted in the hopes of creating a new image of prosperity."[18]

The principal stereotyped images of the small town, the "Main Street" town identified by Meinig, have been drawn on and highlighted in the development of historic districts. The elements of the small town were—and are—highly standardized: the big houses of the gentry, the middle-class environment, distinctive areas occupied by minorities, parks as places of ritual, schools, libraries, and churches.[19] All these elements feature prominently in the ways historic districts are interpreted and structured. The landmarks within them are reinforced and memory of their significance is revived through such devices as the walking tour, the nomination of individual structures to the National Register, and the removal of the aluminum or stucco false fronts so often put up to "modernize" stores and conceal the Victorian and early-twentieth-century facades.[20]

The emphasizing of one period of significance would not have gained such force were it not for a substantial coincidence between, on the one hand, perceptions of historical significance as embodied in landscapes and streetscapes and, on the other, fashions in the aesthetic appeal of certain landscapes and streetscapes. The approach to the past that has so strongly influenced the development of historic districts owes much to an impulse to tidy up what remains of those aspects that are not aesthetically appealing or socially acceptable. In this regard too historic districts need to be placed in historical perspective. The approach to the past on which they are based is not a new phenomenon. It is in a tradition that long predates the 1966 legislation, and the historic district phenomenon would not have gained such headway and appeal had it not been building on these historic cultural foundations. "Beautification" is one name given to similar earlier manifestations of the desire to "improve" America's urban environments. It is an important predecessor of some aspects of the historic district phenomenon. Indeed, it helped to create some of the historic landscapes that historic districts are now being designed to preserve. This is because beautification has long functioned as a historicizing influence: in this sense the idea of making a district historic has a long ancestry. The "historic" appearance of some places is often attributable to decisions made at some time after the primary era of historical significance for which they are now remembered. The appearance may have been changed then to make the district conform more closely to the styles appropriate to the very same period of significance that is now the object of Historic District designations and design controls. Changes made both then and now may have made the district conform more completely to aesthetic ideals that appear to flow out of that historic era and the values for which it is now honored. For instance, Oglethorpe's squares in Savannah would have been very unkempt in the eighteenth century and not at all the way we see and admire them today. "They were mostly surrounded by unpretentious wood houses and were not landscaped."[21] It was only in the nineteenth century that the ideal townscape began to be realized. For example, it was then that the live oaks so admired today were planted.

The beautifying of New England villages in the nineteenth century is a well-known phenomenon. A "colonial" image was bestowed on many of them in accordance with contemporary perceptions of the styles of the colonial era. New England village historic districts can trace their ancestry to this era. Under the influence of the colonial revival, many village greens were transformed by beautification.[22] There are certain similarities between impulses behind the creation of historic districts and the village improvement movement of the nineteenth and early twentieth century.[23] It was in the post–Civil War years, Rifkind tells us, that the towns of New England, western New York, and Ohio "achieved their unique beauty."[24] A major difference is that the earlier movement had a largely negative attitude toward the past, which it saw as responsible for much ugliness. In *Main Street*, Sinclair Lewis demonstrated that Carol Kennicott's concern for the "improvement" of Gopher Prairie was linked to her despair at the horrors of the architecture of Main Street, an urban landscape that preservationists are working so hard nowadays to preserve. But, of course, in many villages and small towns the past that is being preserved today is the past that the "improvers" created.

Beautification is a tradition that has molded a wide range of landscapes. The attractiveness of many mill and mining towns today is often criticized as a falsification of the historical reality. But the beautification of some of these places too set in well before historic districts were ever thought of.

Dickeyville near Baltimore (NR 1972), for instance, is a mill town whose origins go back to the mid-eighteenth century and whose mill operations ended only in 1967. But in the 1930s, following the town's sale to the Maryland Title Guarantee Company, it began to appeal as a commuter suburb. In 1937 the Dickeyville Improvement Association was formed, and its impact is very evident in the landscape of today. "As one walks along the falls today, the feeling of the town is different. The mills are gone and the houses, with their black shutters and white picket fences, have been altered to a condition they probably never enjoyed in mill days." Yet this is the "historic" ambience that many people now find so agreeable in Dickeyville.[25]

History that Is not Represented in Historic Districts

Aspects of the Past That Are Not Preserved or Restored

When an era or event or personality has been determined to be of primary significance in the history of a district, two major issues must then be resolved. The first is whether features believed to be characteristic of the era are to be *restored* and, if so, which ones. The second is what to do about the evidence surviving from later (or, sometimes, earlier) eras that are not considered of prime relevance to the predominant historical character.

The restoration of the earlier era is bound to be highly selective. There is much that has been lost and much also that present-day tastes would not want to see restored. In 1969 Richard S. Hagen, writing about Galena, Illinois, pointed out, "It must be remembered that historic business streets have always included the commercialism abhorred today. The old buildings of Galena's Main Street were covered with signs. Should these, as well as wooden sidewalks, store barrels and dirty streets, be restored in an attempt at totally accurate historic preservation? One should answer positively, but it is more realistic to accept that present-day standards of cleanliness and taste will be imposed. Thus preservationists tend to restore the past to what they think it ought to have been, not to what it was."[26]

Signage in historic commercial districts is an example of the sort of issue that causes controversy. On the one hand, many modern-day signs do not belong within a restored Main Street setting. On the other hand, the use of signs in commerce is a traditional and historic practice. Review boards try to take enlightened attitudes to signs and issue detailed guidelines as to what will and will not be permitted.[27]

Fort Worth is an example of a place where there has been support for keeping aspects of the more recent past. Some property owners wanted to retain false board-and-batten fronts on commercial buildings. These false "Colorado fronts" dated back only to the 1950s when the area first tried to attract tourists with wooden awnings and walks. One restaurant hung signs proclaiming itself the site of Annie Oakley's wedding and other fictions. The fronts will probably remain, as they are being acknowledged as part of the city's legacy. Gordan Kelley of the historical society is quoted as saying that "cowboys have come along and carved their initials and whittled on them until they look more antique than the actual structures. They've got their own history now."[28]

There has also been debate on the extent to which areas such as the Stockyards in Fort Worth should be cleaned up. Some have insisted that "part of the hub's history is its very seediness."[29] There can be resistance to clearing away the accumulated aging of a town. Seediness itself can be perceived to have "charm." There were similar attitudes in Seattle to keeping transients in Pioneer Square. Bill Speidel, a Pioneer Square entrepreneur, said, "We're not Newport, Rhode Island; we're an old gold rush town and the original skid road. If we didn't have the bums around, we'd have to hire them from central casting."[30] We shall be seeing further evidence of this assumption that a historic district should be treated as a stage or film set.

Another controversial issue is whether overhead wiring belongs in a historic district. As anyone who has attempted to photograph historic buildings in a city can testify, they often obtrude most jarringly into an otherwise seemingly pristine "historical" scene. The beautification of some New England villages had involved putting the utility lines underground at the outset.[31] The restoration at Williamsburg also involved putting the overhead utility wires underground.[32] In Port Townsend the wiring has been retained for historical reasons: "Overhead wiring is part of tradition as well as necessity in Port Townsend. Undergrounding is appropriate in areas built before overhead wiring was invented; in these cases, it eliminates the incongruity between the ages of the buildings and the wires. From the late nineteenth century, however, overhead wiring was very much a part of town atmosphere. Undergrounding of wiring in Port Townsend is not essential on historic preservation grounds, although it may be desirable on more general urban design grounds."[33] A similar decision was made in the Ballard Avenue Historic District in Seattle (NR 1976): "An unusual aspect of the [urban design] plan [by Folke Nyberg] is that the electric street wiring will not be put underground. The architect and the community felt that cheap power from the overhead wires had contributed much to Ballard and should be preserved as a historic feature."[34]

The restoration of the past in mining towns has been highly selective. Restored houses in Columbia City, California, were to be made available for tenants "who will maintain uses generally in keeping with the activities of the inhabitants during the town's now-vanished heyday. . . . [But] presumably sin and gambling, two of the major industries, will not be reestablished by the public authorities concerned."[35] The people of Georgetown, Colorado, were unwilling to let the railway return to the town even though it had been so significant in the town's development. Tom Bennhoff, a local probation officer, was quoted as asking, "Does an attachment to history mean that we want to rebuild all the old whorehouses?" The proposal to revive the railway (now a major tourist attraction) was regarded by some as likely to lead to the destruction of "Georgetown's quaint life-style." There were similar attitudes in Georgetown regarding the possible renewal of mining activity, even though the town recognized the role mining played in the town's creation "and the opportunity of reestablishing this link with history."[36]

History as Change over Time

A major difficulty has been the seeming inability of historic districts to represent change.[37] There are many influences that have reinforced the bias inherent in the criteria in favor of a focus on one period and episode. For instance, the emphasis in historic preservation on built structures has often produced at least the appearance of a static community, especially when there is a preoccupation with styles and a desire to highlight the finest, "purest" most high-style examples of each.[38] A highly significant and commonplace aspect of urban history that receives minimal recognition through the process of designation of districts as historic is the history of "decay" and "deterioration." The understanding of history that has underlain so much of the development of historic districts represents the very reverse of urban history as the record of continuum, change, and process. The concept of the historic district has to a large extent been based on a commitment to a representation of history as static, a series of points in time artificially frozen and then immunized to a substantial degree from the impacts of change. This is not only un- or even antihistorical. It is also profoundly antiurban in the sense that it denies the diversity that is the very essence of urban life and the source of its greatest challenges and enjoyment. For change is the essential and only constant characteristic of the history of many American city districts. If a district has remained prosperous, it is likely that the character of its built environment—on which historic district classification is necessarily so dependent—has kept changing to reflect and serve the needs of the economy that is generating that prosperity. This may mean that the creation of a homogeneous historic district representative of one particular era is no longer possible. Too much "history" has been removed. The changes that such districts have undergone are history of another kind, the history of adaptation and change. But that is a history that is not easily captured in the format of a historic district. A particular problem has been the relationship between architectural history and the representation of change. The inclusion of architecture in the 1966 criteria, and the enormous growth of expertise in architectural history, brought it to the forefront of appraisals of historic buildings and districts. This has probably been inevitable in a situation in which the emphasis has been on the appearance of the external physical fabric of built structures. Architecture has also become dominant in large part because it has provided the easiest (the most physically visible) and least controversial way to define historical identity for a district. In addition, it has often been the architecture — the Queen Anne houses, the brownstones, the Georgian row houses — that has led to restoration and gentrification. The tendency has been to favor the surviving representations of particular styles that have been least altered. This runs contrary to another feature of the history of perceptions of American urban development. Change in buildings was not always regarded in so negative a light. In the nineteenth century there was a disposition among those promoting the claims of fast-growing new towns in the United States to welcome incongruity in architectural styles and in the sizes of buildings because of what this denoted about the town's evolution.[39] The changes indicated growth: the town was manifestly not standing still, which tended to be the image associated with sleepy New England villages with their homogeneous and outmoded architecture of the pre-Victorian eras. The town was making rapid strides toward its destiny as a great metropolis, which its founders and boosters had claimed was "inevitable."

Not just change but also multiple pasts are neglected. Towns and cities of any size are bound to have many interlocking and overlapping histories in their past. Rare indeed is even the village that has been naturally frozen in time so that only one history awaits interpretation. Such a place, if it did exist, would be profoundly "unnatural."

There is also the very common situation where the history in a historic district, as that history has been conceived, and the ways in which a district is now being used differ widely. The history does not relate to what is happening now. Only the architectural facades may bear any significant relationship to it. How can one present here the history of disruption or absence of continuity? Districts of this type are the rule rather than the exception. A predominant feature of the history of American cities has been the frequency of change both in the uses to which districts are put and in the type of people who live in them. Historic preservation does not readily represent this salient feature of American life, this propensity for "moving on" shown by Americans, a very mobile people who have, as de Tocqueville said, "a restless temper." Constant movement of people in and out of districts has been a commonplace of American urban history. Seeking new housing in new districts to reflect enhanced socioeconomic status has always been part of the American way of life.[40] Throughout American history the upwardly mobile have abandoned homes and districts for new locations, and their former homes have been occupied by nonelite people. This is particularly true of the "zones of transition" that so many inner-city districts have become. Many districts that once housed the elite have subsequently been occupied by the very poor—and then perhaps at a later stage nearer our own time by gentrifying young professionals. Many one-time elite districts have become home to people of different ethnicity and socioeconomic status from those who first built the houses and lived there. The history of many city districts is a complicated story of the constant turnover of social and ethnic groups. And that history continues.

One result is that there are many historic districts in which the history that is being remembered is not the history of the ancestors of the people who now live in them. This is particularly the case with two kinds of district, those that have been abandoned by the white middle classes and those that have been occupied—often reoccupied—by them through gentrification. Such districts raise the issues of whose history historic districts should represent and of who "owns" the history within them. Many districts that have undergone gentrification, one of the more recent episodes in the seemingly endless flow of tides of American residential and social mobility, have had a complex history. Often the initial settlement of these districts had been by affluent people who built homes to reflect their status and then abandoned them and the district for the suburbs. Then came occupation of the houses (in a much more intensive way and usually as tenants) by lower-income people, often African Americans. Gentrification, most notoriously in Georgetown, has seemed too often to result in the displacement of these people by affluent whites who were returning from the suburbs.

These latest occupants of districts that have seen many other kinds of residents in bygone eras have been criticized for their attitudes to the history of their new neighborhoods. Many people who move into gentrifying districts have preferred to identify with the affluent lifestyles of the builders of the houses. Much of what is done to "restore" such a neighborhood is designed to remind people of that era and to blot out what had happened to the houses and the district in the intervening years, or to describe it as a regrettable period of decay and deterioration that is fortunately about to end. Brett Williams accused the gentrifiers in Washington, D.C., especially Georgetown, of trying to create an artificial and baseless community of memory out of a sanitized past. She argued that they have no real roots in their new neighborhood and yet seek to cling to an invented history in which they have not shared. Many of them have lodged their own histories in other places and among other people. The history of their new district is not theirs. Because they can identify with it only in a nonpersonal way, it has become "heritage."[41] Another historian, T. H. Breen, has concluded that for recent arrivals seeking to define a historical identity for their newly acquired neighborhoods, the appearance of a tradition and a heritage seemed to be all that mattered.[42] In contrast, a bulletin in the National Trust's Information Series has pointed out that changes of occupation of a district have characterized the history of many communities, especially in large cities, for a long time, "and there is ample evidence that people need not be the original settlers to value a neighborhood's historic character as a part of contemporary life."[43] It does acknowledge that issues will and do arise as to who owns the "history."

Many districts that were once the locations of the homes of the rich and that still have an architectural legacy from that era have not been gentrified—"regentrified" might be a more appropriate term—and are still occupied largely by poorer people of nonwhite ethnicity. Michael Tomlan has pointed out how much of the nation's cultural heritage is now in black care.[44] In 1976 Richard Ortega wrote of the consequences for preservationism of the lack in ghetto areas of "strong cultural and social identification with the once-elegant townhouses of an earlier era's bourgeoisie. . . . Designation and its protection must substitute for the culture that previously kept the areas vital."[45] However, one black conservationist saw an opportunity: he described black people as having become the custodians of the nation's architectural legacy and urged them not to desert it but to use it to their own advantage.[46]

There is a history in all this. It is the history of transience and mobility and of their impacts on community structure and stability. It is not a history that historic districts have been conceptualized to convey, and yet it is a history in which there are substantial continuities that underlie and transcend the apparent flux and impermanence. Change itself is a constant, and the experience of in- and out-migration is shared by generations of people, although of different ethnic and social backgrounds. Sherry Olson, in her analysis of the pattern of living in Baltimore, has argued that "the physical patterns and variations designed in earlier generations are differentially occupied and maintained. The scale, grain, and texture built into the landscape continue to provide the set of sieves by which today's society sorts people in terms of income, race, occupation, and age."[47] The type of resident may have kept changing, but the district's fabric frequently retains homogeneity and is still acting at any given time as a container for people of one particular social grouping. In architectural terms a district may continue to be homogeneous enough to be eligible for historic district status.

But the social history will be something very different. Matching the two is one of the most vexing issues confronting the agencies involved with establishing the character, identity, and purpose of historic districts.

Another aspect of urban diversity that is revealed in debates over which history historic districts should represent is generational. It is often newcomers who are attracted to "historic character" in places whose history is neither theirs nor their ancestors'. Older people may take a jaundiced view of the romanticizing, myth making, and historicizing that accompany historic district development, in particular the support for it by people who did not live through the actual history that is to be remembered in this form. An article about Park City, Utah, in *Historic Preservation* reported that older residents "have not always favored attempts to revitalize the older area of town." There were adverse reactions to a proposal to put back the original streetlights. "Some old-timers think the newcomers are a bit too romantic about what the town really was. They remember how jerry-built many of the plain wooden houses were—thrown up to keep up with the mining boom—and wonder whether there is much worth saving." It was also reported that some of the newer residents "feel that the unimproved homes and peeling paint contribute to the aging charm of the historic district."[48]

Five

Selecting History

*I*T IS NOW MORE THAN THIRTY YEARS SINCE PAS-
sage of the National Historic Preservation Act and establishment of
the National Register. The historic districts that were brought into being as
a result of these initiatives are themselves passing into history. The history
they represent is something above and beyond the history in whose name
their creation was justified and of which the structures within them are
claimed to be a legacy. They are also embodiments of certain ideas, values,
and preoccupations of the era in which they were created. For most of them
this is the 1970s and 1980s, an era in which they were at the forefront not
only of historic preservation but also of strategies to save neighborhoods.
The more we become distanced from that period, the more the districts will
be seen as a part of its history and studied from that perspective. Indeed,
there was a certain peculiarity about the notion of interpreting the "history"
of a district as having come to an end and turning the district itself into a
sort of commentary on or summation of its own historical development.

Historic districts are historical artifacts much more than timeless com-
mentaries on a finished history. Their significance should be seen to lie as
much in what they tell us of the perceptions of the "historical" predominating in the era in which they were created as in the history they purport
to record, represent, and commemorate. That history arrives to us in this
guise in such a filtered, selective, and manipulated form that its usefulness
as a way into what "actually happened" in the past is open to question. Dis-

junctions are bound to emerge between newly dominant historical interpretations and preoccupations and those that were embodied—seemingly
for all time—in the structure and raison d'être of many of these historic
districts formed in an earlier age. A likely forerunner of the way in which
interpretations of historic districts will focus more and more on them as a
product of their age is what has been happening in Colonial Williamsburg.
Much of our interest in it now concerns what its restoration reveals of the
way the past was interpreted and understood in the early part of the twentieth century.

As the fifty-year cut-off point extends beyond 1966, it is conceivable
that a historic district might ultimately qualify to become a historic district
all over again because of what it reveals about the history of our own times.
A gentrified district will surely in time be of historic interest in the same
way as a New Deal planned community is today. Already in many districts
the historic preservation and restoration associated with gentrification have
become part of the history that is on display, perhaps the predominant part.
If one visits a historic district such as Old Town Triangle in Chicago (NR
1984), the phenomenon that presses itself most on one is not the history of
the people who once lived there and built the houses but the remarkable
feats of restoration that have been carried out.

Yet few descriptions of historic districts in architectural and other
guidebooks comment on either the consequences or the significance of the
processes that led to their transformation into historic districts. Already we
have noted the scant awareness of what happened to districts in the era of
"survival" between the original time and the point when a different generation decided that what was left from that era should be deemed "historic."
The history of what happened to districts in the often lengthy period between the original history that is being emphasized and the present is seldom being told. But, in addition, what is conspicuously absent from the
presentation and interpretation of most historic districts is historic preservation itself. There is little description of the feats of historic preservation and restoration that have gone into producing districts as they appear
today. Visitors are frequently invited to experience the historic environments as if they "were really there then"—wherever and whenever "there"
and "then" might be. There is an emphasis on what is now, not on what
is no longer and why it is no longer—although some places do provide
guides to what has disappeared, usually to make a point in a campaign for
preservation of what is left.

This chapter brings us to the third phase of the history of historic
districts, their creation. There has been much debate among sociologists
as to the significance of this phase. It deserves more attention also from

urban historians. In particular, it has been asked whether historic districts, in which regimes of control over changes to buildings and townscape elements have been established, block "normal" urban evolution and, if so, whether this is a good thing. Is historic districting a form of detached observation of history or an intervention into it, deserving to be seen as part of history and judged as such? Preservationists have come in for a good deal of criticism for their form of interventionism. They have been urged not to block normal, organic processes of change by turning dynamic, living cities into static museums.[1] Walter C. Kidney in Pittsburgh likened that form of preservationism to urban renewal against which it had itself been a rebellion. It too threatened to "stop the neighborhood's historical process, albeit only as regards what the eye can see."[2] His qualification acknowledges a point that frequently occurs in these arguments: *social* change cannot be halted even if the architectural shell within which it is continuing to occur is frozen.

Is it wise or safe, some ask, to intervene in allegedly "natural" processes of change in towns and cities? This raises the question of whether there *are* normal, organic processes or whether all change in cities has been the consequence of some form of human intervention, planned or unplanned. If the latter is the case, preservation is but one form of intervention and is in no way abnormal. Albert Hunter, in a study of community life and changes in the structure of communities in Chicago published in 1974, claimed that local community organizations were increasingly trying to "control ecological structure by aiding or altering the processes of invasion, succession, and competition."[3] The many organizations concerned about urban renewal and rehabilitation had been, in his view, "specifically oriented to *planning* a reversal" of what had hitherto been "*natural* processes of invasion, movement, and decay." These processes were being countered by "planned processes of change and maintenance of a specific ecological structure for the local community."[4] Historic districting is clearly relevant to this argument in that it aims to counter the particular "natural" processes to which Hunter refers. It is, of course, allied in this respect to all the different forms of zoning that have been established in American cities over the course of the twentieth century. Indeed, we have seen the close relationship between historic district development and zoning controls, beginning with Charleston in the 1930s. The difference is that this kind of zoning is being justified in the name of "history" and therefore invites comment on the divergence between the historical interpretations that it seeks to establish and the realities of urban change that it frequently seeks to counter or reverse but that themselves are part of a community's history.

A couple of examples may be used to illustrate the issues surrounding historic district creation as a form of intervention in urban change in the name of history. One concerns ghost towns. Their decay is sometimes "arrested" by park and other authorities in subtle and "invisible" ways that leave the impression that the town is perpetually hovering on but never quite reaching the point of disappearance. One of the most spectacular ghost towns in this state of arrested decay is Bodie, California.[5] According to one preservationist in 1974, it "would be a mistake to restore Bodie. Leaning buildings, broken windows and sagging roofs are an asset and must be retained if the ghost town atmosphere is to be preserved. Stabilization of the buildings, however, will be important to keep them from disappearing entirely. The intent is to crystallize Bodie exactly as it was when acquired."[6] What was done at Bodie remains controversial. There are pressures today for renewed mining near such ghost towns. The reaction at Bodie has been to attempt to expand its boundaries as a historic district and thereby stop renewed mining activity. In 1991 a preservationist wrote to *Preservation News* querying the decision to stop the evolution of a place—even one such as Bodie, whose history did seem to have come to a definitive ending. Why should Bodie, he asked, be protected from the latest boom-and-bust episode in its history? The impulses leading to such an episode now—an episode of "bust"—were just the same as those that had operated throughout the town's history. After all, if the state had decided to freeze Bodie's development in 1882, it would not be the historic landmark it is today.[7] Of course, mining technology today is very different, and the areas where gold is sought would no longer be as isolated as Bodie and innumerable other gold rush settlements were. Therefore, it is most unlikely that Bodie would revive in anything like its original form even if gold were again being mined in its vicinity. A town of that sort simply would not be required. But a new kind of mining landscape would emerge. Fifty years from now that too would be "history." Who are we to stop it from happening in the name of history?

A second example concerns the role of large mansions or estates in a historic district. The authors of the 1977 report, *Values of Residential Properties in Urban Historic Districts*, commented that in Georgetown the large mansions and townhouses "contribute importantly to the character of the district as a whole." Indeed, the notable houses with their landscaped grounds were "pivotal properties within the area" because the strategically situated open space they provide "relieves the otherwise intensive development" of the district's residential blocks. The report argued that to maintain Georgetown's "delicately attuned ambience," it was critical that the remaining land parcels of significant size remain intact. The problem was that a rapid and disproportionate rise in land values had "increased incentives to divide these larger parcels." The authors acknowledge that the subdivision of such estates has been a feature of the history of Georgetown since the very beginning. "It is interesting to note that of the 194 sites in Georgetown improved with structures built before 1825, at least 147 are divisions from original lots."[8] So here a trend that was part of the "historic" era itself, and helped to make the historic district what it is today, now has to be checked to help maintain the "historic" nature of the district.

Explanations for why some "historic" districts are not accorded recognition are to be found in the history of our own times.

To find an example of the paramountcy of contemporary considerations, one needs only to ask why there was such a rapid growth in the number of historic districts. One of the most important reasons was the federal tax credit regime established in 1976 by the Tax Reform Act. Tax credits encouraged and rewarded investment in the rehabilitation not merely of individual structures but also of large numbers of structures within districts. The development of historic districts since has closely followed the fortunes of federal policy on tax credits, which has undergone repeated changes. Three examples of the significance of tax credit policies may be drawn from one very small, one medium-size, and one very large community. At Weston, Missouri, historic district designation in 1972 is seen as having led to new interest in the downtown business area. Eventually, in 1982, the Weston Development Company was formed. It worked with the Historical Museum and the Board of Aldermen to secure the Historic Building Ordinance, which preserved the integrity of Main Street.[9] In Philadelphia the Center City has twenty National Register districts, "the largest concentration of National Register districts in the downtown area of any major American city." Philadelphia is described as having "found rehabilitation tax credits to be an important urban revitalization tool" and as having "led the mid-Atlantic region in its use of the tax credits."[10] When the tax credits were substantially reduced by the Tax Reform Act of 1986, Philadelphia was undeterred: its new Center City Plan of 1988 actually recommended that the boundaries of its National Register districts be expanded "in order to make more buildings eligible for the federal investment tax credits allowed on the rehabilitation of historic properties." The city "want[ed] to be in a good position to take advantage of the credits in the event Congress decide[d] to restore their usefulness."[11] In Harrisburg, the city council, seeing historic preservation as a response to the city's seriously depressed state at the beginning of the 1980s, inaugurated formal historic preservation programs in 1982. Since then, Harrisburg's proactive historic preservation program has included creating historic districts—each National Register historic district was nominated by the city, and there are municipal historic districts as well—and taking maximum advantage of tax

credits. There has been an enormous volume of certified historic rehabilitation investment in Harrisburg since 1983.[12]

Another way to appreciate the limited role of purely "historical" factors is to consider the phenomenon of districts that appear to be just as
"historic"—in first-stage terms—as those that have received official designation in their vicinity yet have not been designated. The reasons for their
omission often turn out to have little connection with official criteria or au-
thoritatively stated definitions of what should be regarded as historic.

Frequently there is considerable debate—and even controversy—in a
community over whether to seek or accept historic district designation,
especially the local kind where controls over private property are involved.
"History" does not play a conspicuous role in these debates. While sup-
porters have tended to place great emphasis on the probability of increased
property values, there are many fears and concerns that sometimes carry
the day.[13] For instance, there has frequently been considerable concern over
the displacement of the poor and the elderly, who cannot afford the increased rental costs that often seem to result from the impact of gentrification on property values. Historic preservation received a bad name in some
quarters for being associated with this sort of thing. Low-income minorities
have been replaced by affluent middle-class newcomers in places such as
Georgetown, Alexandria, and the Church Hill section of Richmond, Virginia. It has often been pointed out that gentrification and displacement
have occurred in many places that were not designated historic districts,
and indeed there are many causes of displacement. But instances emerged
of residents of districts that were starting to undergo gentrification organizing to oppose historic preservation and, especially, historic district designation. In Charleston, where the historic district phenomenon might be
said to have begun, an expansion of the historic district was rejected because of fears of displacement.[14] There fears have been real, but real estate
interests, who want free rein for their development activities, have often
been all too ready to join in and fan the flames. The same has been true of
politicians when they have seen political capital in opposing historic preservation. Historic preservation, intended as a means to stabilize and protect
neighborhoods, has been depicted as destroying them.

There is inescapably a major political dimension to historic district development. Miller's conclusion, after several years of service on Cincinnati's
Historic Conservation Board and the Ohio Historic Preservation Advisory
Committee, was that "politics is a critical if not the crucial factor in determining historic district boundaries, despite our elaborate discussions of
architectural integrity, historically significant events, persons, groups, institutions, and urban design and aesthetic issues."[15] The political dimension is

by no means confined to considerations of the impact of historic district designation on property rights and values. History itself enters substantially into this area of contemporary politics. This is because the struggle over historic interpretation is often a struggle to acquire the predominating influence over a community's future direction. The history in whose name preservation is justified and developed can become highly politicized. This is why the substitution of a long past, even mythical history that has little relationship to anything in the present except impressive old buildings is often preferred.

An example that has been extensively documented by Miller is the struggle over the interpretation of the past of the Over-the-Rhine district adjacent to downtown Cincinnati. By the early 1980s there were four documents projecting four different futures for this neighborhood. These were based in part on different views of its past or rather different emphases on facets of what had been a complex past. Which of these interpretations prevailed mattered a great deal because each had relevance to current planning and ideas about community development. While each construed the meaning of ethnicity differently, "all of them treated the history of ethnic groups in a way that made control of the past crucial to the control of the future of the neighborhood."[16]

History can also be seen entering into another area of concern that appears at first glance to be basically economic. When the Borough Council for Upland, Pennsylvania, repealed the local historic district ordinance, William McGlaughlin of the state's Bureau of Historic Preservation, commented, "It's a classic breakdown of new arrivals who liked historic character versus long-time residents who didn't think they could afford all this stuff."[17] But there is more to these concerns than just economics. They appear also when people who are going to be affected are themselves part of the history in whose name the preservation is to be undertaken. Ortega sees "an inherent conflict between the way people and neighborhoods age and the way preservationists measure time." Hostility can result from attempts to relegate a community's recent past to "history." "The imposition of historicism on a district whose life, vigor and character were intimately intertwined with the longtime residents' own lives could not but impose on them the label which their neighborhood had acquired—they too were historical, they too were designated."[18] The intertwining of these economic and generational sensitivities has been brought out in a study of two districts in Philadelphia.

Many newcomers are interested in the preservation of old housing styles, and have had the facades of their dwellings restored to the "original" appearance. In Queen Village, the older of the two neighborhoods, historic certification of houses is popular among new residents. By contrast, more old-timers prefer simple and functional structures, and have covered their facades with artificial stone and have added aluminum storm and screen doors. Problems arise when well-meaning newcomers suggest to neighbors that they fix up their house "the way it is supposed to be." This is more than an insult about the appearance of a house; it is also indicative of an attitude that consciously promotes neighborhood change. Old residents resist such suggestions because they are well aware that tax reassessments generally follow in the wake of highly visible improvements. Many have thus come to consider renovated exteriors, be they historic or modern, as symbols of unwanted intrusion and unwelcome change.[19]

Usable and Nonusable Pasts

One of the principal reasons why some history has been selected for commemoration in this form and some has not is that historic districts are a form of usable history. A wish to use the past, as it can be portrayed and commemorated in historic districts, to help towns, cities, and neighborhoods cope with the challenges of the present and the future has frequently been a motivation for seeking historic district designation. What might be called pure commemoration of the past is rare. History has been put to a wide variety of contemporary uses. As a result, the past that is usable has tended to be favored over that which is not.

The reasons for which designation has been sought vary widely. Some historic districts have been promoted for "internal" reasons, for example, to aid with housing rehabilitation, to promote neighborhood stabilization, or to protect properties from undesirable intrusions that will disturb the established character of a neighborhood. Others are concerned with a desire to attract the interest of outsiders, especially tourists. The latter desire is often, perhaps usually, not present at the beginning but may emerge—or be imposed on a district—as a town or city becomes aware of the income-generating potential of its historic districts. Lowell, Massachusetts, is an example of a town that, by means of a major commitment to development and marketing of heritage, has gone from being a place of minimal appeal to a major tourist attraction. Yet while some historic districts advertise themselves, others are far more discreet, having sought designation as a source of protection from intrusion and not as a means of inviting it.

Creating pride in community, and a sense of community identity and "uniqueness," has been a constant theme in justifications for seeking historic district development. This is seen particularly in the involvement of modern-day boosting and urban promotion in historic district development. The status of a historic district and the prestige of having a district accepted onto the National Register are often cause for considerable local pride, especially when preceded by enormous effort to assemble and make the case for recognition.[20] Plaques and notices frequently advise visitors and residents that they are in a National Register Historic District. Numerous towns regard their historic districts as status symbols and like to boast about how many they have. There is a tradition underlying these attitudes: the development of historic districts has a connection to some of the principal and most abiding themes of urban boosting in the United States. Those traditions survive in the conceptualization and promotion of historic districts. An example of this is the significance of the prominence that has been attached to prestigious elite districts. Old reputations and images of districts are being revived or perpetuated via historic districts.[21]

The ability to create and manage historic districts is being put to use in the promotion of a wide variety of community goals. Historic district nominations have often been the result of the implementation of neighborhood and district rehabilitation strategies.[22] For instance, the designation of commercial districts has commonly come through involvement in one of the now numerous Main Street programs.[23] Making the business district a historic district and taking advantage of tax credits have been major components in many packages of Main Street rehabilitation strategies. An example of a small town whose historic preservation program has had as its principal purpose the refashioning of its image is Okmulgee, Oklahoma. The image that had developed was of a traditional western town, "a rough-and-tumble sort of town." In 1986 Okmulgee applied to become part of the Oklahoma Main Street Program. The new image that was chosen derived from the boom era of the 1920s, and restoration was organized to focus on the architectural legacy of that era. By 1991 there had been extensive facade restoration and a "new sense of pride."[24] In 1992 Okmulgee's downtown was placed on the National Register.

The prominence of community rehabilitation strategies in the development of historic districts derives in part from the role of local organizations that have taken the initiative in arranging their nomination. "In the United States, citizen pressure plays an important role in determining what gets designated. . . . Grass roots agitation has played a significant role in getting an ever wider array of places protected as historic districts."[25] Indeed, some states provide for citizen approval of the establishment of historic districts via referenda.[26] Much historic district development has been the result of reaction to some traumatic event in the life of a community. One of the most common of these has been the actual or impending destruction of a landmark structure whose significance is seen not so much in architectural terms as in the associations it has had over the years with the community. At Grand Rapids, Michigan, for instance, the Heritage Hill Association was formed following the destruction of the city hall in 1969.[27] Another catalyst has been a threat to a neighborhood, whether from urban renewal or from the expansion plans of an institution such as a hospital or a university.[28] The strongly district-oriented preservationism in San Antonio is largely the work of the San Antonio Conservation Society, which originated in campaigns in the 1920s to save first the old Market House that was threatened with demolition and then the downtown portion of the river—now the Paseo del Rio—that the city was going to cement over to create a parking area and a storm sewer.[29] At Pullman the catalyst was a proposal in 1960 to rezone the area for light industrial use. In Guthrie, Oklahoma, the destruction of downtown buildings led to the formation of organizations to stop more demolitions; historic district designation came in 1974, and the historical society persuaded the city to pass a historic preservation ordinance in 1978.[30] Another catalyst has been concern over the impact of the growth of nearby metropolitan areas. This often threatens to overwhelm the traditional character of small, hitherto relatively separate and isolated communities through, for instance, the acquisition of properties by city commuters or the development of facilities to cater to the recreational needs of the metropolitan population.[31] At Steilacoom, Washington, pressure came from the expansion of Tacoma-Seattle and the influx of new residents. Preservationists were stirred into action by the bulldozing of old sea captains' homes.[32]

Often, especially in smaller towns, the inspiration and community enthusiasm for district preservation have originated in the efforts put into the restoration of a landmark building. Such campaigns can become the focus for a sense of restored community identity and purpose.[33] The threatened destruction of a landmark structure can rally preservationists and suggest the possibility of using that building as a focus for urban rehabilitation. For example, in 1981 the Norfolk and Western Railway bought the station at Richmond, Indiana, and proposed to tear it down. "The outcry from preservationists and city officials has thus far prevented its destruction. Projecting the station as the keystone of Richmond's new Enterprise Zone and the proposed Fort Wayne Ave. Historic District, the city purchased the property from Norfolk and Western in 1985 and is holding it for future sale and development."[34] The Richmond Railroad Station Historic District was entered on the National Register in 1987. Restoration of the Opera House at Granbury, Texas, sparked interest in restoring the square in which it was located—and this restoration was in turn a major source of inspiration for the National Trust's Main Street Program.[35]

Disasters can inspire efforts to renew a town through strategies of preservation and restoration of the historic areas that remain. Destructive, traumatic events such as tornados and hurricanes heighten awareness of the vulnerability of heritage. They tend to produce the same effect as urban renewal, the concentration of surviving heritage into "fragments" that stand out dramatically, almost defiantly, from the surrounding swaths of destruction and are valued as representations of so much else that has been lost. Hurricane Agnes in 1972 was a catalyst for renewal in many places, especially when followed by allocations of government funds for restoration.[36] In Harrisburg the Historic Harrisburg Association was formed in 1973 in the aftermath of the devastation caused by Hurricane Agnes. Federal funds were used following Hurricane Agnes to refurbish Market Street in Corning, New York.[37] At Ellicott City, Maryland, the hurricane arrived just as the town was embarking on its bicentennial celebrations, and celebration of the latter provided extra force to the already existing desire to restore the old town.[38] A tornado raced through and devastated the Old Town Historic District in Petersburg, Virginia (NR 1980), on August 6, 1993. Although still in its early stages, recovery is taking place, and it will be of interest to see to what extent the theme of renewal and recovery becomes worked into the refashioning of Petersburg's self-image as a community.[39] Here a historic district that has been established for fourteen years has now had a powerful new element of history injected into it, an element that other communities have exploited to give a new theme—and a new urgency—to historic preservation strategies.

The "heritage" townscape that is highlighted in modern urban planning and rehabilitation reawakens echoes of some of the booster-inspired, but seldom realized, visions that underlay much of the early development of towns. To a remarkable extent, sometimes quite consciously, agencies responsible for schemes of urban rehabilitation have reached back to ideals that were formulated when a town or district was first settled. They have used buildings and townscape features that are legacies of those ideals. An example is the heightened emphasis on elite houses and elaborate, aesthetically pleasing public buildings at the expense of humbler dwellings and less pretentious halls.

The promotion of historic districts has often involved reviving images from the glorious pasts of the towns concerned.[40] Centennials and other kinds of historical commemoration have frequently given a boost to the consciousness of the history of a district and provided incentive and funds to do something about it.[41] Obviously the history selected for attention on such occasions will be highly selective. A common theme is that of rebirth and revival—just as the phoenix symbol was used in nineteenth-century boosting after the numerous fires and other calamities that towns experienced. Modern-day boosters are just as anxious as their nineteenth-century predecessors to find ways of making their towns and cities distinctive in relation to their rivals. The nature of the rivalry may have changed somewhat, but history has a role to play. For example, the steering committee for the Lower Downtown Historic District in Denver "determined that if the city lost the valuable buildings in this area, it would lose a treasure that set Denver apart from not only its suburbs, but other cities as well."[42]

There are echoes of the booster era in some of the publicity surrounding historic districts today. Anderson, Indiana, for instance, boomed after 1887 with the discovery of natural gas. Many years later, after the boom era had long since passed and urban renewal had done its worst, the citizens rediscovered the street that was the very epitome of that era: West Eighth Street (NR 1976). The Historic West 8th Street Society was formed after residents donated gaslights and organized a gaslight festival in 1973. The society's aim was to restore it to the grandeur it had known as "Anderson Street [its name then], The Center of Culture for Anderson, Indiana, the Queen City of the Gas-Boom Era."[43]

A town's "golden age," when its elite district or districts last looked their best, was often the time when it enjoyed its fullest prosperity and when nineteenth-century urban boosterism was at its peak. There are some striking links between the publicity associated with historic districts and the themes and aspirations of those earlier eras. For example, a brochure issued to publicize the historic district of the former Missouri River port of Weston (NR 1972), left high and fairly dry when the river altered course, declares, "With this guarantee of preservation, almost 15,000 square feet of retail space has been restored and many new businesses have begun to recreate the bustling pre–Civil War era of business activity." The aim of the city boosters is to "reestablish the city of Weston as the active center of commerce that existed before the Civil War."[44]

In some towns and cities the drive to create historic districts has come from concerted initiatives in which restoration of pride in the community is seen as linked to the restoration of buildings and districts whose features exemplify eras when there was pride and confidence. At Muncie, Indiana, for instance, a historic district strategy came out of its Pride Task Force in 1987. Four of Muncie's six National Register historic districts came after 1987, and a fifth, originally designated in 1980, had its boundaries extended in 1989.[45] It is often stated, or at least implied in much preservation activity,

Downtown Syracuse, New York. One way in which historic districts come into be-ing. The removal of fronts that were added later reveal Victorian facades.

that there is a relationship between buildings and levels of economic optimism. In this way buildings can be given modern relevance. The idea is that somehow the mood of the original boosters might rub off via restoration of the buildings they created to display their wealth and their confidence in the town's future. There seems to have been a resurgence of belief in the inspirational impact of architecture—something inherited, perhaps, from the time when the focus of historic preservationism was on the houses of the famous. This reached a peak in the enthusiasm for restoration of the mills at Lowell. According to a 1978 report, *A Future from the Past,* "A tremendous dynamism and community spirit surrounded and supported the construction of the mills, and the legacy of this spirit was written into the architecture of that same period. It is a thoroughly human document of what these places have meant to people in the past. Today it can become a model for the regeneration of community spirit and faith in the future, and a source of pride and confidence in the present." [46]

Much of the emphasis in the Main Street program has been on finding strategies to counter moods of "pessimism." [47] An example of this approach is a "socioarchitectural account" of the buildings of Westminster, Maryland, undertaken by Christopher Weeks as a prelude to devising a conservation program for that town. His aim was to rediscover the social meanings of the architectural styles that had been used. He pointed out that buildings can be seen as symbols of "faith in the community." In his view, there is continuity between past and present in, for instance, decisions by banks to renovate and adapt old downtown buildings. He argued that the styles of downtown commercial buildings "reflect the optimistic dynamism of a century ago." [48] Much the same theme has been picked up in a book on the Upper West Side in New York City. "New Yorkers of the nineteenth and early twentieth centuries had a tremendous gift for accomplishment," it says, "and an enviable belief in themselves and their future, and their buildings are a physical embodiment of that energy and optimism. Maybe preserving them will help keep *us* optimistic and energetic." [49] And this approach often does seem to pay dividends—at least in the short term. The energy and the funding that are devoted to urban renovation do inject, even if only temporarily, new currents of enthusiasm and activity into downtown business life.

The notion that the past can be put to use in these ways causes some confusion because it conflicts with the basic evolutionary ideas that, as we have seen, have supplied a framework for understanding not only urban development but also its representation in historic districts. Business people often have difficulty understanding what relationship there might be between progress and an emphasis on the past via historic preservation. [50] In 1969 Arthur P. Ziegler, Jr., reported that South Side merchants in Pittsburgh were very hesitant to support restoration of Victorian buildings: "It baffles their notion of progress which to them has always meant discarding the past and modernizing."[51] After all, that was what happened in the Victorian Era itself: the very buildings that were now the focus of preservation campaigns often stood as proof of that. The Victorians were energetic "modernizers" of the buildings *they* had inherited from the past. Negative attitudes to the past led then, and can lead now, to a readiness to see old buildings go. In Scranton the Architectural Heritage Association (AHA) of Northeastern Pennsylvania recently fought to stop the demolition of twenty downtown buildings in the Lackawanna Avenue Commercial Historic District (NR 1983) to provide for a shopping mall. Cynthia Zujkowski, an AHA board member, commented, "This is a town that was poor for so long and does not have a good sense of self worth. . . . [T]here is no pride in the past." The old buildings are "a symbol of failure."[52] More commonly, evolutionary ideas about the "inevitable" course of change in towns and cities have led to an assumption that old buildings are destined to go. There have been serious conflicts between modern-day boosterism and preservationism. By the mid-1950s the businessmen of St. Joseph, Missouri, for instance, had "grown discontented with the old buildings and the sleepy river-town image." The message of the chamber of commerce campaign was, "Think proud. St. Joseph is changing horses [also a theme from the past]. We are shaking off the past for a brilliant future."[53]

One of the major themes of the use of history in modern-day boosterism is the exploitation of inspirational examples of how in the past towns responded to times of crisis. Emphasis on past trials and crises to show how a town survived them is a common theme in explanations of the significance of historic preservation today. Barbara Rasmussen, chair of the Historic Landmarks Commission of Morgantown, West Virginia, writes, "I hope to see the local understanding of our town's historical significance take on an appreciation of the municipality's resilience, having survived difficult transitions of its own, through the nation's many changes."[54] The guide to the historic preservation program of Harrisburg states, "In the development and growth of the Nation, many communities have risen and fallen based on the events and fortunes of a single era. Harrisburg, a key transportation center since the mid-18th Century, has endured and, with a diverse economy, is today the region's center."[55] It is common for people to be invited to look at a city's stock of historic districts and buildings and draw a lesson about the character of the community from the fact that so much has survived and in such good condition.

An example of the way in which connections are made between a town's current needs and a history of survival in the face of adversity is a walking tour brochure issued by the Bangor Historical Society. Old booster slogans are revived: the historic districts of Bangor are described as "a proud reminder of the time when the Queen City was the Lumber Capital of the World." Thoreau is quoted as having described Bangor as a "shining light on the edge of the wilderness." The city is described as a survivor, and the historical record is invoked to prove this. The town's many trials are referred to. "And, yet," it points out, "throughout the 19th and early 20th century, in the best and worst of times, Bangor aspired economically, politically and culturally to a standard of excellence, unsurpassed in most areas of the nation. . . . Today, Bangor continues to survive. It is adapting to a changing society, exploring new directions and, yet, while looking toward the future, the city seeks to recapture the vitality of the vision that created and sustained it in the past." Much is made of the city's response to the Great Fire of 1911, which devastated the business district. "The city refused to be defeated. . . . The Great Fire District is an architectural monument to the dynamic spirit and will to survive. . . . The City seems determined to expand and prosper, as it has often done in the past. And by embracing those tenets of excellence that have guided the city through much of its history, Bangor will be ready to gracefully confront the 21st century, like a dignified old lady who gratefully acknowledges her past but looks to the future." The last phrase captures the essence of the booster perspective on history. At Bangor survival of multiple catastrophes has been made the theme in particular of the West Market Square Historic District (NR 1979). Seven commercial buildings remain here as a fragment not just from the Great Fire but also from urban renewal in the 1960s.

Past, Present, and Future

Themes that set up relationships and lines of continuity between past, present, and future are frequently used in the promotion of historic districts. A brochure supplied to visitors to the old river town of Columbia, Pennsylvania, is typical in emphasizing its history and then inviting the visitor to "come away with both a feel of the past and pride in the future." Attitudes to the past as reflected in historic preservation are markedly future-oriented. In historic preservationism the past is also the future. It is common for those responsible for publicizing a "historic" town to explore the paradox that the town's future "lies in [its] past."[56] At Waycross, Georgia, the aim has been described as being to "build our economic future on the quality of our past."[57] This phrase has been frequently used in connection with Lowell. It is a theme that has also been taken up by preservationist promoters of the Main Street program. Antoinette Lee has written, "Many communities wish to frame their future in terms of their past."[58] In 1984 Mary C. Means wrote, "The National Main Street Center's emphasis on quality in design for buildings of *all* periods addresses the need for a sense of continuity, linking the town's past with the present and positioning it for the future."[59] Carol Galbreath referred thus to the significance of historic preservation in one small town: "With its revival, Jacksonville [Oregon] . . . illustrates the small town paradox: Small towns change in order to stay the same. The town was rejuvenated—it grew younger—by showing its age."[60]

Historic districts have often been a significant part of strategies to create or reinforce desired images. *Conserve Neighborhoods*, a 1978 National Trust newsletter, said that a key factor influencing a neighborhood's future was its public image and that historic district status could help in this regard.[61] Thus the neighborhood associations that wished to revive the Historic Hill District of St. Paul believed that one of their principal tasks had to be to dispel negative perceptions about the neighborhood. Designation of the area as a historic district was a significant opportunity to do this. House tours were held each year, and a video was made and shown extensively. "The new, positive identity of the Historic Hill District began to grow as the negative impressions were erased."[62]

T. Allan Comp is one prominent preservationist who has strongly advocated the use of history to restore community pride. His experience had been in mill towns, where he observed that learning about their town's past had helped to make the local people more confident about the future. Claremont, New Hampshire, for example, "wanted to hold onto the industrial buildings that had helped to create it, and its history became a way of learning how Claremont once used and could again use those mills as both symbols of its past and a promise of its future." In his view the same had happened in Augusta, the "Lowell of Georgia." "Again, Augusta found in its own history, in an understanding of its own past, a kind of promise for its future." Other kinds of community had been similarly affected. For instance, Lockport, Illinois, had "literally turned its back on the canal that created it—physically lost touch with its own roots. Its history became a way of reorienting the perspective of a whole town and giving it a great deal more pride in itself." Comp is one who believes that architecture can convey inspirational messages to struggling communities. In the great mining city of Butte, Montana, he writes, "the boastful structures built by some of Butte's famous entrepreneurs as well as its small businessmen still speak of a pride and a kind of affluence that Butte can still build toward." There he learned "the real binding power of a shared historical perspective in a community."[63]

The most celebrated case of using historic district and historical park development to help to revive a town's pride in its future and thereby its economy has been Lowell. The complex of mill structures, dams, canals, and civic and institutional buildings at Lowell is regarded as one of the best surviving examples of the kind of industrial community established in the Northeast during the early stages of the American industrial revolution. By 1846 the mills at Lowell produced in excess of one million yards of cloth a week. By 1850 ten large mill complexes employed more than 10,000 people, and Lowell was the second-largest city in Massachusetts. From a population of 2,500 in 1826, it had grown to 33,000 at midcentury. The methods of production and the management of a largely female workforce attracted nationwide and indeed worldwide attention. A particular distinguishing feature of Lowell was its rows of brick boarding houses that accommodated female workers, many of whom had migrated to the town from rural areas. Most of these were eventually demolished as they fell into disuse. In the second half of the nineteenth century Lowell lost its primacy in textile manufacturing to new centers such as Fall River. Its inland river location, once a major asset, declined in significance as compared with seaports. Lowell did continue to be an important industrial center. But the feature for which it was now best known was the arrival of foreign immigrants to work in its mills. This characteristic of being a diverse ethnic community, attracting people from a remarkably high proportion of the successive waves of working-class immigration into the United States, has remained with it to the present day. The textile industry in Lowell went into decline in the early twentieth century as the mill owners failed to modernize their operations and machinery, often preferring to relocate in the South. The depression had a particularly devastating impact: by the mid-1930s most of the large mills had closed, and total employment in the textile industry was down to 8,000. Many of the buildings were completely or partially demolished.

Lowell Historical Park and the Lowell Historic Preservation Commission were established by Congress in 1978. The Boott Mills, one of the last surviving mill buildings (the company closed in 1954), have been extensively renovated. The building is now a museum: one room, the weave room, has been fitted out with scores of machines operating to produce fabric. When these are working the noise is deafening, and visitors are urged to wear earplugs while walking through. The aim is to reproduce at least one part of the original environment in which the work was carried out. Lowell is much more than just a historic district. The "historic" core of the old mill city is treated as both museum and park. The "heritage" buildings and canals are landscaped, and there is much sculpture and symbolic representation of aspects of the city's past. There are many festivals throughout the year and a strong emphasis on use of the amenities surviving from the industrial era, especially the canal network, for recreational purposes.

The theme employed at Lowell was revitalization through the rediscovery of heritage—at least of those facets of the city's heritage that could be used to give it a new, positive image. The aim was to replace Lowell's image of decline.[64] But using the past to do that was a complex exercise. For there were many negative features of the past, and these were all too evident in Lowell's highly depressed condition. There had been pride in achievement, but there had also been suffering and conflict. It was an ambiguous legacy, which meant that treatment of it would have to be careful— and selective. As noted in a 1977 sociological study of what had happened at Lowell, many of Lowell's problems could be attributed to "the legacy of its past." Yet paradoxically that very legacy was now to be used to give the town a new lease on life.[65]

In 1978 the U.S. Department of Housing and Urban Development and the Massachusetts Department of Community Affairs set out a rationale for the use of history for community revitalization in circumstances such as those at Lowell:

> Perhaps the single most important problem facing the New England mill towns is the problem of *image*. The overwhelming decline and collapse of the textile industry in the North has tarnished the image of these cities, not only in the eyes of people from the outside but also in the eyes of the citizens themselves. The discouragement experienced by people as a result of "hard times" has simultaneously destroyed their faith in the future of their communities and paralyzed their belief in the value of their own resources. The loss of confidence is understandable, considering the adversity and the bleak prospects for the future which these communities have faced for the last half century. Nonetheless, the negative outlook can have a debilitating influence on a city's future *economic* prospects. In other words it can be a circular situation with people's attitudes affecting the economic health of a community. Some people tend to forget that economics is in fact a *social* science.[66]

The emphasis at Lowell was therefore on the *achievements* of the past. Pat Mogan, an educator who spearheaded the campaign, said later, "We needed a strategy for the revitalization of the city and that strategy had to come from Lowell's heritage. Until a city has a past, it has no future. We were sowing our own seeds of destruction by denying our own background."[67] The phrase "until a city has a past, it has no future" is reminiscent of one of the major booster themes of the nineteenth century. Boosters had been as interested as Mogan now in effect was (through a different medium, that of historic preservation) in having "histories" of their towns compiled so that a line of development and progress could be established and one could discern the direction from which the future would come.[68]

The image seemed the key to solving Lowell's problems.

> In the face of economic decline, Lowell's residents were acquiescent. They were paralyzed by hopelessness and a preoccupation with the way things always were. In 1970, many middle-aged Lowellians had never seen Lowell in any condition except decline and had little reason to believe that things would or could possibly change in the future. . . . The greatest indication of the depressed nature of the city was what the people thought about themselves. The continual feeling of defeat brought on by half a century of economic decline created a mindset that had become self-perpetuating. . . . According to [Paul] Tsongas (the individual frequently cited as most responsible for Lowell's revitalization), "It was difficult to be proud of your home-town if you came from Lowell."[69]

Mogan said, "Too many people inside Lowell viewed the city in a negative frame of reference. This attitude permeated the schools, hampered the learning process, and prevented people from seeing beyond their immediate situation."[70] Lowell's assets—the positive, usable parts of the historical legacy—were seen as including in particular the human story of immigrants and labor embodied in the city's industrial heritage. "Mogan believed it was possible to look to the past for a vision that could be used to unify and energize the city. His idea was to create an historic park that would tell the story of Lowell's people and industry, and, at the same time, provide a theme around which the city could build a new future."[71]

Students and academic researchers from Harvard University and the Massachusetts Institute of Technology were recruited by Mogan to write theses on Lowell, using Model Cities Program funds. This research highlighted the city's rich history, the significance of the canal system, the historical value of the mill buildings, the strengths of the local labor force, and the cultural diversity of the population. "Documenting the past gave Lowellians insights into the future. A key benefit of documenting the past was to increase awareness of why industry was first attracted to Lowell and what it would take in the future to attract new industry to the city, including an available labor force, sound infrastructure, and local leaders promoting the city."[72]

Obviously, such rejuvenation does not work automatically or by merely reminding people of selected portions of their community's past. There must be effective leadership, substantial commitment of resources, and a single-minded vision of the future and of the relationship of the past to it. It has been pointed out that although New Bedford, another declining and demoralized New England industrial city, has also had a rich history, a history at least as significant as Lowell's, it has not been able to exploit it to the same degree.[73] Other old industrial towns in Massachusetts have been adopting Lowell's "park" model with state support in an effort to replicate that city's success. But the jury is still out on the extent to which even the great Lowell enterprise has succeeded in revitalizing the city. The restoration has been a splendid achievement, and there now exists a park that attracts large numbers of visitors every year. But Lowell itself continues to suffer from high unemployment and crime rates, and its major revival as an industrial center is still to come. The park has an atmosphere that is far removed from the hurly-burly of the industrial era, and in spite of some efforts to reproduce that atmosphere—for example, the noise made by the roomful of operating looms—the very quality of the museum displays only serves to accentuate the irretrievable pastness of Lowell's industrial glory days.

The image itself has had to undergo considerable and constant modification and supplementation. In the late 1980s Wang, the computer company whose willingness to invest in Lowell had been made so much of, scaled down its operations and laid off many workers. In 1992 the National Park Service produced a guide to Lowell and did its best to update the historical interpretations. The theme now was "boom and bust" as a perennial characteristic of Lowell's economy. What was happening could be interpreted historically as the downturn in a cycle. This acknowledged adversity but suggested grounds for continuing optimism: Lowell would take advantage of the next upturn in economic conditions. For if the economy was temporarily depressed, a countervailing force had been instilled by the creation of the park: "The city's new pride recalls the spirit of the milltown's boom days."[74]

Ambivalent Attitudes toward Emphasizing the Past

Looking to the past for inspiration is not a strategy that commands universal support. The worry is that emphasis on the old may give the wrong impression. In Jacksonville, Oregon, some longtime residents saw long-established buildings as representing the status quo: "preservation meant no growth, no progress, no profit."[75] Because of the concentration on using historic district designation as a tool of neighborhood and downtown rehabilitation, a perception has developed that only decayed areas need designation. If an area receives designation, the assumption is that it must be in trouble. Richard I. Ortega has explained why some people do not like their towns or neighborhoods being turned into historic districts: "Like it or not, preservation carries with it connotations of protection from decay and spoilage, old age and decline. There is no need to preserve life, people reason; preservation is directed toward the dead and the dying."[76]

A dilemma for modern-day boosters has been to avoid emphasizing the past to such an extent that people will conclude that their town has abandoned aspirations for the future. For example, a brochure publicizing Belle Grove Historic District in Fort Smith, Arkansas (NR 1973), after recalling the town's boom days, argues that the buildings of Belle Grove "are more than reflections of the past, for these are the foundations upon which Fort Smith will stand as it continues to move into the future."[77] Some nervousness can also be detected in publicity for Madison, Indiana. A brochure notes that Madison is called the "19th Century Williamsburg" but goes on to assure readers that "unlike Williamsburg, Madison is a real, vital, modern city, providing homes, jobs and recreation to thousands of people living here."[78] This ambivalence toward Williamsburg reflects a desire both to exploit its celebrity and to distance Madison from the negative connotations associated with its image. A brochure produced by a variety of local organizations in Bellows Falls, Vermont, including the chamber of commerce and the historic preservation commission, is entitled "Building on the Past." "Although many village buildings are listed on the National Register of Historic Places," it says, "Bellows Falls is not a village captured in a museum. It continues to build on its past."

Tourism and Historic Districts

Strategies involving historic district development may be focused on tourism. The recent history of historic preservation at Lexington, Virginia, shows the course taken by towns whose historic areas appear to have the potential to appeal to tourists. Threatened destructions of historic buildings led to the creation in 1966 of the Historic Lexington Foundation, which developed a program of house tours and other activities focusing on individual buildings. The chamber of commerce arranged for a report by the Colonial Williamsburg vice president on how the town could be developed as a tourist attraction. Gradually the foundation itself moved from a primary concern with individual houses to undertaking a study of a Main Street block. It bought and resold properties in this block. In 1971 it was instrumental in getting the council to adopt a Historic Area ordinance. A project for laying herringbone brick sidewalks throughout the historic district was begun, and unsightly utility poles were eliminated. A historic district inventory, for which the foundation offered the city a matching grant, was begun in the early 1980s.[79] A major post-1966 divide has been between places such as Lexington that have sought to attract tourists by emphasizing, protecting, and exploiting their "historic" assets and those that, while also possessing and valuing such assets as central to their community's identity, have wanted to protect them and have seen keeping tourists out as a necessary strategy to that end. Historic districts have been developed in both sets of circumstances. What has emerged in those places that assign a high priority to attracting tourists is a constant attempt to shape, control, and manage their historic environments so as to make them more attractive and consumable. This often means having to protect these environments from some of the more damaging impacts of tourist interest. Robert Whitelaw, director of the Carolina Art Association, put it thus in 1939: "We [Charleston] have become a tourist city and in all likelihood will become more so, but unless we protect ourselves with a plan for the future this source of revenue and individuals who are interested in us will work to destroy the very things that made us attractive."[80]

In some historic districts the residents go to considerable lengths to avoid publicizing or promoting their districts as "historic." They want to keep tourists away. An example is Harrisville, New Hampshire (NR 1971), originally a company town and manufacturing village, which preserves its brick-granite mills. Harrisville has many of the attributes of the archetypal New England village: "brick mills straddle Goose Brook and small ponds lead one to another in a postcard scene."[81] But no effort has been made to promote the village as a tourist destination. Instead the villagers have striven to find an alternative to tourism and other forms of commercialization of heritage in order to combine historic preservation with ongoing economic viability. In 1971 an organization named Historic Harrisville Inc. bought six structures and then sought tenants for the premises from a variety of industries ranging from traditional weaving to modern high-tech enterprises. One can visit some historic districts today without realizing that that is what they are—unless one has checked first in the National Register. For instance, the central historic core of Mount Pleasant, South Carolina (NR 1973), struggles as a quiet residential district to preserve its anonymity and placid lifestyle in the shadow of the frenetic tourism of neighboring Charleston as well as the suburban growth surrounding it. The history preserved there is given little publicity.

The Strengthening of Community

Historic districts represent the tradition of valuing and seeking to strengthen "community" and "permanence" as against the impermanence associated with Americans' rootlessness and restlessness, the "frontier" side of the American experience. One recent commentator, Mitchell Schwarzer, has claimed that the dominant philosophy of historical preservation "has perpetuated a mythic bifurcation of American society into the permanent metropolis and the transient frontier." The creation of historic districts, he says, results in "the polarization of American cities and towns into zones of static monumentality and unregulated market activity." The "myth of permanence . . . contrasts the deep-seated meanings of high, traditional architecture with the allegedly ephemeral buildings associated with frontier, or mobile culture." The latter and the districts that contain them are dispensable. "Especially in its association of architectural traditions with original meanings, the myth reinforces the cultural values of social groups dominant during the nineteenth century. . . . The practice of dividing built culture into preserved or unpreserved segments is a result of the opposition between the myths of permanence and transience."[82]

This suggests that historic districting has been associated predominantly with strategies to solidify the bonds of permanence in community structures. However, there is one critical respect in which urban historic preservation has endeavored to synthesize the two poles of the American tradition. This is the involvement of what is called the "pioneer spirit" in the restoration of historic districts. One writer has gone so far as to describe "the pioneer spirit, long a basic element in the American culture," as "the *genius loci* of historic districts."[83] This interpretation moves us a long way from the pejorative connotations of the term "gentrification," which, interestingly, was derived from *English* sociology. It imposes a distinctively *American* interpretation on the phenomenon. An emphasis on the new "urban pioneers" appears in much of the literature on the rehabilitation of old houses. In 1974 James Biddle said, "It seems that getting back to the city, or staying there, is the goal of many 'urban pioneers.'"[84] He repeatedly used the phrase to describe preservationists.

Impermanence and transience have been associated with rejection of the past and with moving on to new opportunities and settings. In this respect at least urban renewal was in accord with traditional American "frontier" attitudes to the past. The reaction against it favored reestablishing contact with the past in the interests of restoring continuity and stability to American society. For example, Kidney, a veteran preservationist from Pittsburgh, aligned himself with those who preferred stability and wished "to live in one place." He criticized the "Pittsburgh Renaissance," the massive plan for the rehabilitation of downtown, for having been "committed to a historic rootlessness that wanted to put the past almost wholly behind."[85]

Another commentator on preservation who has seen the frontier tradition as antithetical to what preservationists are hoping to achieve is Larry E. Tise. He wrote in 1981 that many Americans think they are still on the frontier. "We have never discovered the meaning of tradition, place, and historical continuity. Our migrating habits in America push against and annul the creation and maintenance of tradition."[86] It was this culture that preservationism resolved to counter. The 1965 Special Committee on Historic Preservation, whose report was a major prelude to the 1966 Historic Preservation Act, found as follows: "Our nation began with migrations, grew with migrations, and remains a nation of people on the move. Few of us have had close ties with the land and with places and buildings. The natural result in too many cases has been a neglect of starting points and an indifference to our cultural trail of buildings and places. This is what we are trying to correct."[87] The report concluded: "The United States is a nation and a people on the move. It is an era of mobility and change. Every year 20 percent of the population moves from its place of residence. The result is a feeling of rootlessness combined with a longing for those landmarks of the past which give us a sense of stability and belonging." It then gave the preservation movement a mission: "It must attempt to give a sense of orientation to our society, using structures and objects of the past to establish values of time and place."[88]

Historic districts have been accorded a role in the achievement of this objective. The transience that has been so prominent a part of American life and has been lamented by some as corrosive of community values is ignored or countered in a number of ways. For example, the emphasis in walking tour guides to many historic districts is on the families who have lived in the houses. It is common for a house to be described by a name that is a composite of the families who have occupied it over the years. To take one example among many, the publicity surrounding the Harry S. Truman Historic District, the area adjacent to the former president's house in Independence, emphasizes a particular interpretation of Truman's significance. The focus is on the Truman home as a family home, and this is linked to an association of Truman with all-American, middle-class, family-oriented values and the theme of the stability of family-based neighborhoods.

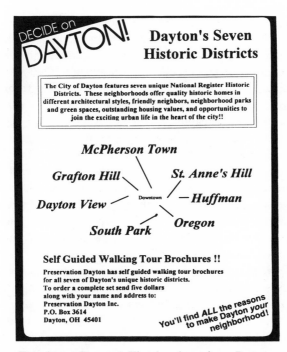

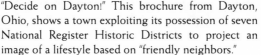

"Decide on Dayton!" This brochure from Dayton, Ohio, shows a town exploiting its possession of seven National Register Historic Districts to project an image of a lifestyle based on "friendly neighbors."

Nostalgia for Lost Community

Historic districts are a resource for community rehabilitation in that they embody various examples and models of community structure that, for a number of reasons, are believed to have worked well in the past. Reference to and use of "history" enables the decay of community that set in after the period of historical "significance" to be cleared away and the original firm lineaments of actual or planned community cohesion and identity to be rediscovered and restored. Pre-1900 districts in particular are representative of eras of strong localism, eras before the development of nationalizing and standardizing forces. Their historical identity is often traced back to those eras and restored from them. They indicate a desire to revive the onetime strength of what has been described by Thomas Bender as the most common American mode of defining community—that of having a territorial base, meaning that one can take a district and find in it a "microcosmic example of the larger society."[89] Bender's thesis about changing attitudes to community in America can be applied to the enthusiasm for the creation of historic districts. His view is that whereas today community can be defined better as an experience than as place, between about 1820 and 1870 society was remarkably decentralized. "The local units of life were replicated across the landscape." Americans "tended to live in local communities that took pride in their parochialism and idiosyncratic ways." A local perspective predominated. "The successful, whatever their route to this success, typically identified with the town that gave them their success—and their status."[90] The consequences of this can be seen in the elite residential districts of this period that are now so conspicuous among historic districts. As Bender argues, by the late twentieth century the connection between success and local status had been largely severed. Yet the historic districts harken back to that earlier and now irrelevant era. Why? Bender suggests that an "unspecified feeling of loss and emptiness . . . makes Americans vulnerable to the manipulation of symbols of community."[91] Another way of putting this is that historic districts embody what has been called the "neighborhood of nostalgia."[92] Nostalgia has certainly played a substantial part in the historic preservation movement, and it has undeniably been an ingredient in the enthusiasm for creating historic districts. Richard Guy Wilson, commenting on the Old West Side Historic District in Ann Arbor (NR 1972), claimed that people want to live in communities again. It is not just a matter of simple nostalgia but represents a reaction against modern conditions. People need to feel that they are "part of a community and, more importantly, a neighborhood, rather than being simply statistics in another homogenized housing development."[93]

Modern planning and trends in modern lifestyles have encouraged not just the maintenance but also the exploitation of the bias in the criteria to emphasizing the character of historic districts as emblematic of certain community types. In a study of the modern development of neighborhoods with reputations and images, Christopher Winters sees the phenomenon of neighborhood "character" as a significant feature of the modern urban scene. According to Winters, several distinctive neighborhood types emerged in the 1970s. The relationship between this and historic districts appears in his discussion of neighborhoods that are being rejuvenated. He argues that historically neighborhoods have had shifting locations and even names, and most have had imprecise boundaries. He identifies a distinctive modern development in the rehabilitation of districts that draw on history for support. His observation is that each neighborhood "tends to acquire a *different* reputation. . . . [N]eighborhoods undergoing rejuvenation are particularly likely to acquire a special social character because these neighborhoods experience a great deal of voluntary and highly self-conscious in-migration in a short period." Self-identification has been important in choosing a district to live in. In his view we should not ignore "the cultural meaning of rejuvenation for the participants."[94] Although Winters does not explicitly deal with historic districts, their relevance to his argument is clear: they define a much sharper identity for a district and create protection for that identity. And they differentiate areas from one another on the basis of identities selected from the multiplicity of pasts that any city is bound to have had. This differentiation has opened up the possibility of providing a wide choice of lifestyle environments. As cities acquire and agencies plan for a range of historic districts, these are being seen as offering a variety of lifestyle options, depending on what type of community structure one prefers. A 1980 report on the Vieux Carré argued, for instance, that one of the goals of historic preservation in New Orleans should be to keep alive environments where alternative life styles can flourish: "Older neighborhoods, with their small parks and interesting architecture, provide for a choice in lifestyle."

> The life of a city is reflected in the various styles of development which predominate at any given time as a city moves through each succeeding period of its history. . . . Though each cycle of a city's history produces a predominantly similar environment inclusive of architectural style, it is the collection of a variety of such environments that produces a viable city. It is the collective variation reflective of each historical cycle and its continuance as an intricate part of a community offering a different way of life that produces the substance of the city. It is this variation in life style and the choice that is offered its citizens which provide a community with its uniqueness, with its viability. Therefore, a fundamental role of local government is to see that this opportunity for a variation in life style — this choice of environments — remains as a viable part of a dynamic urban area. Conversely, the City must ensure that no one pattern dominates to the point that it replaces or eliminates others. . . . The assurance of diverse environments is a goal fervently recognized as well as fervently challenged in most American cities. Each city . . . must insure that . . . attention to one specific environmental pattern is not achieved to the detriment of other patterns.[95]

This certainly suggests the imposition of a modern approach to neighborhood differentiation on the patterns of the past. It also suggests the possibility of reinforcement for the traditional approach to historic districts as enshrined in the National Register criteria, of making each district embody "significance" that relates to a particular era or episode in history.

The development of historic districts can be related to the renewal in the 1960s of concern for restoring the strength and vitality of the neighborhood as a fundamental unit in cities. The extent to which the ideal of the neighborhood remained important in people's lives was revealed by the reactions to the destruction of many of them during phases of urban renewal. Their significance was a theme in the influential sociological work of Herbert Gans, which introduced the concept of the "urban villager," as well as in the writings of Jane Jacobs. In 1963 one commentator described the historic district in larger cities as an attempt "to keep alive the village within the city."[96] Neighborhoods have certainly seen cycles of emphasis and neglect. The development of historic districts coincided with one of the major upswings of neighborhood consciousness. But it was not just coincidence. History was being invoked as a major source of inspiration, a way of rediscovering the roots of neighborhood identity and restoring coherence to neighborhoods.

There was a swing away from the master plans that had been imposed on neighborhoods without the consent of its residents or their involvement in the planning and decision-making processes. Instead, neighborhood planning came into vogue and there was a growing emphasis on citizen participation.[97] "Neighborhood revitalization" was the new slogan. Planning studies began to take heed of "neighborhood dynamics and potential rehabilitation strategies." The new emphasis was on cultural and social values and the importance of not destroying "neighborhood," which was seen as a particular and precious repository of such values. And the emphasis was also once again on territory. Indeed, one historian describes planners as having now elevated territory to being the preeminent element in the definition of a neighborhood.[98] It has remained preeminent. All the definitions of neighborhoods that have emerged since the late 1960s stress the importance of locality. Neighborhood became a principal focus of programs whose purpose was urban revitalization.[99] By the 1970s a strident localism had emerged. The 1970s were referred to as the decade of the neighborhood. "The virtues and charms of the neighborhood [were] everywhere trumpeted as the answer to urban decay and the solution to urban anomie."[100] By the time of the National Neighborhood Policy Act, passed in 1977, it was being assumed "that the nation's neighborhoods are a national resource." The aim of the legislators was to "promote community continuity and heterogeneity."[101]

Much of the theory behind creating districts of the historic district type to foster and strengthen a sense of neighborhood and community can be found in arguments advanced in an influential book, Albert Hunter's *Symbolic Communities*, published in 1973. Hunter does not specifically refer to historic preservation and historic districts, but his work is clearly relevant to their conceptualization. Hunter drew on the work of Kevin Lynch, as well as on a considerably earlier study by Walter I. Firey on the relationship between land use in cities and moves to protect the distinctive character of city districts.[102] Hunter concluded that "it appears that the spatial order itself may be a central and persistent component of the cultural and symbolic order of local urban communities." In his view what studies such as those by Firey and Lynch had established was that "for local urban communities to operate as objects and arenas of meaningful social action their residents must possess some conceptual image of them. . . . [T]hese symbolic images must be shared or collective representations, and . . . individuals must have the means, varying needs, and abilities to draw on this local culture to define and delimit meaningful symbolic communities."[103]

Msgr. Geno Baroni, president of the National Center for Urban/Ethnic Affairs in Washington, D.C., told the National Trust annual meeting in 1976 that the development of a "new sense of neighborhoods" must become a much more significant part of the historic preservation agenda.[104] By April 1977 the issue was clearly assuming urgency: *Preservation News* published a supplement on neighborhoods that contained many instances of inner-city neighborhood rehabilitation. Grassroots experience showed preservationists that neighborhood restoration was becoming one of the principal routes to historic conservation. Because of the funding available and the high level of public and governmental support for action to preserve older districts in the cities, this was the area in which historic preservation was most likely to achieve success. And this, of course, pointed the way to a predominant emphasis on preserving *districts* rather than individual buildings. In the forefront of these developments was the Pittsburgh Landmarks Foundation. In 1971 Ziegler, its director, discussed what he called "the problem of neighborhood self-determination." He advised preservationists that "today community self-determination has become a dominant, even a militant theme."[105] This development represented a reaction to the way neighborhood perspectives and sensitivities had been overridden and ignored in the planning associated with urban renewal. Now neighborhoods had to be involved in the planning process.

There was a sense of going back to a golden age when homogeneity and stability had been characteristic of local residential groups. Gerald D. Suttles has suggested that this owed much to the emphasis in the work of the Chicago sociologists Robert Park and Ernest W. Burgess on the "natural," "ecological" character of neighborhoods in a city. In his view, the assumption that there had been this sort of golden age had been virtually unchallenged by sociologists and fostered a romantic image that was used by those interested in "deriding the present" to negotiate "a return to the past."[106] It is significant that to rebut this idea Suttles draws on the work of historians concerned with communities in the past.

Yi-Fu Tuan has referred to "the multifaceted and often ambiguous nature of the neighborhood concept." Ziegler, the influential Pittsburgh preservationist, observed how hard it is to say where a community or "neighborhood" begins and ends. "Even if you are able to pinpoint the boundaries, are the people across the street from your perimeter not going to be affected by whatever happens in your neighborhood? Are they therefore not also to be considered? . . . Second, what about the transient quality of urban neighborhoods of all kinds? . . . Third, does an urban neighborhood have the right to this kind of autonomy, as if it were not 'part of the main'?"[107] Many nonresidents participate in the life of any district. But, if all this is true today, it has to be recognized that it has often been true historically as well. Any attempt to use history to help "restore" neighborhood cohesion and stability has to encounter these aspects of historical reality. For instance, Kenneth A. Scherzer, describing the immense complexity of districting in nineteenth-century New York, refers to what was then "the highly transitory nature of symbolic space, a psychosocial dimension of neighborhood that is forever changing as urban subcommunities constantly change and are redefined—even when the original buildings survive."[108]

The alternative view of neighborhood is that in the modern age it is not and cannot be restricted to one territorially defined district. People seek—and through modern technology and forms of transportation and communication can seek ever more easily—their community and social interactions across wide areas. They are not restricted to their immediate vicinity. The idea of the district as a self-contained neighborhood is anachronistic and based on nostalgia for a way of life that has long since gone and can never be retrieved even if the "historic" dimensions of a district are retraced and highlighted. Modern lifestyles mean that the old type of neighborhood can seldom if ever be re-created. The "historic" element in neighborhood restorations is bound to be somewhat limited. For example, the Hyde Park Historic District in Kansas City (NR 1980) is a district whose renaissance began in the mid-1970s when individuals discovered that once-fine old houses could be acquired fairly cheaply. New owners were thus enabled to invest in their rehabilitation, often returning interiors to single-family occupancy. There were annual festivals with home tours, and historic preservation appeared to be a significant aspect of what was happening. "Even so," commented the local architectural historian, "without the traditional anchors of true neighborhood schools and clusters of local shops for daily needs, Hyde Park (which in fact is three neighborhoods: north, central and south) is different than it was in the 1920s or 30s."[109]

Groups of residents who are concerned about actual, impending, or threatened changes to the character of their neighborhood often seek the protection afforded by historic district designation. In Dallas, for instance, initiative for the Swiss Avenue district came from a group of nine residents who thought historic district designation might solve some of that neighborhood's problems.[110] This concern is linked with the history of the district in communities where a strong sense of ancestry is felt by members of families that have lived in the neighborhood for many generations. Their commitment to maintaining the historic character of the district may provide the motivation needed to have it designated as a historic district. Publicity for a number of historic districts draws attention to the fact that descendants of original or early families are still living there. At New Paltz, New York, descendants of the original Huguenot families, although now widely scattered, have played a large part in contributing to fund the resources—the Huguenot Historical Society, guided tours, a visitors' center—that maintain a "live" historic district for Huguenot Street, "the oldest street in America with its original houses" (NR 1966).

However, in many restored districts those seeking "historic" designation are not the descendants of the people who actually made the history and built and lived in the houses. They are the owners of properties they have restored, and they are interested in protecting their investments through the maintenance of an overall historic character for the neighborhood. This is a common pattern, for instance, in districts with large houses that were subdivided into apartments owned by absentee landlords. Deterioration often followed, but the houses survived. The new owners invest a great deal of time and capital in their restoration. A common pattern has been for outsiders to start buying property for renovation and then put pressure on the city authority to establish an official historic district with architectural controls and a design review process.[111] Some of the neighborhoods close to the city center at Lynchburg, Virginia, illustrate this phenomenon very well. Diamond Hill was an exclusive neighborhood until the end of World War II. Then came decades of neglect, as many of the original owners moved away or died. Most of the fine old houses stood vacant or were converted into apartments. The Diamond Hill Historical Society, formed in 1974 by concerned home owners, has been a catalyst in the "rebirth" of "the Hill." One of its achievements was to gain acceptance for the district on the State and National registers. Nearby is Garland Hill, from which the original families had gradually moved as it ceased to be fashionable. Many of the larger homes were then converted into apartments. Uncaring absentee landlords took over in the 1960s and 1970s. In the late 1970s new owners began to move in, several homes were reconverted to single family dwellings, and neighborhood organization developed.[112]

In the 1970s lifestyle considerations and the energy crisis brought younger professional middle-class people back into some inner-city areas. When they moved into districts with deteriorated housing that had been the homes of poorer people, the process became known as "gentrification." The marketability of a historic ambience has been a major feature of the relationship between historic district development and gentrification. Districts that have a "historic" image and atmosphere, or can be enabled to acquire one through such devices as historic district designation, have had a strong appeal for the "gentrifiers." The relationship has worked both ways: gentrification may have come first and then been a stimulus for seeking historic district designation.[113]

The Appeal of Design Review

In many places that have become historic districts a primary motivation for seeking designation has been the appeal of the design review and control processes associated with it. Design review is an integral, indeed the central, feature of the management of local historic districts throughout the United States. The detailed protection and enhancement of a district's historic character are ensured largely through the establishment of design guidelines that set out criteria to be considered when an application for an alteration, addition, or demolition is reviewed.[114] Design guidelines may be only advisory or they may carry various incentives. In some cases they are mandatory: their requirements must be complied with. A section of the guidelines usually describes the important visual characteristics of the existing buildings and environment that should be preserved.[115]

Design review is another instance of rendering the past usable. We are told, for example, that historic district status was sought for Lafayette Park in St. Louis not to commemorate the history or architecture of the district but as "a tool to preserve buildings and build public interest in the restoration of a residential community." A new group of people wanted to become residents and saw historical significance and the design review processes that went with it "as a way to reimpose some level of social control on the community and thereby make it more attractive to urban investment and potential home buyers."[116] Historical meaning became a tool for regeneration. At Charlotte the people involved in the revival of the Fourth Ward obtained its designation as a historic district because the historic district law was "the only legislation providing for design review in North Carolina, and most of the South."[117] James Marston Fitch put it this way when discussing why people like historic districts with design review boards: "It is not so much a matter of preferring 'Georgian' at Annapolis or 'Creole' in New Orleans or 'Spanish Colonial' at Monterey, it is rather the sense of blessed relief that such controlled environments give [them] in escaping from the visual and sonic chaos of the typical, uncontrolled American streetscape."[118] In 1977–78, Ellen Beasley surveyed nine communities in which there was a design review process for historic districts. She returned to them eight years later and found that eight of the nine had enlarged their districts and/or added new ones. Her conclusion was that "this was not because people were so enamored with historic districts but rather, because they saw the accompanying design review as a means of having some control over change and development, and the quality of change and development, in their neighborhood or community." In her view, the underlying motivations for historic districts today are "issues of growth and design, not historic association, as suggested by the fact that several boards have been given responsibility for design review in outlying, undeveloped areas."[119]

The Emphasis on Usability and the Presentation of History

We can now see some of the reasons why certain aspects of the past are favored for remembrance in this format and not others. Presenting a historic district in terms of *all* the facets of its history and in terms of its history as continual change is likely to be difficult, confusing, and unpopular. This is especially so if one of the principal, present-oriented aims of historic district designation is to enhance and strengthen neighborhood or district identity. The more multiple pasts are emphasized the more complex—as well as realistic and genuinely historical—the message and the interpretation of the character of the district have to be. In many cases, this will militate against certain other objectives now commonly associated with creating historic districts, notably the stabilization of neighborhoods. This is not always the case. For instance, drawing out and highlighting evidence of African-American history within a historic district that might originally have been designated "historic" for quite different reasons may also serve that objective by increasing pride in the achievements of the African-American community.

As for change, the problem is that if an attempt were made to represent and highlight it as a predominant characteristic of the evolution of the built environment of today, homogeneity would almost certainly have to be sacrificed. Loss of clarity and consistency in style and theme would almost invariably be the consequence of portraying accurately the actual character of change in a fast-growing urban environment. This would be to the detriment of the image of neighborhood stability that it is so often hoped the restoration of themes from the past will enhance. If evolution is linear and orderly, well and good. But if it is a mess—and the state of many inner-city areas today allows no easy and comforting belief in orderly progress toward better urban living—then the "real" past is no use and an invented past has to be substituted.

One particular kind of change, the occurrence of "deterioration" on a substantial scale, has been a major reason why designation has been sought. But it has not been sought so that that phase of the district's history can be remembered. Many districts that have been accorded historic status have gone through a period of "decay" that has been a significant part of their history. Now evidence of it is suppressed as much as possible.[120] Modern-day boosters try to blot out those intervening years of decline, the survival era, in their use of history to promote their towns. For example, a brochure made available to visitors to Hollidaysburg, Pennsylvania, outlines its history down to the Civil War era and describes the development of industry, stressing the availability then of raw materials and experienced mechanics, machinists, and tradesmen. Then it goes straight to the present day: "Hollidaysburg offers an unlimited supply of trained labor, space for building and expansion." Another brochure takes seven paragraphs to get to the Civil War and its stimulus to industrial growth and then covers the next 130 years in one sentence: "The community adapted well to the growth and economic changes that heralded the dawning of the 20th Century."[121]

Lynch and others have raised the question of whether history *should* have anything to do with issues of neighborhood rehabilitation. Is history, they ask, better kept out of the purposes for which many people have supported historic district designation, or at least given only a subsidiary role? Lynch criticized the assumption that a sense of place must always be founded on history. In his view, some history is better regarded as irrelevant "to the study of seemliness, either because it happened too long ago or because it is better forgotten. The fact that sensory quality has best been managed, up to now, in areas marked for preservation is a weakness in the field rather than a natural limitation."[122] Emphasizing the history of particular places, and making that the basis for community reconstruction, can give rise to conflicts with those who are indifferent to a sense of history or are even actively opposed to its expression. There is also, Lynch warned, the likelihood of conflicts over whose history is to be saved and which version of past events is correct. In other words, "history" is not a neutral force that can automatically be relied on to provide relief and distraction from present conflicts. It has the power and potential to divide communities—whereas the purpose of historic preservation is often said to be the rediscovery and strengthening of community identity. Zane Miller has detected a reaction against an emphasis on history as a binding, community-strengthening influence. He has pointed to a trend among planners in the 1970s toward a new definition of "culture," one that would give less weight to history. According to this view, people should be empowered to define their own culture and in the process to neutralize the characteristics of place, including the history of the place.[123] What happens is that "history" tends to be confined to the relatively safe ground of architectural style, while the fifty-year cut-off point for National Register listings throws some sort of insulation around more contemporary controversies.

The adequacy and appropriateness of a history-oriented approach to district definition have also been queried in debates on the relationship of history to the "sense of place" that many critics have seen as lacking in historic districts. If one wants to incorporate this rather intangible attribute, is it simply a matter of adjusting and broadening "historic" assessments? Or does "sense of place" imply a different approach to defining the characteristics of a district, an approach in which "history," instead of being the controlling element, should take its place alongside aesthetic and environmental criteria?

Six

A New Format and Strategy
for Historic Preservation

THE HISTORIC DISTRICT STRATEGY, IN ADDITION to helping to achieve community goals, has become a principal feature of the modern historic preservation movement. This chapter considers their development from this perspective while recognizing the close connection between preservation and community rehabilitation strategies. Preservationists have learned that coalitions with city planners are effective and necessary for the achievement of preservation objectives. And because city planners work at the level of districts and zones rather than individual structures historic preservationists are drawn into the same spheres of action. More and more their energies have had to be focused on district and neighborhood preservation and rehabilitation. After all, if a proposal for the preservation of a building or a district cannot be given a rationale that conforms to current planning criteria and priorities, it is likely to be greatly weakened in the competition for allocations of public funds.

Since 1966, within the framework created by the National Historic Preservation Act and by state initiatives, there has been a strong trend toward organizing the protection of "historic" structures as much as possible within historic districts, making a district the protective shell around threatened structures of historic value. This was not an accidental and unplanned development. When, following the passage of the 1966 act, regional conferences were held to publicize its provisions and map strategies for its implementation and a campaign was begun to sell the concept of the historic district to traditional local historians, Murtagh and his colleagues at the Office of Archeology and Historic Preservation made it known that they "hoped to implant in their history-oriented constituents an apprecia- tion for . . . historic districts preserved as living communities."[1] In 1974 Murtagh urged states to "think in district terms whenever possible" when submitting National Register nominations.[2] Increasingly they have.

Such arguments coincided with growing enthusiasm for the historic district strategy for historic preservation on both administrative and man- agement grounds. This strategy emerged out of a growing emphasis on the efficient, economical management of historic resources.[3] In many cir- cumstances the creation of a historic district and the establishment of appropriate controls appealed as the most efficient form of management of the resources that had traditionally been the focus of historic preservation: individual structures. As concern for preserving historic buildings grew, many communities were faced with serious problems managing these re- sources. During the 1960s many found themselves at a crossroads in terms of historic preservation strategy. Some decided to take the "heritage vil- lage" route, to collect as many of the endangered buildings as possible and move them to a "village" where an artificial but secure "historical" environ- ment could be created. This strategy—which does *not* gain historic district recognition for the resulting area—is to collect and concentrate the re- maining historic houses of a town or city in one place and call it a "pioneer village" or give it a name such as "Heritage Square" or "Old Town." This has often seemed the only alternative if a town's architectural heritage is to be properly cared for. Looking after individual buildings at a dozen dif- ferent locations over a large city is very difficult and expensive. Houston's Heritage Park is one of the most celebrated examples of the "village" alter- native. There a number of old buildings are concentrated in one location and boost the city's modern image in their contrast with the skyscrapers at whose feet they appear to nestle. This strategy has not been without controversy. In 1994 local preservationists in Houston were reported to be angered by a decision of the city and the Harris County Historical Society to move a house from the Fourth Ward into Heritage Park. The concern was in particular about the implicit abandonment of the Fourth Ward as a historic neighborhood through the removal from it of one of the key structures that defined its "historic" character. Margie Elliott, the executive director of the Greater Houston Preservation Alliance, argued that "the plan sends the signal that the city is giving up on a depressed neighbor- hood desperately in need of investment." "We're opposed," she said, "to taking a significant landmark out of a district, especially when there's an opportunity to do neighborhood preservation that hasn't existed before."[4]

The city responded that it had had no choice: the former owner gave the society the house but not the land, and it therefore had to be moved.

Other communities rejected this kind of historic preservation and started on an alternative route toward creation of one or more historic districts in which buildings deemed worthy of preservation would retain their location among others that by traditional criteria would not have been judged so worthy. For example, the catalyst for the commissioning of a full-scale preservation study, *Marshall: A Plan for Preservation*, by the historical society of Marshall, Michigan, was a plan to move some of the older houses into a "historic display area" and create a museum village.[5] The chamber of commerce then organized a downtown restoration program and a substantial part of central Marshall eventually became a National Historic Landmark.[6]

Through the channeling of federal funding for historic preservation into neighborhood contexts the 1966 act revolutionized the possibilities and made it a great deal more feasible to contemplate leaving buildings in situ and attending to the preservation or restoration of their environments. Some museum villages were left in a somewhat ambiguous position in the new world that gradually took shape after 1966. For example, the origins of Strawbery Banke, Portsmouth, New Hampshire (NR 1975), predated the act, and now it sits awkwardly within the world and the framework created by the act. This ten-acre site once was a seriously deteriorated area that had been scheduled by the local urban renewal agency for total demolition and clearance. It was saved, and it is now an enclosed area with an admission charge. One can visit a variety of displays in historic houses with guides, some in costume and role-playing.[7] Like Heritage Park in Houston, it is becoming a refuge for houses unwanted or endangered in other parts of the town. But, unlike the park, it is regarded as acceptable for the National Register.

The heritage village was not, of course, an option for the saving of huge and often loved, or at least familiar, landmarks such as town halls, courthouses, and larger churches. They could not be moved. But in many communities urban redevelopment and other changes in the urban environment had left landmark buildings of this type dangerously exposed and vulnerable. For instance, many railroad stations, churches in inner cities, and old-fashioned city halls were now isolated as fragments or disparaged as "white elephants." Urban redevelopment had left many "historic" buildings standing forlornly alone and isolated in seas of urban devastation. Their contexts and therefore much of their meaning and appeal had gone beyond recall. Awareness of the limitations and risks involved in focusing on and trying to protect single buildings in isolation[8] laid the basis for a more comprehensive approach that would involve in particular the identification and creation of historic districts.[9] It was thus a strategy that also struck a chord among traditional preservationists whose primary concern was and usually remained with the preservation of individual structures.

In many places of major "historic" interest, particularly the concentrated walking city cores of the older towns, the point was arriving where many buildings within a small compass were either going to have to be deemed worthy of preservation and protected by the sorts of controls associated with historic districts or else they would soon disappear as a result of demolition or neglect. Rather than mount a laborious research effort and a campaign to justify separately the preservation of each one, it has often proved to be more efficient to deal with them collectively and embed the case for them within an argument about the district as a whole. There was therefore a strong element of promoting administrative efficiency in the growth of interest in historic districts.

During the 1970s and 1980s historic preservation moved from its traditional primary concern with individual structures to an emphasis on the contexts of structures. Indeed, beyond that there has been a transition from interest in contexts essentially as supports for individual buildings toward a concern for protecting the "historic" character of precincts and other types of urban settings, irrespective of whether they contain structures deemed worthy of preservation on their individual merits. Contexts are becoming recognized as worthy of preservation in their own right.[10] The focus is increasingly on preserving areas in which there are no individual buildings that would have been considered worthy of preservation in accordance with traditional criteria.

Why has this happened? The major problem with concentrating on individual structures has always been that it ignored what was happening to their contexts and settings. Those who have maintained the traditional preservationist concentration on individual buildings have been obliged to recognize that many of the structures that they wished to save are being rendered vulnerable by changes in their surroundings that deprived them of much of their meaning. Around a building there often exists a hitherto neglected zone of protection afforded by all sorts of other features of the townscape that individually have not been seen as worthy of preservation according to traditional criteria. Many preservationists have been converted to the district approach as it has become clear that a focus on individual buildings is too narrow and that it would be in the interests of the survival of individual structures themselves that an effort be made to protect their contexts. Once those deteriorate or are transformed into the settings for incompatible buildings or activities, buildings can lose a great deal of their meaning. They are then made more vulnerable because their historical meanings are much harder to understand. The context can—and, preservationists came to appreciate, should be allowed to—perform a fortifying and validating function for "historic" structures. In 1975 James Biddle explained thus the trend toward preserving the environment of landmark buildings: "While we are still concerned about saving an individual landmark, the preservation movement has gone beyond that stage to the concept of preserving the landmark's setting or an entire ensemble of historic structures and their background buildings. After all, it does not make much sense to save a historic house and then find it surrounded by gas stations and fast-food franchises. Thus, for example, the houses around a town green might be included in a district to preserve and maintain the well-planned ambience created by a town's founders years ago."[11]

In this, as in so much in the preservation sphere, Massachusetts—and New England in general[12]—led the way. A forerunner was the creation of the Beacon Hill Historic District in 1955. The spring 1956 issue of *Old-Time New England* commented on that development: "In [Charleston, New Orleans, Alexandria, Winston-Salem, Georgetown, and Annapolis] it has been recognized that the preservation of historic monuments involves wider responsibilities than saving the single surviving old building, forlornly hemmed in on all sides by later structures and completely shorn of any meaningful context."[13] Yet a few years later Boston was to provide an object lesson in what could happen to a landmark building when its context was destroyed. When fifty acres of buildings were erased in West End in 1958–60, the first Harrison Gray Otis house (1795–96, designed by Charles Bulfinch) was left intact. It had already been moved back forty feet on its site and deprived of its front terrace in 1926 when Cambridge Street was widened. In its earlier existence, it had been a rooming house with ground-floor shops and had "participated fully in the life of the street." Now that life has gone, traffic sweeps by outside on the widened thoroughfare, and the shops are no more. "Today the Otis house seems lost in the hodgepodge that remains."[14] As if to prevent this sort of thing from happening again, section 2 of the Massachusetts Historic Districts Act (1960) described securing the "maintenance and improvement of settings" as one principal means of preserving and protecting "buildings and places significant in the history of the commonwealth and its cities and towns or their architecture."[15] The very first sentence of the Massachusetts Historical Commission's publication, *Establishing Local Historic Districts*, reads as follows: "In Massachusetts, local historic districts offer the strongest form of protection for the preservation of historic properties."[16]

In retrospect we can see that the emphasis on historic districts as a way of more effectively protecting landmark monuments sometimes operated as a tactical necessity, a bridge that took traditional preservationists into acceptance of a new approach to historic preservation.[17] But it also meant that for some time historic districts were likely to be mainly districts where significant "historic monuments" were located and in peril. Providing better protection for landmarks was one significant justification for the creation of historic districts. For example, the body that was given responsibility for designating historic districts (as well as historic structures) in New York City was called the New York City Landmarks Commission. Two parallel trends transformed the historic preservation agenda. The central significance of landmark buildings began to diminish as more and more districts that had no such structures in the traditional sense were designated. At the same time, as we shall see, there occurred a profound reinterpretation of the meaning of the concept "landmark." Today the following statement is typical of those that routinely appear in historic preservation handbooks: "Cities and counties with the most successful preservation programs are those which have strong local control and apply it to neighborhood-wide areas containing historic buildings. . . . Historic buildings do not merely exist as individual isolated structures, but remain in cohesive neighborhoods whose integrity and character should be protected."[18]

What has been increasingly appreciated is that even monumental civic, commercial, and institutional structures did not stand alone historically. Civic buildings, for instance, usually stood in a complex of such structures. Such buildings were often designed to impress, to dominate streetscapes, to convey by their relationship to surrounding buildings and to the streets certain images of authority and prestige. Remove or change that environment and much of their historic meaning is gone. Numerous historic districts embody the environmental significance of famous buildings. They have also contributed to changes in understandings of the relationships between architectural significance and historical significance by showing architecture in context.[19]

The environmental movement has also had an impact. During the 1970s there was pressure for broader environmental considerations to be introduced into historic preservation, and an emphasis on historic districts and landscapes fitted in with this. In 1974 a planner, Jon Pohl, pointed out that buildings are only part of the environment: "The atmosphere in many of the areas that stand out as potential historic districts is the kind of pleasant informality one finds in small-town America. The landscaping that embraces Evanston's much-loved elms and other large shade trees, the carefully tailored lawns and parkways, and the straight streets and sidewalks all contribute to the overall visual character of the community." The emphasis must be on maintaining "the character of our visual surroundings."[20]

Urban renewal was a significant contributor to the transition to a historic district-oriented strategy for historic preservation. While the 1966 act did give formal federal recognition to historic districts and a register on which they could be recorded, there are numerous respects in which it is best understood as a facilitator of continuity in areas in which development had long been occurring. One of these was the shift toward the preservation of buildings within the district structure. Independently of the act, initiatives taken under urban renewal programs and supported by urban renewal funding laid foundations for the management of a "historic district" approach to historic preservation. For example, urban renewal enabled fresh life to be breathed into some of the existing historic districts. The report on College Hill in Providence was undertaken in the urban renewal era and had a considerable impact after 1966 as a result of its reissue in 1967. It was then used in the development of historic districts in places such as Newburyport and New Bedford.[21] HUD's Urban Renewal Administration helped to fund a demonstration study to develop a preservation plan for the Vieux Carré in New Orleans. This was completed in 1968. Aspects of the history of this report reveal it as a transitional phenomenon. A primary objective of the study had been to classify individual buildings within the district in terms of their importance or value. But the report itself recommended that preservation planning should be directed at the total environment—referred to as the district's "tout ensemble"—and not just at individual structures. The phrase "tout ensemble" had been used for some time in New Orleans to justify a preservation strategy that went beyond individual buildings to take in the preservation of the entire style or character of a district. It has had considerable currency as a definition of a holistic approach to historic preservation. Even so, the Vieux Carré Commission acted only on those parts of the report that dealt with the survey and rating of buildings.[22]

There are risks in a historic district strategy. Other areas that are thereby seen as nonhistoric may be neglected or even abandoned by historic preservationists. The alternative would have to be a phasing out of the selective historic district approach. The authors of *Legacy of Minneapolis* write, "The effort to preserve—that is, to fully maintain—a small number of selected structures and districts is still set in a vast sea of marginal and sporadic maintenance. Could the preservation movement produce a small collection of monuments shining against a large, dull background of neglect and decay? Or will there be a gradual merger of the historic preservation movement into a widening, deepening stream of improved maintenance and adaptive reuse?"[23] The scale of preservation action involved in the creation and maintenance of entire districts reflects a great growth of resources, knowledge, and expertise. The organizational infrastructures underpinning campaigns to obtain historic district designation have changed considerably.[24] The history of the creation of historic districts from Williamsburg and Charleston at least to Pittsburgh and Savannah in the 1960s is replete with the achievements of strong and sometimes controversial personalities, determined and single-minded individuals with a flair for publicity or organization or both.[25] However, this dependence on local initiatives and the personalities who put energy and imagination into making them succeed has diminished. The world of historic preservation has increasingly become a world of committees, boards of architectural and design review, historic preservation commissions, and complex town planning procedures. The processes of achieving, implementing, and managing historic district status are now strongly bureaucratized.[26] "Organizations and agencies are charged with or assume responsibility for identifying and caring for an entire community's valued landscapes. They develop scientific criteria, inventory local resources, and designate those places that best fit the criteria."[27]

Historic districts reflect, and have further stimulated, interest in and knowledge about architectural history. Over the last two decades there has been an outpouring of field guides and other books designed to facilitate ready recognition and appreciation of architectural styles.[28] More and more people are visiting districts and looking knowledgeably at well-preserved or restored examples of major styles and epochs in architectural history. The more sophisticated architectural guides help us to appreciate changes to the style and usage of buildings over the years. In particular, there has been a major growth of appreciation of the "High Victorian" styles that were so prominent in the mid- to late-nineteenth-century boom periods of urban growth. Numerous books and articles, for example, the series *Painted Ladies*, guide and encourage the restoration of Queen Anne and other spectacularly styled Victorian residences.[29] There has been an awareness of the contributions of architects to the distinctive characteristics not just of single buildings but of whole districts.[30]

There has been a rapid growth in the historic preservation community and the "preservation support industry."[31] It is estimated that there are as many as three thousand organizations in the field and 600,000 individuals belonging to some type of historic preservation organization. By 1986 the National Trust for Historic Preservation had 185,000 members and by the early 1990s over a quarter of a million.[32] Its annual conference, which attracts approximately 2,500 attendees, is a mind-boggling demonstration of the breadth and complexity of this community. In 1974 Paul Sprague wrote, "One special problem confronting persons wanting to form historic districts is that districts cannot easily and effectively be defined by volunteers working alone, especially if they are without architectural or historical expertise."[33] Therefore professionals must be used. This restraint on expansion may be disappearing, to judge from reports of the critical role played by volunteers in doing architectural surveys prior to historic district nominations. For example, the Fan Woman's Club of Richmond did a survey of Richmond's Fan Area in one day, covering more than three thousand buildings. "The day ended with a community celebration in a neighborhood park."[34]

A host of nonprofit preservation organizations are now playing a significant role in developing historic districts. To take one example from many, Historic York, an organization formed in York, Pennsylvania, in 1975 in response to the threatened demolition of a house, has been responsible for nominating ten historic districts to the National Register.[35] The formation of such organizations has tended to be the next step taken in a community after the growth of interest in the restoration of individual houses. These organizations combine the provision of advice, guidance, and inspiration for individual house restorers with attention to the context, fabric, and environment of the district as a whole. In large part this is because the individual property owners appreciate that the value of the property into which they have invested much capital and hard work is very dependent on the quality of the environment. Neighborhood associations of property owners organize campaigns to secure historic district designation to protect these investments. At Elmira, New York, for example, an informal group of neighborhood residents who had grown concerned about encroaching blight and lack of historic preservation activities began meeting to share their concerns in 1977. A year later, the Near Westside Neighborhood Association was established. The city then designated the Near Westside as a target area in need of community development programs and activities. The association has since been active in a wide range of projects.[36] Residents of Elizabeth Boulevard, Fort Worth, seeing deterioration setting in by the early 1970s and single-family residences being broken up into apartments, formed the Ryan Place Improvement Association. It initiated National Register designation. Once that was secured local government was lobbied for a protective preservation ordinance.[37]

Nonprofit and neighborhood organizations are newcomers to the business of local history. Historical societies of the traditional kind have not normally seen the development of historic districts as one of their core responsibilities. Their main involvement in this area has often come through efforts to protect the integrity and appeal of the environments of the historic houses and house museums of which they are the custodians. Local historians and historical societies and their libraries have often played a key role in the research needed for historic district designation and in the subsequent efforts to keep alive informed awareness of the history of a historic district.[38] But there has been an evolution in the activities of some traditional historical societies so that they have eventually assumed the character of preservationist pressure groups. A new breed of historical societies has developed as part of the preservationist movement. These societies—sometimes the older societies given a new purpose in life—have assumed a much more activist role in preservation. At Tecumseh, Michigan, a popular house tour program was organized by the historical society. It is credited with helping to mobilize the awareness of architectural heritage that persuaded the city to pass a historic district ordinance and have a district placed on the National Register.[39] The historical society in Birmingham, Alabama, is now in large part a preservationist organization—and a very active one. At Galesburg, Illinois, it was a grassroots preservationist movement that formed the Galesburg Historical Society in the 1970s for the express purpose of protecting architecture through zoning regulation. In 1976 the society began developing a strategy to preserve the Public Square, the city's historic core. It was the society that took the initiative in getting the Public Square nominated (successfully) to the National Register as a historic district.[40]

The Existence of Districts as Historic Districts

There is a fourth phase in the history of historic districts, the history of what happens *after* they have become "historic." A district does not pass out of history just because it has been given this label—unless it is a walled-off museum. Districts that are designated as historic continue to be part of the ongoing history of the towns and cities in which they are located. Historic districts, unlike museum villages and heritage parks, are places where people continue to make their homes.[41] Inevitably, therefore, compromises between the past and the present have to be made to accommodate the requirements of modern living. After thirty years it has become apparent that historic districts are not functioning just as add-ons to the variety of neighborhoods in cities. They are themselves part of the texture of the modern city. Much of this is attributable to the alliances that have been forged in so many cities between planners and historic preservationists. Policies for the conservation of existing housing stock in particular have brought planners and preservationists together at the district level. Historic preservation has frequently become involved in the development of strategies that have favored the conservation of buildings and housing for other than historic reasons. Planners and the many others involved in historic preservation projects have often had agendas of their own in which the achieving of historic preservation of the traditional kind, giving priority and primacy to the sorts of considerations embedded in the National Register criteria, has not always been the principal objective. A recent study commented that "historic preservation has become less a separate movement and more a philosophy of urban planning and design." The lines are becoming "increasingly blurred between preservation, neighborhood planning and growth management."[42] This means that heritage preservation can become, and has become, a feature of wider city and even regional planning.

Historic Districts and Ongoing Change

Historic districts do not simply either reflect or ignore changes that have already occurred. They also have a relationship to the continuing history of districts. No issue has been more hotly contested in the discussions about historic districts than the matter of the extent to which change should be controlled in the name of the district's "historic" character after designation has occurred. There are innumerable forms of influence constantly being exerted over the character of a district. These continue regardless of regimes of historic district controls that are largely over design and architecture. Other major forms of control are in the realm of planning and zoning. Internal changes in buildings are normally not regulated, and so through adaptive reuse the character of a building's function in and relationship to its context can change fundamentally while facade features remain protected. And there is the social sphere, "the natural evolution of life" as one historical society person perhaps despairingly had to admit when witnessing change that went contrary to the image portrayed by the architecture.[43] Being designated a National Register historic district certainly does not stop change. Lacking the protections of local designation, National Register districts sometimes disintegrate and even disappear. Change can erode the "historical" character of a district to the point where it has to be removed from the National Register, as has happened in the case of Underground Atlanta. The Olive Street Terra Cotta District in St. Louis is another example. It was placed on the National Register in 1986, but by 1988 all but one of the contributing structures had been demolished.[44] A notorious instance of demolition of most of the major structures shortly after designation is Jobbers Canyon in Omaha. Jobbers Canyon, a district of early-twentieth-century warehouses, was destroyed between 1987 and 1989 after it had been designated a National Register historic district in 1986. The city's business leaders, desperate to retain a major food-processing company, ConAgra, proposed a vacant site adjacent to Jobbers Canyon. But ConAgra decided that the "big, ugly red brick buildings" of Jobbers Canyon were not compatible with the kind of development they wanted on the site and insisted that they be removed. The city resisted this demand but in the end had to give way after the company threatened to take its development, much needed by Omaha, to another place.[45]

Locally designated historic districts, however, are distinguished by the establishment of regulatory processes with regard to changes in buildings and other features of a district's historic character. Here the question of controlling change arises with particular frequency in the design of new buildings.[46] Historic preservation commissions have constantly to consider the "appropriateness" of proposed designs. This is the aspect of historic districts that most impinges on people's lives—and on their finances. Design review processes mean that one cannot do what one likes with one's property. From one point of view this is itself an "unhistorical" development. Many historic districts show the consequences of people having been free to do what they liked with their property before the district was designated "historic"—the "modernization" or "Victorianization" of Federal or Georgian houses, for example. These are part of the "history" that is now subject to protection and controls. Some guides to historic districts pretend that this did not happen or deplore it if they do mention it. "In Manchester [Vermont], a house that had been 'modernized' in the Victorian period, so that the residents were quite used to its revised appearance, was sought to be restored to its original architecture; there was a good deal of resistance from people in the town. However, the Manchester authorities agreed to approve the restoration."[47]

What are referred to as "modern intrusions" are often frowned on, and there has been a great deal of debate as to the extent to which "modern" styles can be permitted in a historic district. A typical National Register nomination—for Dorset, Vermont—approvingly describes that village's lack of modern intrusions. This sort of language is common in historic district nominations. "Nonconforming" and "noncontributing" are the most commonly used terms.[48]

Alexandria has proved to be one of the most controversial examples of a strict stand against new styles. For many years the city council wanted all new buildings in the central historic core to be in traditional styles, and most are. On one occasion, when the Board of Architectural Review approved some "modern" designs, it was reconstituted. Its backers said that the city should not be "a museum frozen in time."[49] Another city where the perceived effects of the emphasis on "design preservation" have been controversial is New Orleans.[50] In such places concern develops over the confusion caused by the proliferation of copies that have appeared to be the result of insisting on using only traditional styles. It becomes less and less easy to distinguish between the authentic and the imitative "historic" buildings.

Historic districts are in essence manufactured and historicized districts. Once a district has been designated as historic, all sorts of changes are usually made to its appearance—often through the workings of design review and the observance of design guidelines—and it becomes more and more self-consciously and unmistakably "historic." The design of signage proclaims the district's "historic" identity. And old buildings from elsewhere are often moved in to fortify this identity. All this may create a district that bears little resemblance to what the locality has ever actually been like. But it *is* "historic."

Design review processes tend to entrench the fixation with one segment of the past of a town which is encouraged by National Register criteria. Helen Edwards, owner of a real estate firm with offices in the downtown of the Concord, Massachusetts, Historic District (NR 1977), was reported in the *Boston Globe* as commenting thus on why they could use only certain colors for their signage: "The center of town has to look as much like it did in Colonial times as possible, to maintain both the visual and cultural integrity of the town. . . . But Edwards doesn't seem to mind. 'Because we're in the historic district, our sign ended up in the background of the movie *Housesitters* when they came to Concord to film in 1991. It made it worth it,' she said. She points out that the town's concern for the preservation of its historical legacy is part of what attracts visitors from around the world. And, it keeps Concord ranked as one of the most desirable, and high-priced, communities in Greater Boston." Alfred J. Lima, director of planning and land management, is quoted as saying he would like to see the tough preservation standards strengthened. "Concord has done a good job of preserving its character, but as development pressures increase we're going to have to be more diligent. The birth of the nation occurred here. To many people in America, this town is like a shrine."[51]

The transformation of a historic district into a "historic" district is well captured in Larry Millet's description of the Minneapolis warehouse district (NR 1989): "The old Minneapolis warehouse district north of Hennepin— occupied by a lively mix of artists, antique dealers, and restaurateurs—is the closest thing left to a spontaneously created urban environment in either downtown [of the Twin Cities]. But as developers move in and rents move up, the warehouse district threatens to ossify into one of those packaged 'old towns' that are so often a substitute for the real thing in American cities."[52] This historicizing reflects the enormous upsurge in recent times in the interest of the marketplace in the use of "heritage" as a motif to promote a wide range of commercial enterprises and products. The Bicentennial of 1976, by heightening consciousness of "heritage" as commercially exploitable, was particularly influential in that regard.

This exploitability is manifesting itself in the growing tendency to use historic districts as film sets. Colonial Williamsburg set a precedent by becoming and remaining the prime example of the historic district as stage set, in its case particularly for political occasions and as the backdrop for meetings of international leaders.[53] As early as 1933 H. I. Brock complained in the *New York Times* that at Williamsburg "a stage set had been set for living figures. . . . [T]here was an uncomfortable sense of newness about the whole thing."[54] The interest of towns in making their historic areas available for filmmaking appeared early on. In 1938 the publisher of the Tombstone *Epitaph* announced that the citizens of that western town were willing to sell the entire town to a movie company for $75,000.[55] Film companies have come to value historic districts as settings for their movies. Jacksonville, Oregon, for instance, is a popular location for scenes in westerns; and Charleston, South Carolina, for antebellum epics. A recent account of the meticulously restored central historic district of Lexington devotes much space to its use for the filming of the movie *Sommersby*.[56] The use of historic towns and districts for movies helps to reinforce their historicity both by inserting additional authentic-looking structures into the landscape — structures that, as at Eckley, Pennsylvania, are not always subsequently removed[57] — and by creating a financial motivation for not interfering with a town's desired historic character. It seems nowadays that, in addition to the test of the number of antique shops, one can also tell a "historic" district by the frequency with which it is being used as a setting for a movie or a television series.[58]

Another aspect of the place of historic districts within the modern city is the influence that they exert that ranges far beyond their own boundaries and the exclusive, special character of the history that they are supposed to represent and protect. A major source of such influence has been the operations of design review boards, the watchdogs over architectural change and the guardians of historic legacies. The development of historic districts and the massive restoration of old buildings have meant that there are now enormous reservoirs of historic style examples in a purified form and a protected environment. Within historic districts, competition from "nonhistoric" styles has been limited not just because of the surveillance exercised by design review boards but also because, as Ellen Beasley puts it, the general public "has always viewed pseudo-historic styles as the preferred design solution for new structures in historic districts" and the marketplace "identified imitative-style structures as being the most marketable for historic areas."[59] Beasley has shown how widespread has been building in traditional styles in historic towns and districts. The results of all this in terms of the replication of historic styles well beyond the boundaries of officially recognized historic districts are becoming obvious—nowhere more so than in the latest form of revival architectural style, postmodernism, which draws on historical motifs and echoes the features of the architecture and design of older buildings in the vicinity.[60]

In particular, design controls have produced a new and distinctive form of architecture. This is because they are intended not just to protect the historic character of existing structures but also to control and monitor the styles in which new buildings are designed, the buildings that constitute the "infill" among the "historic" structures. Analysts of the operation of design guidelines and controls have discussed whether they stifle or stimulate creative design. It is clear that sometimes they do have an inhibiting effect.[61] However, Nathan Weinberg's description of how by the late 1970s in Santa Fe "some architects working with the indigenous styles and design elements required in the historic zone have produced residential and commercial buildings of great merit and of an appearance unique to New Mexico" can be confirmed now as characteristic of the experience in numerous localities that have been subject to regimes of design control.[62]

There is a tradition here which helps to explain the ways in which American architecture has been affected by, as well as has influenced, historic preservation. The revival of historic architectural styles has been one of the major features of American architectural history. In the nineteenth century, there were Greek, Gothic, Romanesque, Queen Anne, and classical as well as all sorts of exotic (Moorish, Egyptian) revivals, all using motifs and forms derived from foreign sources. The twentieth century saw more of these, for example, the Spanish and Mediterranean revivals. But from the early twentieth century what were seen as distinctively American styles—colonial, Georgian, federal—began also to be revived and ultimately acquired a dominant position in American architecture, especially house design. Historic preservation itself can be seen as in this tradition of revivals. It is quite literally a revival in, for instance, the removal of aluminum false fronts to revive nineteenth-century commercial facades[63] as well as in the restoration of Victorian houses to something more than their original splendor. A historic district of such buildings is a district that has undergone a form of architectural revival similar to those of the past where what is revived is not the past as it actually was but an idealized or distorted version of it. This kind of revival is capable of being spread well beyond the areas that are initially designated and set aside as historic.

Boundaries

One of the most critical issues affecting the development of a relationship between historic districts and the towns and cities in which they are embedded relates to their boundaries. The development of historic districts coincided with and reflected the emergence of new thinking about how urban districts in general could be better structured. That there was a linkage between these trends and historic district development undoubtedly owed a great deal to the influence of two groundbreaking books published during the 1960s. In *The Death and Life of Great American Cities* (1961), Jane Jacobs, wanting to restore and strengthen the neighborhood in the American city, gave much thought to what would be an appropriate structure for "effective districts." The problem, as she saw it, was that most cities "possess many islandlike neighborhoods too small to work as districts. . . . [T]hese include . . . many unplanned neighborhoods." Parks, squares, and public buildings should, she argued, be used as part of a street fabric "to intensify and knit together the fabric's complexity and multiple use. . . . Few people, unless they live in a world of paper maps, can identify with an abstraction called a district, or care much about it." A city cannot "be mapped out in segments of about a square mile, the segments defined with boundaries, and districts thereby brought to life." Physical barriers to easy cross-use should be the boundaries. "The fact of a district lies in what it *is* internally, and in the internal continuity and overlapping with which it is used, not in the way it ends or how it looks in an air view."[64]

The other book was Lynch's *The Image of the City* (1960). Lynch was particularly concerned about the lack of distinctiveness in Boston's districts and likewise provided much discussion of what a district was and might be. He argued that "if Boston districts could be given structural clarity as well as distinctive character, they would be greatly strengthened." Among the major difficulties that he identified in that city's "image" were "confusions, floating points, weak boundaries, isolations, breaks in continuity, ambiguities, branchings, lacks of character or differentiation."[65] He attached great importance to landmarks and nodal points when he analyzed what planners needed to do to secure what he argued was essential, a clearer, stronger definition for urban districts. "A city district in its simplest sense," Lynch explained, "is an area of homogeneous character, recognized by clues which are continuous throughout the district and discontinuous elsewhere. The homogeneity may be of spatial characteristics, like the narrow sloping streets of Beacon Hill; of building type; . . . of style or of topography. It may be a typical building feature."[66] The reference to Beacon Hill is significant. Lynch took this recently established historic district as a good example of a neighborhood that was effectively structured in the terms of the criteria

Plaque commemorating the creation of the West Gardner
Square Historic District, Gardner, Massachusetts, in 1985.

that he had been emphasizing. In turn, as if in accordance with his point of
view, the interpretation of what is distinctive about historic districts usually
emphasizes their streets and focal points, such as buildings, parks, squares,
and boundaries. These are, for instance, the skeleton of the walking tour,
which is one of the principal ways in which historic districts are experienced. Nominations of districts to the National Register frequently use
Lynch's set of requisites—nodes, landmarks, edges, paths—as measures of
the extent to which the place that is being proposed is indeed a district.

Having identified "weak boundaries" as one of the major difficulties in
Boston's image,[67] Lynch maintained that a district is "sharpened by the defi-
niteness and closure of its boundary."[68] In his view boundaries give a district
an essential islandlike character. One of the principal tests used to decide
whether to grant historic district designation has been the clarity of the
proposed boundaries. The edges of historic districts are frequently marked
by prominent buildings that serve as landmarks. Their presence there plays
a large part in the determination of the boundaries. For example, in Mott
Haven Historic District, New York (NR 1980), both ends of the east side
of Alexander Avenue terminate with a church, and both ends of the west
side terminate with a public building.[69] The edges of Hamilton Heights
Historic District, New York (1983), are described as being "anchored" by
three churches.[70] A historic district is required to have clear, logical, and
defensible boundaries. When it is designated, its boundaries are defined
and drawn on maps. Markers and plaques are frequently displayed to advise passersby that they are entering or leaving the historic district. Usually
these boundaries did not exist before, at least in this explicit way. They sel-

Lawyers Row (1870s), adjacent to the courthouse on the Public Square, Bedford, Pennsylvania. Part of National Register Historical District (1983). The offices are still used today by attorneys.

dom correspond to boundaries used for other purposes, such as local government. Their definition causes historic districts to stand out as distinctive entities, sometimes more so than in their original "historic" phase and certainly more so than in the intervening "survival" era. The creation of these boundaries, especially where they have not existed before or for a long time in so clear-cut a form, or where intangibles such as neighborhood identity are expected to be taken into account, frequently attracts controversy.

The issue of boundaries emerged during the shift in emphasis in historic preservation away from individual buildings. A significant contribution to the evolution of the historic district was made by the desire to preserve the environment of landmark buildings. Historic buildings, it has become clear, gain added validation through the identification and protection of their historical contexts. Today there are efforts to create wider historic districts in the vicinity of hub railroad stations that will include warehouses, hotels, and other facilities that were integral to the operation of those institutions.[71] "Lawyers' rows" adjacent to courthouses are another example of buildings that, if incorporated into a district surrounding the sort of landmark structure that has hitherto been the stand-alone focus of historic preservation, enable one to understand much more clearly the significance of that structure itself and its relationship to the community. But when attention turns to the context of buildings, the boundaries of that context have to be defined. And it has not always been easy to discover or rediscover and then define these contexts in such a way as to secure general acceptance for them. As the determining of historic districts reaches out beyond the fairly easily defined confines of individual structures, the fixing of appropriate and defensible boundaries becomes a complex matter. This was even more the case as interest developed, via the writings of Lynch, for example, in mental or cognitive maps, that is, maps drawn by people which reveal the associations that particular buildings and landmarks have for them as they live and move about in a city environment. Elasticity of boundaries derives also from people's less easily definable notions of the dimensions of their neighborhoods. Larry Ford pointed out that mental maps constructed by locals far exceed official historic districts in size.[72] Neighborhoods are not neatly self-contained and clearly separated entities. They overlap and interrelate, and people's perceptions of what is their neighborhood will vary considerably according to their personal circumstances and experience. It is seldom possible to structure a city as a series of self-contained historical contexts for landmark structures. These contexts are bound to overlap, and what is deemed appropriate as the setting for one landmark may well not suit another. And as the focus on landmarks fades and concern for the integrity of the district itself grows, different kinds of understandings of the relationships of the buildings within it and between them and buildings in adjacent districts may emerge.

There are many possible definitions and categories of boundaries. An important analysis of edges and boundaries was undertaken for the National Trust for Historic Preservation in the 1970s. In April 1973 the trust was awarded a grant from the National Endowment for the Arts City Edges program for a study of twenty historic districts. This was in effect a major exercise—virtually the first—in creating a working description of a historic district. The 1966 criteria were so general that this work remained to be done. The purpose of the study was "the identification, description and analysis of the elements that form the edges of these historic districts." The results were published in *A Guide to Delineating Edges of Historic Districts*, intended as "a guide to those individuals and agencies legally responsible for delineating the edges of historic districts yet to be created, for revising existing district edges and for facing problems caused by the boundaries of existing districts." The study provided much detailed advice on features that should be considered in the determination of boundaries. These included not just the traditional architectural inventory but also natural features, archaeological, historic, and cultural sites, and the townscape itself—"the form and image of a community." Historic factors in delineating edges were discussed. The boundaries of the original settlement or of a planned community were recommended as "a logical boundary line for historic districts, easily understood and enforceable." Edges might be based on topographical considerations. They might be drawn to include gateways and entrances. Physical edges such as railroads, expressways, and major highways could be used "to define and structure areas otherwise lacking in visual identity." Edges could be made also by major open spaces, such as parks and cemeteries, and by rivers, marshlands, and other natural features. An example of the impact of strong edges given in the report was Pullman, the famous company town south of Chicago. The distinctive architecture is described as having created highly visible edges, strong physically and spatially. The way in which the railroad embankment had acted as a wall is related to the history of the district: "This edge was originally planned to provide vistas of the company town to railroad passengers, with most of the important public buildings facing the embankment." The conclusion was that this district and the citizen organizations "[had] achieved a real sense of community and place, reinforced by the clear visual edges."[73]

The report recognized that the boundaries of historic districts might have to reflect political constraints and tactical considerations and exclude, at least initially, institutions and property owners who resist inclusion. "A compromise at best, this is usually a negative edge factor used to insure swift passage of an ordinance."[74] The case studies in the report bear out the view that political and strategic considerations were having a good deal more to do with determining the shape and content of historic districts than purely historical aspects. The report is revealing on how historic districts were being constructed at that critical formative phase—what was being put in and what was being left out, and why. It emphasizes the role of politics, compromise, and the attitudes of property owners. For example, in Charleston major commercial buildings were excluded because of lack of concern for protection of nonresidential areas and a desire to forestall any opposition from local merchants. At Beacon Hill, where the north slope was added after the destruction of the adjacent West End, legislators kept the State House out even though it is historically and architecturally an integral part of Beacon Hill. The historic district of Santa Fe, New Mexico, was enlarged when property owners petitioned for inclusion. At College Hill, Providence, the key determinants were the limits of concentration of pre-1830 buildings and the location of properties owned by the opposing institutions (Brown University, Rhode Island School of Design). The purpose of using 1830 as the cut-off date was to ensure acceptance of the district. "While the importance of Victorian and later 19th-century architecture in Providence was recognized in the demonstration study, the aesthetic and historical value of these later buildings had not been widely accepted by the community in the 1960s."[75] There was also a desire not to appear in conflict with urban renewal projects. In connection with Pioneer Square, Seattle, for instance, a major role was played by political, social and individual pressures. There was opposition on the part of some property owners—but also a desire on the part of others to be included.

Boundaries of historic districts often change, as a scrutiny of entries in the National Register reveals. This occurs, for instance, where for tactical reasons a district has deliberately been started on a small scale. The 1973 report advised proponents of historic districts to start with a small, easily defensible core district and expand it as the concept gained acceptance. The creation of even a modest historic district is seen as a way of giving people nearby time and opportunity to appreciate its benefits. Historic home tours in historic districts seem to have this effect. "Neighbors watching the whole process across the garden fence are motivated to fix up their own properties, and the process moves from house to house, block to block, until new historic districts are formed."[76]

In addition, once a district has been created, there has often appeared to be a constant need to protect it and its boundaries by expanding them or by creating buffer zones between them and threatening influences—a process that is somewhat reminiscent of the way empires, notably the British Empire, expanded in the nineteenth century. An example is the Huning Highlands Historic District in Albuquerque (NR 1978). There has been concern for years over a sadly deteriorated high school on its borders. "When this building . . . is rehabilitated," we are told, "the entire neighborhood will be buttressed."[77] Action is also often taken in rural areas to protect villages from the encroachment of developers, especially if a large metropolitan area is nearby.[78]

Boundaries have proved to be both firm in terms of the criteria and porous in terms of the influence that seeps out beyond them. Once a historic district is created, there is often a diffusion of its influence.[79] A significant spillover effect into contiguous areas—"creeping Old Townism"—has been observed in places such as Providence, where it took the form of restoration activity and a sense of pride in owning a historic building.[80] Two geographers have written of German Village, Columbus, Ohio, "The rehabilitation of German Village has had a contagious effect since the 'villagizing' process seems to be spreading to areas immediately outside the Village, particularly on the east and south, and many people refer to a German Village area that far exceeds its official boundaries."[81] Boundaries are permeable from the opposite direction as well. Historic districts increasingly are

Old Main, Old Albuquerque High School (1914), New Mexico. Its deteriorated condition has led to concern about the damaging impact it makes as the focal point of a historic district.

functioning as a sort of island or refuge, drawing into themselves unwanted and endangered buildings from other areas where they may possibly have served as a nucleus or catalyst for historic district formation. As Beasley has pointed out, several communities, such as Indianapolis and Mobile, "have had success moving buildings into historic districts. . . . The relocated buildings have been of an age and style compatible with the buildings in the districts." However, her view is that in these instances the buildings "would not have survived in their original locations."[82]

The interest in renewal that is aroused in adjacent areas often causes districts to expand until a boundary such as a highway or business district is reached.[83] Rampart Street is a six-lane divided highway one hundred feet wide, but it was also one of the original boundary streets of the Vieux Carré in New Orleans. It traditionally separated the Vieux Carré from other districts in terms of development. Faubourg Marigny on the other side of Esplanade Avenue was excluded from the historic district. The influence of the Vieux Carré on it became so marked, however, that there was much talk of the Faubourg Marigny itself having acquired the characteristics of a historic district.[84] The *Guide to Delineating Edges* reported interesting effects on nearby areas in Santa Fe—and consequences for the integrity of the original historic district. The existence of the district influenced the appearance of the contiguous area. Despite the lack of controls requiring such action, many property owners elected to preserve and restore their existing buildings, or to build in a manner compatible to the Santa Fe style. "This spread of similar architectural styles, forms and building materials, coupled with the generally irregular edges, has created a minor problem of identification, whereby it is often impossible to define the edges of the district in the field except for the Plaza core area."[85]

This shows how influence, having originally spread out from a historic district, can start to flow back in the reverse direction. This process of imitation may then begin to threaten the integrity of the original historic district. *Delineating the Edges* recommended including a buffer zone in a historic district to shield it from possible "new housing, shopping centers or industrial parks that may overreact in a quaint or fake historic way to the features of the historic area."[86]

A problem that arose in Cincinnati's Dayton Street Historic District illustrates the care that has to be taken in creating, reviving, or emphasizing boundary or edge features. The Dayton Street Neighborhood Association (DSNA) angered long-term black residents by its reconstruction of a historic arch on Linn Street. "To the DSNA, it is an ornate reminder of the neighborhood's cherished architectural past, salvaged to serve as a boundary marker for the Dayton Street Historic District." In fact, it used to be the archway to the police department and as such held many bad memories for the older residents.[87]

There has also been concern over the possible social impacts of the creation and enforcement of boundaries. It has been suggested that there is a danger of repeating and reinforcing the extreme social differentiation that was a feature of suburbanization.[88] Larry Bennett has commented on the closed-off character of the new middle-class residential areas in cities.[89] Historic district boundaries and their often explicit physical representations may reinforce this tendency. Because of their formal and indeed legally recognized status and the apparatus that has been constituted to protect them, they may be more resistant to the adjustments of relationships among people that were once possible across what used to be informal boundaries. Features that are relied on to structure historic districts have certainly not been a neutral element in the situation. They have themselves been of great significance in highlighting and entrenching existing barriers and boundaries, some of which may over time have become relatively weak and insignificant or forgotten in the life of their community.

What's In a Name

When a locality is designated a historic district, it receives not only boundaries but also a name. This is another distinguishing feature, a form of boundary. This may be the first time that a district has had such a clear-cut and authorized identity. Hunter described names and boundaries as of critical importance for communities because they confer a sense of identity and status and define a new reality that may be usable in a variety of contexts. He suggested that such symbols of community have been created and manipulated by those who wish to heighten and then exploit a sense of community solidarity.[90] This latter insight was followed up by Suttles some years after the publication of Hunter's book. Suttles looked again at the situation in Chicago, the city that had been the subject of Hunter's study. He found that the evolution of names and identities for Chicago communities had continued at an unrelenting pace. There was a constant "sub-nucleation of the urban landscape" in which people sought to establish "defensible space" so as to "try to regulate the process of redevelopment." He recognized that some of the smaller areas with fancy names were "little more than the invention of real estate entrepreneurs." Then there were "partially contrived 'ethnic neighborhoods' (Ukrainian Village, Lithuanian Plaza) which have been invented or revived through a political process in which some evidence of ethnic presence has been seized upon to promote a commercial district or increase local control." "Andersonville," for example, was a name devised on the basis of a long-vanished Swedish presence. It was being used to distinguish a district from an adjacent neighborhood that had developed a reputation for being populated by "drunken hillbillies, bums, street people, and transients." Apart from this revival of "old" ethnic areas, other districts were trying to find "a niche in the market for a distinct housing preference" or "some suggested ambience." Suttles suggests that the historic designation of some twenty-one residential areas was "probably the most advanced stage of this kind of local exceptionalism." He refers to numerous local groups that had erected eye-catching banners "giving the name of the neighborhood and suggesting something of its aspirations ("Buena Park: An Historic District")."[91]

Real estate developers have been using names in this way for many years, as can be seen in the numerous historic districts based on suburban real estate promotions and now bearing the names of their developers. Suttles points out that "local boosterism has always contributed greatly to neighborhood names and reputations."[92] This manipulation of perceptions through names can be traced back to the origins of America's towns.[93] The naming of places in America has been strongly influenced by boosterism since the days when tiny hamlets were called "cities" or named after Paris, Rome, or Athens.

By the 1890s most towns were developing neighborhoods with "visible economic similarities among those who lived in them and differences from other neighborhoods."[94] Sam Bass Warner has pointed out that "in the United States, sometime between 1850 and 1880, our cities began to mean many different things to many different people, and urban imagery then multiplied accordingly." There were "the Gold Coast, Fifth Avenue, and Euclid Avenue, the streets of the rich and the millionaires; the skyscrapers of New York and Chicago. . . . [E]very big city had its little Italy, its Lower East Side, its Germantown, its cabbage patch, its Dear Old North End, its Honkeyville and Niggertown. The class and ethnic imagery and vocabulary were rich and varied, some complimentary, some pejorative. The late-nineteenth-century city was no longer a small Illinois Central Railroad town with its right and wrong side of the tracks; it was a place of multiple images, and it has been ever since."[95]

Over the years districts in American cities have been given many nicknames, for example, "the Hill," "Quality Hill," "Millionaires' Row," "Mansion Row," and "Silk Stocking Row" for the wealthy sections.[96] "Pill Hill" was a common name for districts inhabited by doctors.[97] The Gold Coast Historic District in Chicago (NR 1978) was identified many years ago in a classic Chicago school of sociology study.[98] There were also many stock names for poorer neighborhoods. Atlanta has its Cabbagetown District (NR 1976). The original Skid Road is commemorated in the name of the Pioneer Square–Skid Road Historic District in Seattle (NR 1988).[99] Some of the images and reputations that areas acquired are being revived and entrenched in the names of historic districts. However, one must be careful: some of the names now being employed look "historic" but are in fact modern inventions. An example is the Cobble Hill Historic District in New York City (NR 1976). In the late 1950s "an enterprising real estate dealer rediscovered the Revolutionary War name, Punkiesburg, a redoubt at today's Atlantic Avenue and Court Street. Translation into English as Cobble Hill transformed the community in both name and desirability."[100] Memphis has a Central Gardens Historic District (NR 1982), which covers an area of early-twentieth-century residential development. We are told that the name itself is of relatively recent coinage and was meant to "invoke the splendors of nineteenth-century New Orleans."[101] The name Farrington's Grove Historic District (Terre Haute, Indiana [NR 1986]) sounds old but was in fact invented in 1976 to give an impression of unity to this extensive area.

Entrenching the Form: The Walking Tour, a Modern Version of "Beating the Bounds"

There is a medieval English parish custom known as "beating the bounds," usually carried out on Holy Thursday or Ascension Day, which took the form of a procession of schoolchildren, accompanied by clergymen and parish officers, walking from one end of the parish to the other. The purpose was to teach the children the boundaries of the parish. To make sure that the lesson was properly learned, the boys were switched with willow wands as they walked along the boundary. Fortunately, today's visitors to the historic districts of the United States are not subjected to such drastic methods of inculcating the significance of what they are observing. But in other respects the walking tours they take may aptly be described as a modern-day version of this quaint custom. The walking tour, in the form of both printed brochures as the basis of self-guided tours and tours conducted by guides, is perhaps the most common way in which historic districts are presented and interpreted for visitors. The famous report on College Hill gave a boost to the concept of the walking tour or trail. Historic trails, it argued, "lend greater prestige to the properties along its route, induce owners to upgrade their properties, . . . stimulate the renewal of areas in proximity to the trail [and] attract attention outside the city to the assets of the historic community."[102] Many towns now have trails with lines on the pavement directing walkers, or symbols outside the historic sites indicating that they are described in more detail in a brochure.

Jacobs argued that it was important to foster "lively and interesting streets."[103] Her influence is clearly seen in the emphasis on the walking tour as the principal way in which people should experience a district. Visitors walking a city's streets themselves become part of the scene and add "life" to a district. And, of course, the presence of people on the streets walking along them and appreciating the streetscapes, buildings, and other features serves to fortify an image in the minds of the townspeople of their towns as interesting places. In some towns and cities walking tours are guided by local people, often retired, who provide a personal view of the city's history — and a fair amount of oral history into the bargain. Good examples are the tours provided in Lancaster, Pennsylvania, Elmira, New York, and Frederick, Maryland, and in the Lawrence, Massachusetts, Heritage State Park. John Meynink began conducting "Portland on Foot" tours in 1983. He is described as knowing the districts "like the back of his hand." "And why not? He worked in them 65 years ago, delivering flour to the ubiquitous corner groceries of the day."[104]

The walking tour entrenches and gives validity to a historic district's structure and form. As they wander around, brochures in hand or under the direction of a guide, the visitors are "beating" particular routes. The better guidebooks describe the route itself and create through the medium of the walk a narrative of the history of the district. Some buildings are observed and commented on; some streets are walked down. Other buildings are ignored; other streets are not included in the tour. A district within a district is formed, and a new plan emerges, one that reinforces some aspects of the existing plan and downplays others. A typical walking tour guide tends to re-create the dimensions of an ideal or desired type of community. It does this through what it draws to the walker's attention and through what it fails to mention. Churches and homes of community and business leaders of the past and their contributions are usually highlighted. Their fine homes are evidence of their commitment to the community and their achievement of rewards through that commitment.

In many historic districts this mode of structuring and facilitating the visitor's encounter makes possible the recovery of a sense of the dimensions of the "walking city." The reasons are explained in a 1973 publication by the New Bedford, Massachusetts, Redevelopment Authority:

> The aesthetic quality of the area as a whole is a direct consequence of the unity of building types, design traditions, spatial configurations and materials produced in a preautomotive, preelevator age. Streets and roadways are relatively narrow, blocks are short, and distances from point-to-point are limited. . . . The scale of the area as a whole was determined by limited distances, restrained building height and bulk, and the combinations and proportions of building parts and materials. Scale, the relationship of parts to the whole, was conditioned by the proximity and position of the observer. In the historic district the observer was intended to move at pedestrian speed. Consequently the details of architectural ornament, textural effects, and combinations of materials were important design elements. Seen from a moving vehicle, these elements blur into an apparent hodgepodge. Perceived at a pedestrian pace they become interesting, varied, picturesque, intimate parts of the urban scene.[105]

Walking tours can re-create the dimensions of districts and define their character and their place in the development of towns and cities. The challenge is to re-create the once-predominant experience of moving about city districts on foot. Unfortunately too seldom is the challenge responded to in an imaginative way. Sometimes the attempt is not made at all: the tour simply leads one from one building to another and explains nothing about the context. Many walking tour brochures simply provide a listing of sites and buildings and describe their history and characteristics. There is no description of the route one takes to get from one building to another or of the neighborhood context and landscape. A sense of place is weakly conveyed, if at all.

Almost all the early historic districts were districts of the walking city type, small and compact enough to be experienced on foot. Districts such as the one in Charleston were created in part to protect such places from the inroads of the automobile. One of the greatest challenges facing those who manage historic districts today is to prevent those inroads from once again destroying the integrity of the historic district. Traffic often totally destroys the historical illusion and sense of place. Walking the streets of a onetime walking city can be difficult and even hazardous. One comment on a historic district goes as follows: "The character of Great Road [Historic District] is best appreciated on foot, today a near impossibility given the heavy traffic routed through the historic district. The speed and volume of automobiles must be counted as the single greatest disruption in the historic district."[106] An example of the impact of traffic on the historic district environment is the fate of village greens, which have functioned as foci and centers in so many towns and villages. In many places they have developed into traffic islands that the pedestrian tries to reach at his or her peril.[107] This is not an entirely new phenomenon. One thinks, for instance, of the sad fate in the mid-nineteenth century of the Indian mound that was the original centerpiece and determinant of the unusual town plan in Circleville, Ohio. Gradually it was eroded and a regular grid imposed because of the inconvenience it constituted for traffic. Circleville has long ceased to have a circle.[108] A modern equivalent is Emmitsburg, Maryland (NR 1992), which began in the late eighteenth century with a plan that included a square as the center of town. The square became a beautiful place, and the center of it became ever more ornate: a well was converted into a magnificent fountain. Now little of this is left. The fountain "had to be removed to facilitate the flow of modern-day traffic."[109] It can be argued that the car is a more appropriate means of appreciating the more extensive historic districts in suburbs created after the advent of (and in their spatial dimensions accommodating), the automobile. But even there the pace and volume of modern traffic renders the experience of driving through such districts very different from when they were first created and fine mansions lined the boulevards to be admired by the relatively slow-moving carriages and cars. In these circumstances the original form cannot be appreciated as it was designed to be, and important features in it deteriorate.

Management of traffic in historic districts has been a concern since the beginning. In a controlled environment such as Williamsburg cars could be banned from the principal streets and the illusion of stepping back into the seventeenth century enhanced. But a living city was a different matter. As early as 1940 the Olmsted report on Charleston was suggesting one-way streets and "off-street parking spaces." Olmsted also suggested widening a few alleys to "channel tourist traffic."[110] Here we can see the origins of the self-guided tour—often originating from a large parking lot or garage adjacent to a visitors' orientation bureau where the brochures are available—as a way of managing tourist impact on a historic district. The aim is to limit traffic so as to enhance the walking tour experience. A 1973 report for the Maryland agencies responsible for establishing historic districts took Chestertown as its example: "Perhaps the single most important facet of the Historic Preservation Plan for Chestertown is an orientation toward attracting the tourist. The movement of traffic is limited to encourage pedestrian movement on walkways throughout the historic district. The visitor information center is in the business district and the historic sites are on an easily accessible walkway system."[111] The visitor to Chestertown today can experience the results of such planning in a remarkably pleasant walking environment—apart from one challenge, crossing Maple Avenue, which bisects the historic district and, as US 213, carries a fair volume of traffic.[112]

Sometimes photographs are displayed around a town or district to enhance the experience of a walking tour.[113] Walking tour brochures frequently reproduce historic photographs or even provide a guide to the locations of buildings that used to be there as well as those that still exist. The latter is particularly common in guides issued by preservationist organizations that wish to make a point and arouse indignation and concern about a lost particular building.

Rival groups sometimes have their own ideas as to what the bounds ought to be. "Historic district" tours are not always of locally designated or National Register historic districts. The term "historic area" or "historic district" is sometimes used loosely to refer to a part of a town that is perceived to have historic attributes or associations. Often, when visitors go to a town and seek a guide to the "historic district," they will be provided with a guide to this kind of area. Reference may be made to the existence and perhaps even the boundaries of local or national districts, but the shape and dimensions of this district may be quite different. It may reflect an alternative community view of the historic area, one that may be less confined, for instance, by architectural considerations. It may represent, in particular, the district where the stores and businesses are concentrated. It is often the chamber of commerce that sponsors the town guides for the business community. These direct visitors to areas where they will spend time and money. Sometimes the two kinds of walking tour are combined. For ex-

Historic District marker, Holland, Michigan.

ample, the visitor to Easton, Maryland (NR 1980), is told, "As you wander through our town, enjoy our Historic District and our many unique shops." The vital thing is to get people out of their cars and into the downtown shopping area. "History" is a lure to this end. The emphasis on the walking tour has fitted in with a trend toward turning some historic districts into what are in effect landscaped urban parks. This is one way to make walking a safe and pleasant experience. At one time there was much enthusiasm for turning "historic" areas within downtowns into pedestrian malls and parks. Examples are downtown Cumberland, Maryland (NR 1983), and Last Chance Gulch in Helena, Montana (part of Helena Historic District, 1972; 1990). In these places one has to park one's car nearby and walk to appreciate the architecture and other historic features. That makes sense historically, but it also means that one walks past the business premises as well as the historic architecture. Some towns are now doing away with pedestrian malls, however, as they find that deterring cars has also deterred potential customers.[114]

Finally, the form that has been established is cemented in place by the erection of markers at strategic entrance points. These may convey basic information about the history of the district or simply proclaim that one is entering a historic district. But, whatever the inscription may be, the message is clear: one is now crossing over into a special place. As regimes of control and protection take effect, the contrast between the two sides of the markers becomes more and more evident.

Seven

Thirty Years On: Do Historic Districts Have a Future?

New Formats in Historic Preservation

*T*HERE HAVE BEEN TWO APPARENTLY CONTRADIC-
tory tendencies at work influencing the place of the historic district
in the modern American town and city. On the one hand, the historic district has become a very special kind of place with the application of a stock
set of items from the vocabulary of historicization that make it easily distinguishable from other, nonhistoric districts. On the other hand, there has
been a tendency to generalize the identification and protection of "heritage" and render less and less relevant the specific historic district format
of historic preservation.

New formats for historic preservation have been emerging. An example
is the growth—or revival—in popularity of the historic park, reconceptualized under the influence of Disneyland as a theme park, a setting for
entertainment, recreation, and the presentation of history in theatrical and
staged formats. At Disneyland several historical themes were used to create idealized settings, at least one of which, Main Street, has been seen
as having a substantial influence on historic district development.[1] There
was a thematic approach inherent in the development of historic districts
from the beginning. Establishment criteria have emphasized predominant
periods, associations with famous people, and historic events. In many of
the classic historic districts, for example, in Santa Fe, a theme has been

identified which has been made the determining influence on their historic environment and ambience. Williamsburg and Independence are historical theme parks. Their examples have been available to keep alive the park concept and provide proof of its abiding appeal. Indeed, one of the most influential features of the Williamsburg model has proved to be the concept of the historic town as a *park*.

Here too there has been an evolution of focus from individual structures to districts. The original tendency was to create parklike settings for landmark buildings. This was a strong feature of early New England preservation. In 1919 Boston city officials wanted to create a park around the Paul Revere House in the North End by demolishing large numbers of adjacent houses, some dating back to the eighteenth century. William Sumner Appleton, the leading preservationist of the time, wrote, "They have an attractive sketch showing the Paul Revere house standing free in the park. How fine that would be." Although this plan was not implemented, the creation of the Paul Revere Mall nearby in 1933 did involve considerable clearance of buildings.[2] Appleton even favored rebuilding the long-since-demolished John Hancock House on Beacon Hill, complete with its terraced gardens, even though that would have meant demolishing a large number of houses in Joy Street.[3]

This idea of establishing parks as settings for landmark buildings had died away as the nation wrestled with the formidable problems associated with creating, protecting, and managing historic districts within living cities. But an episode in Alexandria in 1970–71 showed the continuing appeal of this kind of park. The issue was whether a historic building of one era should be pulled down to enable a greater focus on a building of an earlier era, the one that has predominated in the desired overall image of the city's historic district. The advisory council said no. But the Northern Virginia Regional Park Authority (NVRPA) wanted to make the Carlyle House (1752) the focus of a small historic park. This meant pulling down the Carlyle Apartments (1855), which were now regarded as "substandard housing" and on which $2 to $3 million would have had to be spent for renovation. No private developer was interested. The NVRPA director called the apartments "an obstruction and an obtrusion." The advisory council said that the apartments helped to define the newly created Market Square, "preventing the space from visually flowing out and destroying the sense of enclosure. In removing the building, an important aspect of the integrity of Alexandria Historic District would be lost."[4] Nevertheless, the apartments went, and the Carlyle House was restored in a new parklike setting.

At Nauvoo, Illinois, a massive Mormon restoration effort has set the few remaining structures of the Mormon settlement in a park environment.

But the most dramatic application of the park concept to a historic district in recent times has been at Lowell, which was conceptualized and developed as a theme park. "Train and barge rides," stated the 1977 report to Congress, "will carry people from the visitor center to other parts of the park, connecting various interpretive areas."[5] The Urban Cultural Parks that New York State has been developing also seek to combine a parklike setting at the core with the continuation of a living city. Other features of theme park development are picked up in the emphasis on entertainment, fun, and festivity and the fostering of a theatrical, stage set ambience. The deployment of the carousel theme and symbol at the Heritage State Parks at Holyoke and Fall River, Massachusetts, and the Urban Cultural Parks at Binghamton, Johnson City, and Endicott City, New York, typifies this approach.

The developing concept of the historic district as a theme park has begun to attract the attention of critics. In 1992 a book entitled *Variations on a Theme Park* folded a number of modern historical park developments, especially in New York City, into this broad concept. M. Christine Boyer contributed an article on South Street Seaport and then expanded her views in *The City of Collective Memory*, published in 1994. Boyer sees parts of cities as having been made into "new visual spectacles and revitalized theatrical decors."[6] In fact, she goes so far as to place what has been done in some restored big city historic areas in a centuries-old tradition of theatrical representation of urban life. She refers to the nineteenth-century tradition of the tableaux vivants. City life is vastly complex and confusing, and the history of ways of making sense of this confusion for those who have to survive within it is full of idealized representations. One thinks also of the bird's-eye views that took the viewer up to a height (seldom realizable except in this sort of fantasy) and displayed an order and pattern unrecognizable at ground level. The particular point about historic districts in large cities is, in Boyer's opinion, that they are themselves fragments. The order is created by the addition of all sorts of symbolic and artistic embellishments into which the few authentic surviving pieces are submerged.[7]

Recently there has been an emergence of various kinds of fake, replica, and manufactured historic districts. "Olde Townes," colonial villages, and many variations on such themes have proliferated. One commentator has observed a tendency in Iowa's small towns, for instance, to develop an "urban theme district (a district consciously planned to convey a specific image). . . . [S]mall towns without restorable historic districts have overcome this by fabricating historical villages, instead. . . . These 'villages' are set apart in a world unlike the everyday life of the community. Their designs express the idea of pure imageability, the same calculus as that used in advertising. They do not serve the community's real needs or its traditions; neither do they satisfy the tourist's desire for a genuine experience of place."[8] The distinction between the real thing and replicas can sometimes be quite blurry. An example is a development at Addison, Texas, where a dozen thirty- to forty-year-old structures were torn down to be replaced by an "Old Town" that re-creates a late-nineteenth-century downtown.[9] A 1977 article in *Historic Preservation* traced the complex interactions between real and fake historic districts that appeared to be going on in Connecticut. New suburban shopping centers and condominiums were described as "lamentable imitations" of "genuine" historic districts at Farmington and Canton. But in turn the fake "Connecticut colonial" features that were being adopted were being introduced into the redesigning of the old company town of Collinsville to make it look "as antique as possible." Preservationists were urgently working to make Collinsville a protected historic district.[10] Sometimes historic districts, as a result both of their incompleteness and of their success and appeal, stimulate the creation of a matching replica that supplies the completeness but is fake, and an interesting relationship develops. The preservation of the historic core of Jacksonville for instance, was followed by the creation nearby of Pioneer Village, a reconstructed gold rush town. It offered stagecoach rides into the "real" western town.[11] Preservationists' concerns about these imitations is summed up in the following extract from a 1968 report on the Vieux Carré: "Authenticity, above all, distinguishes a genuine historic district from a 'true-to-life' simulation. Because they are subtler, ersatz restorations and pseudo-historic reconstruction pose, perhaps, the most critical threat to the preservation of an area like the Vieux Carré."[12] This would be true if historic districts *were* authentically historic, but they are not because of all the history that is excluded in their manufacture and also because of the historicization that controls their management. If the line between them and "fakes" is sometimes blurred, one has to acknowledge the degree of fakery that often goes into the representation of history in this medium.

It might be thought that the historic districts that have been the subject of this book have had nothing to do with trends of this kind. The sort of replica or fake district that has developed in many places where there is no foundation of "authentic history" to start with certainly does not gain acceptance to the National Register. But matters are not quite that clear-cut any more. Let us take museum or heritage villages as an example. Once upon a time there did seem to be a clear distinction between the historic district that satisfies National Register criteria and the museum village that does not. Preservation Park in Oakland, California, belongs in the latter category. It has been described as "a meticulous recreation of a late-nineteenth-century neighborhood." Its landscaping duplicates that of Victorian-Era neighborhoods, "based on careful documentation by local historians."[13] Of the sixteen historic structures in the park, five were originally on the site and eleven have been moved from elsewhere, including several rescued from the path of a freeway. Preservation Park is not a historic district. It does not satisfy the criteria. Most of the structures that are there, although authentically "historic," that is, not replicas, have come from somewhere else. The distinction between such a district and a historic district would appear to be clear-cut. Other cities have set aside areas that had no "historic" associations or structures but happened to be vacant and used them as a depository for threatened buildings. An example is Heritage Square in Los Angeles.[14] In San Francisco twelve Victorian houses were rescued from an urban renewal project and moved to fill in vacant lots in a nearby block where there were already houses of a similar type. This was then called the Beideman Place Historic Area.

But more and more districts that have achieved recognition and designation as historic districts are themselves turning into compromises between the district that is authentic in accordance with the established criteria and in which all of the structures are on their original sites and the sort of district that is manufactured, as in the "heritage village" model. The reason for this is the growing tendency to move threatened buildings from other areas into historic districts to supplement the old houses that constitute the original core. In part this is designed to fortify and entrench the overall historic environment of these districts. It has proved to be extremely difficult to avoid this when there are huge pressures on isolated buildings outside a protected zone. What happened at Strawbery Banke in Portsmouth was an early example of this situation. There the moving of houses from other sites into the village's sheltering embrace has occurred and indeed was accepted as part of Strawbery Banke's responsibility from the very beginning. Increasingly, moving houses into historic districts has become a preferred alternative to clustering them in an artificial museum village, although the latter can have the advantage that entrance fees can be charged to help defray costs of maintenance.

The houses that are moved into historic districts are usually sold for rehabilitation and are not treated as museums. An example of this kind of development is the large central historic district at Columbus, Georgia (NR 1969; expanded, 1988). An area of this size—nearly thirty city blocks—is very likely to contain many features and structures that detract from overall "historic" quality. Pressures are certain to arise for alternative uses of portions of the district that appear to be only marginally worth protecting in historic terms. A strategy of enhancing and strengthening historic character is often an imperative in these circumstances. Of the ten houses highlighted by the Historic Columbus Foundation in the walking tour brochure that it supplies to visitors, five have been moved to their present sites from other locations in recent times. In 1994 two churches were proposing to demolish four turn-of-the-century houses to expand space for car parks. The Historic District Preservation Society, having failed to persuade them to save the houses, reached an agreement with the churches to allow the money that would have been spent demolishing the houses to be spent instead on removing them. They now provide "infill on the edge of the Seventh Street Historic District" and "help revitalize a blighted part of the district."[15]

The history of Irvine Park in St. Paul illustrates the significance of moved houses in fortifying a historic district as well as the extent to which the movement of houses is itself a part of a tradition in city neighborhoods that long predates the creation of historic districts.[16] Irvine Park, first settled in the early 1850s, is one of St. Paul's longest-settled residential districts. Its heyday was in the 1870s when it became one of the city's most fashionable districts, and houses were built in the latest styles to display the wealth of their owners. By the end of the century, however, streetcars had opened access to locations farther removed from the river, and Summit Avenue and neighboring streets became the preferred abodes of the well-to-do. A long, slow period of decline, typical of many such districts in America's cities, began. Many of the larger houses came into the possession of absentee landlords and were subdivided into apartments. By 1970 this was a severely blighted district: 96 percent of the housing was classified as substandard. Houses were being regularly lost through vandalism, neglect, and arson.

During the 1970s a restoration plan was devised by the Ramsey County and Minnesota historical societies in association with a residents' association and the City of St. Paul Housing and Redevelopment Authority. They formed the Irvine Park Review Committee. Irvine Park has two major anchoring features that have greatly assisted the process of defining and maintaining its identity as a district. One, already referred to, is the park. The other is the Ramsey House, the home of the family and descendants of Alexander Ramsey, territorial governor and U.S. senator. The house is now operated as a house museum by the Minnesota Historical Society and attracts thousands of visitors to the district each year.[17] One of the main strategic decisions of the Irvine Park Review Committee was that historic houses should be clustered around the park and vacant lots used as move-in sites for endangered houses of merit. In a walking tour guide prepared by the Historic Irvine Park Association thirty-five properties are specifi-

The Alexander Ramsey House, Irvine Park, St. Paul, Minnesota. The house, erected between 1868 and 1872, remained in the possession of the Ramsey family until they willed it to the Minnesota Historical Society in 1964. It is now open as a museum and anchors the Irvine Park Historic District.

cally drawn attention to and described. Of these nearly a third are not in their original location. The National Register designation attaches to the district "exception b," which allows buildings that have been removed from their original location as long as they are "significant primarily for architectural value" (or are "the surviving structure most importantly associated with a particular person or event"). The district then became a shelter for houses endangered elsewhere. Eight of the houses were moved into Irvine Park during the 1970s and early 1980s. For example, one house was moved there in 1982 when its original location was becoming "surrounded by commercial concerns." Another house that was built in 1853 was bought by the Salvation Army in 1979 and then in 1981 moved six blocks to a different site in Irvine Park to make way for a building expansion. Houses have been moved in to fill gaps that had been created by fire and demolitions. A house that developers moved there in 1983 was placed on a site where a house had been razed by fire four years earlier. The era of historic preservation has certainly seen major changes to many of the houses at Irvine Park in the name of restoration. But in this there is nothing new: the history of many of the houses reveals constant change to their appearance and physical fabric over the years. What now appears as a historic district at Irvine Park is nothing like any district that existed previously at that location. Its history is in large part the history of what historic preservation and modern-day strategies of neighborhood rehabilitation have wrought. However, it must also be recognized that what they have wrought belongs to certain aspects of the traditions of neighborhood change.

From the Special to the Representative

Historic districts have evolved from the rare and exceptional to the representative and typical and finally to the comprehensive application of the model and the emergence of the generic. The origin of the historic district was as a very special place, a tradition that can be traced back to the emergence of the concept in places such as Charleston and Beacon Hill. Prior to 1966, although there was no overall national set of criteria, it is clear from the character and very small number of historic districts that had been created that they were perceived as very exceptional places, not representative of anything but worth preserving because of their unique qualities.

The multiplication of historic districts since 1966 has caused this tradition to lose much of its force. In the years following the creation of the National Register, the concept of the historic district moved from the original emphasis on the ideal, outstanding, and nontypical toward the view that it should be a showplace of the "representative" and the "typical," still exceptional, no doubt, but exceptional in relation to ability to represent a type of district that was once widespread but was now to be found in a reasonably intact form only in these relatively rare localities. It soon became apparent that a new type of "historic" district was emerging—one unlike the old prestige places. Richard Guy Wilson wrote, "The principles of preservation long considered applicable to areas with established historical pedigrees— the Vieux Carré in New Orleans or Society Hill in Philadelphia—are being tested in the much more common late-19th-century middle-class neighborhood."[18]

What was unclear was whether all districts of a particular type that satisfied the criteria should be deemed acceptable for inclusion on the National and State registers or whether only some were to be chosen. The trend toward the third phase of historic district development, based on comprehensiveness, was given strong impetus by the opportunities and incentives set up through the regimes of tax credits and the routinization of the process of creation of a historic district through the establishment of bureaucratic procedures and regulations. As the lists of historic districts continue to expand without any established cut-off in place, we seem to be arriving at a situation in which every district that satisfies the broadly in-terpreted criteria and that is in a good state of preservation is a potential historic district.

There were numerous problems associated with trying to maintain a balance between selectivity and the preservation of the typical or represen-tative. The National Register criteria are so general that an enormous range of phenomena can qualify any particular district as typical or representa-tive. This is especially true when the definition of significance is applied at local and regional as well as national levels. Typicality can also lose its force when so much of what is supposed to be typical has disappeared. In addition, there is a shortage of clearly discernible benchmarks or standards against which "typicality" or "representativeness" can be measured.

As "representativeness" began to merge into "comprehensiveness," dis-quiet began to grow. The main current of opinion regarding the trend toward comprehensiveness was initially one of enthusiasm, especially as the growth of historic districts coincided with the development of the neigh-borhood movement in the 1970s. Gradually, however, concern began to be voiced that the best interests of historic preservation were not being served in the way the system was operating. In an article published in 1985 Robert Kuhn McGregor indicated some of these concerns. He was criti-cal not just of the large number of historic districts that were being created in New York State but also of their great similarities. Essentially they came out of the same period of development—a time when architectural trends were predominantly national in scope. As McGregor puts it, "A handful of such districts could be justified, but ninety-one?"[19] McGregor believed that a historic district should have some end beyond the simple act of preserva-tion. It should tell a story. Only those that did should be selected.

One of the principal reasons for the trend toward mass production of historic districts has been the stereotyping of the history they represent. Various influences have been at work here. One has been the concept of "imageability" and the development of more and more sophisticated, and now computer-managed, techniques for creating desired design images. The interest in imageability owes much to Lynch's books, notably *The Image of a City*, in which he analyzed the structure of city districts and showed how features within them could be enhanced and manipulated to create more coherent urban environments. Second, there has been the influence of Anselm Strauss who in books such as *Images of the American City* drew attention to the great significance in numerous spheres of urban life of imagery associated with the city, for example, the long history of the use of visual representations in urban boosterism. The insights of both Lynch and Strauss are reflected in Jakle's comment that "the most attractive cities" have been "the most imageable places: cities where belief and attitude attached readily to elements of landscape. Impressive skylines and bird's-eye views, unusual streets and nodal points, unusual interior spaces and landmarks, and easily defined districts, all contributed as icons to making cities legible and memorable." [20]

A powerful influence attending the production of stereotypes was, and still is, tourism. It both simplifies and enhances stereotypes in historic districts. As Jakle has shown, tourists experience cities in distinctive ways. Certain kinds of districts particularly appeal to them. Elite residential districts, "contrived for display, made ideal tourist attractions." Tourism leads to a tendency to package "history" so that it becomes historical heritage "and not an integral part of the contemporary scene. . . . Historical features in landscape tended to be fenced off in a preserve called History." [21] Most historic districts are not tourist destinations, and the people living in them do not want them to be, except perhaps on carefully controlled occasions such as home tours—which are often aimed rather at other residents to show them how they can restore their own properties. But some of the most celebrated historic districts are tourist attractions, and they have tended to set the tone. Their reputations receive much publicity and influence attitudes to the "historic." Increasingly one sees on interstates notices that seek to lure one off to "the Historic District," and certain preconceptions as to what they will find certainly enter people's minds as they detour to visit these places.

The most entrenched images of historic districts have owed much to Charleston, the Vieux Carré, Beacon Hill, and other celebrated examples of the phenomenon. For instance, it was reported that when design review for the newly designated Fourth Ward district in Charlotte began, "those who took the historic district designation literally wanted old Savannah or Charleston." [22] Such places began their lives as historic districts as very special places, but they too have proved capable of yielding material for stereotypes that have been usable as imagery for the broadening range of historic districts that came into existence after 1966.

A great deal of the history of historic districts since the mid-1970s has been the fashioning of images for them. Historic districts do not just exist ready-made. They have had to be conceptualized, researched, defined and delineated, defended and justified. When the National Register was established in 1966, there was little guidance immediately available to show people what a historic district actually was or should be. Most of the work still had to be done. More and more sophisticated methods for constructing a historic district are coming into existence and being applied. In the process stereotypes become entrenched. An example is what has happened at Paterson, New Jersey. The objective here was to save and re-habilitate the Great Falls of Paterson and Society for Useful Manufacturers Historic District. As at Lowell, the key to revitalization of this town was seen to be through the utilization and exploitation of images associated with the historic but now largely derelict mill areas. In 1971 the Great Falls Project Committee maintained that preservation of the historic industrial district was of vital importance to the city's businesses. The stereotype of a grimy, blighted mill town has dimmed the city's "earlier reputation for growth and pragmatism." The committee hoped to "renew civic pride and reaffirm the old image of the city by halting the spread of blight within the historic district and again making the area a viable economic resource."[23] But fashioning a usable image proved to be unexpectedly difficult and con-tentious. It was not until 1993 that the following announcement was made: "Decades of struggling to envision what a fully restored historic district may look like—one sculpted to authentically reflect Paterson's proud past and its current needs—may finally be at an end thanks to a clear vision for tomorrow presented today to the City by the Great Falls Preservation and Development Corporation."[24] They had conducted a "Visual Preference Survey," in which two groups of interested citizens and officials were shown 220 photographic images of various development patterns, comparative building types, and streetscapes. Some were of current scenes and historic photographs of the district. But the majority were images of other cities, notably the Cannery Row section of San Francisco, the riverfront area of Minneapolis, and Philadelphia's Society Hill. Reactions to the images were scored. An image of row houses in Philadelphia received one of the highest ratings. These efforts to form a historic district by composites of people's images of how it ought to look suggest that by 1993 a stereotypical historic district had emerged. They also show the development of highly sophis-ticated methods of developing images of towns and their possible futures and getting decisions made on this basis.[25]

By such means the tradition of beautification lives on, adapted to mod-ern conditions, using modern techniques, and relying heavily on themes derived from heritage. It now draws on a set of stock historicizing motifs that owe much to the essential elements of the major symbolic landscapes. These can be applied to almost any setting and help to explain why the historic district has become such a readily replicated phenomenon. In the 1970s, as the enthusiasm for historic ambience grew, beautification projects that involved pseudo-Victorian and colonial themes—irrespective of the actual history and architectural heritage of the town in question—were in vogue.[26] Even the "Wild West" began to be "beautified" in conformance with stereotypical images of what a western town ought to look like. In 1973 a plan was produced to change the entire character of Deadwood, South Dakota, through a process described as "beautification."[27]

From the point of view of some critics, there has been a serious diluting and debasing of the concept of the historical as a result of the way in which historic districts have developed. Loosely expressed criteria have been generously applied to a considerable variety of circumstances, moving the idea of "historic" farther and farther away from the exceptional district of outstanding architectural and historical significance. There was debate, for instance, on the creation of the huge Upper East Side Historic District in New York. Some asked whether granting historic status was the right way to go about organizing such an area. "To protect specific buildings is historic preservation; to petrify 60 busy square blocks is urban planning run amok," one developer was quoted as arguing. John Costonis, a prominent land use lawyer, asked, "Will the historic district concept have any integrity if the major problems are really problems of zoning and contemporary design?"[28]

There have been numerous proposals to create alternative categories of district in which heritage, while still being acknowledged and protected, is but one element.[29] The term "historic district" might then be reserved for districts where historical criteria really are going to predominate. Cities have been resorting to an increasing variety of other types of classification to provide protection for neighborhoods and for the buildings within them. These may well not have the word "historic" in their designations. For instance, Nashville has two kinds: the Historic Preservation District, in which exterior alterations to existing buildings, the exterior design of new construction, demolition, relocation, and alterations to property such as fences and sidewalks are regulated; and the Neighborhood Conservation District, which does not cover alterations to property and in which the exterior design of building additions are regulated only where habitable area is being increased.[30]

Pressures for compromise have been particularly strong in business districts. In 1985, for instance, an attempt was made to create a new type of local historic district for East Fourth Street, Cincinnati, meshing new development with historic buildings.[31] In February 1992 the Committee on Historical Preservation of the Chicago City Council voted to designate the Oakland Multiple Resource District "an historic district defined by individual landmarks rather than broad boundaries," thus enabling vacant land to be outside the scope of review and allaying fears of delays in development.[32] Increasingly popular are "conservation districts."[33] While some conservation programs are administered by the local historical agency, others are located in the local planning or zoning agency. Preservation of historic character is usually only one of a number of objectives. The most famous application of the conservation alternative has been in San Francisco via the 1985 Downtown Plan which included block-by-block protection of almost five hundred historically significant buildings within five architectural conservation districts.[34] In addition, there has been development of the "cultural district," especially where there is a concentration of historical theaters. This is being done in Buffalo, Tacoma, and Seattle.[35] In all these ways the concept of the protected district can be universalized and protection integrated into general planning regimes with heritage one, but only one, among numerous values that are taken into account.

Enlarging the Possibilities

The historic district is far from a static concept. It is being reconceptualized in many ways, particularly through strategies that have been devised for preserving or restoring the memory of the history of localities. These have enlarged the possibilities for creating "historic" districts to such an extent that application of the concept does not now need to be confined to a few districts in which have survived sufficient appropriate physical structures. For many years the meticulous restoration of buildings that have disappeared has been regarded as incompatible with a historic district (as compared with a museum village). That has meant that in a historic district there are often many gaps where significant buildings once stood. Guides to some districts are as much about what has been lost as about what still stands. Such guides are particularly common in districts that cannot satisfy the criteria because too much has disappeared.[36] But now the gaps can be filled—in the imagination, if not in physical reality.

Interpreting historic districts was not uppermost in the minds of the early preservationists who were associated with their establishment. Their concerns were more inward-looking, toward protection and restoration. Visitors such as tourists were too often regarded in stereotypical ways, either as easy sources of wealth or as barbarian invaders from whom the fragile historic environments needed to be protected. It is salutary to look back on a report done in 1937 on the interpretive situation at St. Augustine, Florida. This report is unfortunately all too familiar in terms of what still often faces a visitor to a historic district. But it also points the way forward to techniques of management of interpretation, which in some places today are reaching a high level of sophistication.

The visitor, upon his arrival in St. Augustine, is able nowhere at present to secure a comprehensive statement of the principal historical features in relationship to each other, much less to secure more than casual assistance, such as would be possibly afforded in a guided tour, in visiting one after another of these sites in some logical fashion. Confronted as he is with the confusion of badly congested traffic conditions, disconcerting signs, overhead wires and other obstructions to his full appreciation of an historical situation, he is likely to make a timid attempt to enjoy and to understand old St. Augustine, after which he finds relief in driving his car out of the town, probably with the unsatisfactory feeling of realizing that he has not gotten what he came here to find.[37]

At the level of the individual structure, there has been an increasing tendency to challenge and stimulate the imaginations of visitors with museum displays, archaeological evidence, and symbolic representations of the "idea" of the vanished structure. A turning point here was what happened in Philadelphia, when, after reconstructions of such buildings as the Graff House in which Jefferson had drafted the Declaration of Independence, there arose the question of whether the same might be done on the site of the long-demolished home of Benjamin Franklin. Because so little information remained about what the house was like, the arguments on what to do, and whether or not to reconstruct, dragged on until the 1970s. By then a different approach was beginning to be taken to such matters. The house was not restored. The eventual creation of Franklin Court showed a rejection of the Williamsburg style of restoration and the potential of a radically different kind of reconstruction. What one sees now in a courtyard is a large steel frame that re-creates the outline of the house on its original site. This is the "idea" of the house. Beneath it are exposed the remains of the house's foundations, and underneath the courtyard itself is a museum with many exhibits and interactive displays relating to Franklin's life.[38]

The influence of this precedent can be seen in such developments as the Women's Rights National Historical Park at Seneca Falls in New York State. The park is under the jurisdiction of the National Park Service. With its focus on a shrine format within the shell of the old Wesleyan Chapel that was the site of the famous Women's Rights Convention of 1848, it is close in spirit to the type of historical environment that was created at Philadelphia. The building had seen a great deal of history since the convention and had changed out of all recognition. The decision was against trying to restore the structure to what it would have been like in 1848. Instead, an architectural competition was held, and a design was implemented which stripped away all traces of the intervening history and left exposed the few roof trusses, rafters, and brick walls that were all that remained of the chapel as it was in 1848. These were then placed in a pavilion.[39] To look at, the structure at Seneca Falls is very unexciting: most of the original building is gone, and what is left signifies nothing without the enormous weight of interpretation and symbolic significance attached to it in the adjacent visitors' center.

What is increasingly happening is the extension of this approach to try to capture and convey the inner "idea" of a context and a district. At the district level this means attempting to secure a much more substantial and central incorporation of a sense of place. An inspiration for this trend was a revolt—led by social and cultural geographers—against the dominance of architectural and building history and against the limiting consequences of dependence on buildings that had survived for conveying the meaning of the past. Gradually there emerged a demand that preservation move away from a predominantly architectural approach toward broader principles for assessing a community's historical character. In response to the criticisms, and as a result of changes in architectural and preservationist education, architectural historians and writers of National Register nominations have become more skilled in appraising the social significance of building styles and in relating architecture to local social settings, present and past. But the sense of place advocates have wanted to go further than this.

One reason for the reaction against what some saw as an excessive emphasis on architecture was that it made preservationists insensitive to the impact of gentrification on a neighborhood. Ziegler had this to say in 1971 about the consequences of an emphasis on the preservation of historic buildings: "Historic preservation groups across the country from the 1930s up until today remorselessly removed neighborhood residents regardless of their longevity in the proposed historic district or their commitment to that area. They simply replaced them with well-to-do residents who could understand the value of the structures and who could afford to restore and maintain them." This seemed to be the only means available to save architectural heritage. The residents were ignored.[40] In 1985 a social geographer, Robin Datel, advanced even stronger criticisms of the preservation movement, arguing that the obsession with architecture was a major cause of displacement of existing residents.[41]

The new style of interpretation of individual sites has been extended more and more to districts, including those, potentially the great majority, where the history that remains is exceedingly fragmentary, and which could not possibly be considered as "Historic" in the terms of traditional criteria. Much is owed here to the writings and example of Dolores Hayden, now professor of architecture, urbanism, and American studies at Yale University, who in 1984 launched a nonprofit organization in Los Angeles called the Power of Place "to situate women's history and ethnic history in downtown, in public places, through experimental, collaborative projects by historians, designers, and artists."[42] The aim of this project has been to devise innovative ways of preserving not just physical fabric but also memory. Art and festival are used to create invocations of memory. Yi-Fu Tuan, a cultural geographer, is another who has had a considerable influence on the debate about sense of place. He argued that a city "does not become historic merely because it has occupied the same site for a long time. Past events make no impact on the present unless they are memorialized in history books, monuments, pageants, and solemn and jovial festivities that are recognized to be part of an ongoing tradition. An old city has a rich store of facts on which successive generations of citizens can draw to sustain and re-create their sense of place."[43]

"Landmarks": Changed Interpretations

Another development that has greatly expanded ideas of what a "historic" district might be has been the revised understanding of a term familiar in historic preservation, "landmarks." Originally, this term related to monuments and buildings of great prominence. This is reflected in the name of many preservation organizations, for example, the New York Landmarks Commission and the Pittsburgh Historic Landmarks Foundation. In the "classic" pre-1966 historic districts landmarks such as mansions were publicized as a major reason for the creation of the historic district. But Lynch and Jacobs did much to cause a wider, more "popular" definition of a "landmark" to take root. The term has increasingly been used to refer to familiar features in townscapes—symbols of belonging within a community—that have provided a sense of orientation in people's everyday lives. Landmarks of this sort may be very humble and architecturally unimpressive structures. Their status in their communities has often first manifested itself in the protests that have broken out when familiar "landmark" buildings—buildings of little appeal or merit according to traditional criteria—have been demolished or scheduled for demolition. The growth of oral history and cognitive mapping has also been influential in reshaping ideas of which features of the urban landscape really do matter to people. A new perspective on what a sense of place means and how it can be built into preservationist action has begun to emerge. Through oral history there can be a better-informed emphasis on the perceptions of their own history held by people within a community. We can discover the sense of loss people feel when their environment keeps changing. Understanding the significance in the lives of townspeople of "landmarks" defined in this different, broader way has begun to modify the rigor of strictly architectural regulation of "context." Anyone who has attended meetings of historic preservation commissions can testify to the frequency with which attitudes of this type surface in discussions of proposed changes not just to buildings but also to trees, street furniture, and other features of the landscape in historic districts. Harry Moul has reported the development of this new outlook in a place, Santa Fe, where a particularly rigorous insistence on the primacy of a particular style, the "Santa Fe style," had developed. He describes how in 1979 the Historical Style Committee tried unsuccessfully to save two turn-of-the-century houses that were totally "nonconforming." The chairman said that by demolishing these two houses "you're destroying the whole feeling of the neighborhood." Another member said: "Those houses are part of a streetscape in Santa Fe which is vanishing. . . . They are part of the history of Santa Fe, even though they are not 'historic.'" On another occasion a committee member, a historian, said in opposing permission to demolish an old sandstone wall: "Part of Santa Fe is that wall, to me."[44] Various other ways are being explored to make the history that is in historic districts the history of what local people perceive as significant. Using local people to help define a historic district is becoming increasingly common. Schoolchildren have been used to research an area, as in Wheeling, West Virginia, or to explore the history and environment of a neighborhood.[45]

Another new approach can be illustrated by what has happened at Point Arena, California, which had two districts placed on the National Register in 1990: Arena Cove and Main Street Commercial. In January 1988 the California State Office of Historic Preservation assigned two staff historians (with graduate degrees in history) to help with a historic preservation project at Point Arena. They decided to use the project as a test of "context-based planning,"[46] that is, starting with a local historical theme, *not* with individual buildings. Types of properties associated with the theme are then discussed and registration standards devised for examples of each type. Every resource is then evaluated in one or more of these contexts, and the statements about the contexts go into the National Register nomination. This is seen as the best approach for a town with few individual buildings that could be deemed eligible for National Register nomination. Local people played a large part as experts in defining "context." This development is at the opposite point on the spectrum from that at which the development of historic districts began. The context is discovered first, and only then are individual buildings brought into the picture.

There are also changes in the interpretation of historic districts. To a visitor, unless plaques and markers are placed at appropriate locations, the historic meanings of a district are often well hidden. Often this is deliberate: many people who have sought historic district designation for their neighborhoods have not wanted to open them up to publicity and the impacts of tourism. But hidden meanings can now be brought to the surface. One can see this happening in museums and in the orientation centers of historic areas. Visitors' centers have become a way to involve visitors in an appreciation of the underlying culture of a historic district prior to their being exposed to the often fragmentary physical remains that have hitherto been all that a historic district has had to offer.

What all this means for the future of the historic district is a greater capacity to be reinvented. As interpretations of American history change constantly, so does the understanding of the history that should be commemorated in a historic district. These changes will lead both to the creation of new historic districts of a kind that would not have been dreamed of when the concept was first developed and to the reinterpretation of the historical content and significance of existing districts. A good example of how a new history can emerge even within the shell of the old is the network of black heritage trails that are now beginning to crisscross the established "paths" (to use Lynch's term) of older districts in many cities.

What this also means is a potential for an increasing number of historic districts, because both the boundaries of "significance" and the means of discovering and presenting it have been greatly expanded. No one has yet suggested that it would be a desirable or practicable goal for the country to be completely organized into "historic districts." But the potential for this is beginning to emerge. It is possible that a city could become composed entirely of "historic" districts—but only in the sense that "heritage" would be one of the elements of the character of a district or neighborhood to be taken into account by planners in devising controls over its development. After all, even historic districts are not exclusively "historic" in the management of their environments. Other issues have to be taken into account because they are not museums but places where people of today live and work. The difference between them and other districts has become one of degree: they are places where *greater* emphasis is put on the protection of "historic" features. The more numerous historic districts have become, the more difficult it is becoming to see them as exceptional places the purity of whose "historical" character must be protected because there are so few left of their particular sort. A curtained-off corner of a city with a very special character is one thing. A huge downtown commercial district, proclaimed as a historic district, is quite another. The rise of the generic historic district has opened the way to a new era.

Heritage Areas and Urban Cultural Parks

The historic district as the appropriate format for historic preservation has been challenged by another major recent trend. Strategies are now being developed and promoted by governmental authorities and other agencies with jurisdiction over areas with numerous neighborhoods and districts. Many historic districts do still exist in isolation as independently conceived entities, the creation of local initiatives. But many agencies responsible for historic district development have been looking at towns or cities or even regions and states as a whole and planning a strategy and set of priorities that will result in a well-balanced set of historic districts representative both of the community as a whole and of the relationships of the social and ethnic groups that have composed its population. The pattern of distribution of historic districts may still principally reveal the relative strengths and weaknesses of contemporary pressures for and against historic district designation. But as more districts are created and more responsibility for creating them is taken by authorities at city and regional levels this randomness may be diminishing.

In the process a more systematic and planned attempt to represent history through an area format that transcends the medium of historic districts has also begun to emerge. Over the last two decades there has been, in parallel with and overlapping historic district development, an increasing number of attempts to create heritage areas that are larger than the traditional historic district. Comp commented in 1991 that all these shared "a common frustration with our traditional narrow definition of place." He also hinted at a political motivation, a felt need to have a unit more "directly linked to congressional interests."[47] The most notable urban-based examples of such heritage areas are the Heritage State Parks in Massachusetts, encompassing such cities as Holyoke, Gardner, North Adams, Lawrence, and Lynn, the Urban Cultural Parks in New York State, and the Blackstone River Valley, covering such cities as Springfield and Worcester, Massachusetts, and Pawtucket, Rhode Island.

The concept of the Urban Cultural Park (UCP) was first endorsed by the New York legislature in 1977. One of its principal aims was to secure coordination among the numerous agencies responsible for planning, managing, and promoting historic revitalization in the state's towns and cities.[48] The UCP program in New York State was started in 1982 as a joint venture between the state Office of Parks, Recreation, and Historic Preservation and twenty-two communities regarded as "historically significant." Fourteen UCPs are now in various stages of development. Each includes the historic urban core, and each is assigned a theme that displays in the park visitors'

center are supposed to highlight. The parks are operated by the munici-
palities, which receive state funding to assist them. The concept is of the
whole community as the park, and the emphasis is on exhibitions, festivals,
theater, and so on. Those visitors' centers that now exist employ state-
of-the-art display technology to demonstrate their community's heritage.
There are audiovisual presentations and ample opportunities for interaction
between visitors and exhibits. The centers are located either in historic
landmarks in the heart of the downtown area or in modern buildings designed with community characteristics in mind.

The themes that have been assigned to the UCPs can sometimes seem
rather strained. At Ossining, for instance, displays on the Old Croton Aque-
duct and the Sing Sing Prison somehow illustrate the theme of "Reform
Movements."[49] In this respect the UCP differs from the historic district,
which usually—though not always[50]—avoids too explicit a thematic approach. The themes are broad and elastic. They can scarcely be said to do
justice to all the complex features of the communities to which they have
been attached. They tell a sort of story. For instance, the emphasis in Buffalo on the "flowering of culture" seems rather at odds with that city's grimy
industrial past. But it is justified in terms of Buffalo's having been "historically a welcome respite on the tedious journey to the western frontier." The
publicity for Buffalo highlights its Theatre District and its restaurants, again
images at considerable odds with large portions of Buffalo's past. But they
are in accordance with Buffalo's plans for downtown revitalization.

"Celebrate Downtown" is a major theme of the UCP program. The
publicity for it goes as follows:

> Bustling, bright; busy sidewalks, clanging trolleys, street vendors,
> grand hotels and theatres, storefronts, busy stoops, factories. From
> the mid-19th century through the 1940's, the throbbing pace and
> ever-changing skyline of America's downtowns tracked the cities'
> rise. For more than a century, the downtown—be it New York's,
> Saratoga Springs' or Seneca Falls'—was the focal point of Ameri-
> can life.
>
> Now in the 1990s, the New York State Urban Cultural Park
> Program is recapturing the age-old magic of the downtown.[51]

Historic districts with architectural significance are embedded within each
park, but their boundaries usually differ. Visitors and residents can get enhanced access to what the presenters believe is the inner significance of
a historic district via new techniques such as audiovisual presentation and
living history guides. These are intended to provide a much wider range of
insights into how a community perceives its history.

The Heritage State Parks in Massachusetts have developed in similar fashion. They are mostly located in old and now often decaying mill and industrial towns and are closely modeled on Lowell, the first such park, although their funding is well below that of Lowell, which has a National Parks Service involvement and has been treated as the principal regional example of a historic mill town. Interactivity and involvement of visitors in role-playing are encouraged here as in the UCPs. Lowell was the model in this regard too. A 1977 report on Lowell placed great emphasis on visitor participation and interactivity. It envisioned, for instance, that visitors would be asked to compare their own attitude to work with the feelings and values of the mill workers. "Visitors will be encouraged to assume duties of early workers to gain an insight into the skills, satisfactions and frustrations that attended early industrial life." [52]

A more regional concept is the Heritage Corridor. The Blackstone River Valley incorporates towns and cities in a regional interpretation of industrial change. There is a strong emphasis on the environmental impacts of industrial development.[53] Heritage Areas and Corridors may be the wave of the future. Their appeal is as a more efficient and comprehensive way of managing the multiple aspects of "heritage," especially those that are dispersed over large areas (such as canals and mining sites). Their linkage of towns and cities with their hinterlands in a more integrated historical approach corresponds to trends in urban history exemplified by such books as William Cronon's *Nature's Metropolis.*[54]

Preservationists have had to take into account that their town planning allies deal with larger units than the small neighborhoods that have so far been the basic kind of historic district. As the units covered in planning become more regional in scope, historic preservation has had little option but to follow this trend, given the closeness of its integration into urban and metropolitan planning. As urban history itself develops a more regional perspective, this approach will appear more relevant to urban historians than continuing to structure the representation of units of urban historical development primarily at the neighborhood level. Much may also depend on the extent to which historic districts remain linked to strategies of neighborhood rehabilitation. After several decades of experience and high hopes, questions are beginning to be raised as to how effective historic district designation has been in counteracting urban decay.[55] One response to the persistence of decline in the traditional cores of many American cities has been to advocate adopting a more regional approach in line with the new "antisprawl" emphasis and looking at the relationships between inner-city decay and the profligate use of space on the edges of metropolitan areas.[56]

So where does all this leave the history in historic districts? The consensus among interested historians seems to be that history has not had much to do with the making of historic districts. Certainly, historians have not been prominently involved in promoting their development. For their part, academic historians have not taken a great deal of interest in historic districts. The scene for their lack of involvement was set very early in the development of the preservation movement when, as Hosmer wrote, historians were ill-prepared for the opportunities now opening up "because their graduate training had been almost entirely based on the exploration of documents. . . . Trained historians did not really view the preservation and restoration of buildings as part of their work; historians were supposed to teach and write."[57] Historians had very little involvement in the Williamsburg restoration. At the formative stages of the "maturing" of preservationism, a gulf appeared which could only widen as the self-contained professionalism of the preservationist community strengthened. Most state laws relating to preservation commissions mention specific professional disciplines from which their members should be drawn. History is usually one of these.[58] Historians have served on many historic preservation commissions. But the historic preservation profession has become vast and enmeshed in a huge apparatus of bureaucratic processes and therefore necessarily inward-looking and preoccupied with professional concerns. A National Trust annual conference can now draw as many as 2,500 participants, but few of these will be academic historians. The recent arrival on the scene of public history reflects a growth of academic interest in issues connected with historic preservation and other examples of applied history, but much of this newfound interest is attributable to the growth of this area of employment for history graduates.[59] From time to time various reports have urged historians to become more involved. For instance, the 1985 Task Force on Urban Preservation Policies urged historians "to join with the practitioners of the historic preservation movement."[60] Nevertheless, academic textbooks on American urban history seldom give more than passing references to historic preservation, and few articles directly related to the topic appear in such journals as the *Journal of Urban History.*

One reason historians have been rather disengaged from the process of historic district development has been their belief that "history" has not had a great deal to do with it. There was a phase of concern about this state of affairs by historians in the late 1970s and early 1980s, but much less has been expressed in the last decade. By the 1970s the pendulum seemed to some historians to be swinging rather too far away from the "historical" area of historic preservation. There were growing signs of a reaction to the alliance between planners and preservationists that seemed to be controlling the agenda of historic preservation.[61] Preservationists were increasingly criticized for neglecting the historical dimension in their work. Some of the criticism came from academics who had been prominently involved in preservationism and were growing disenchanted with some of the trends they observed. For example, Paul Sprague, a Milwaukee academic and historic preservation consultant, wrote in 1974 that care "should be exercised, whenever historic districts are contemplated, to guard against the temptation to create districts primarily as an aid in stabilizing urban areas. . . . The preservation of delightful old neighborhoods having no sites or structures of historic, cultural or architectural interest should be left to the urbanists, town planners and the like."[62]

There have been occasional efforts to insert more history into historic districts and to make preservationists more knowledgeable about the history of the districts they are working to save. The July–August 1982 issue of the National Trust newsletter, *Conserve Neighborhoods*, was devoted to the history and characteristics of early-twentieth-century neighborhoods. It referred to the work of social and urban historians such as Alan Gowans, who has studied the social contexts of architectural change.[63] In the reports prepared as the basis of submissions for historic district designation, as well as in the nomination themselves, there is in fact an enormous amount of history, local, social, and architectural. Little of this sees the light of day in published form, although there are significant exceptions, such as the two extensive series on towns and districts in Rhode Island and North Carolina. This is a new form of local history, and often more impressive than the old because it is more comprehensive, especially in the ways social and architectural history are linked. While traditional local history sources are drawn on, the statewide coordination of enterprises of this kind offers the potential for a "new," less parochial form of local history. Certainly the work associated with historic district nominations is one of the most significant developments in American local history in recent years.

The debate over where historic districts would go which ensued after the 1986 changes to the tax credits regime revealed the extent of the perception that historic districts had moved a long way from having a primarily historical raison d'être. Some preservationists welcomed the diminution of what they saw as a corrupting and compromising commercial involvement in determining which areas were worthy of historic preservation. There was a feeling that historical considerations ought to be and could now be brought back more into center stage after an era in which financial issues had been allowed to become too dominant. People, it was argued, had come to think that historic district designation was required and should be sought only when capital investment needed protecting, not when there was justification in terms of historical interest and value. Preservationists had found it tactically necessary to stress economic benefits. Now that these were not so substantial, a reorientation of preservationism seemed to be possible and desirable. One survey of the issues facing the movement in the 1990s commented, "There is a real need for preservationists to identify, articulate, and communicate preservation's value in historical and cultural terms."[64] What this controversy revealed was a feeling among historians that the history in historic districting had become compromised and diluted by the inclusion of various nonhistorical objectives in the agendas of those who had been promoting it.

Historical criteria in the promotion of historic districts have been strained to such extreme limits in some places that the historical significance has become hard to discern. The suggestions that the word "historic" should no longer be used as a descriptor are scarcely surprising.

However, the focus of attention recently has been on ways in which the neglected history might be restored. In the process not only are the adaptability and flexibility of the historic district format being further revealed, but real possibilities are emerging for some more organic incorporation within it of at least some of the missing dimensions of history whose absence has been the target of so much criticism.

As we have seen, much thought has been given to how a sense of place might be fostered. Critics of historic districts have been saying for some time that this is above all what they lack. In a contribution to a 1974 conference on historic districts, Richard C. Frank, an architect with a firm of preservation consultants, pointed the way forward when he addressed the less tangible aspects of community character and suggested how they can be discovered and incorporated into the process of defining historic districts.

> In recent years, historic districts have traditionally been conceived as compositions of historically and/or architecturally significant structures existing in concentrations which force consideration of the grouping as an identifiable unit. However, I believe that those who are involved with such areas sometimes overlook the fact that such districts are actually places where people live. As such the history or the architecture may be meaningful, but often there is an additional, intangible "something more" that holds together these remnants of the past. It must be understood that a "sense of place" is just as important as the cultural history and architectural examples that comprise particular areas. And in some cases this sense of place is the most important of the three.[65]

Frank went on to describe an inventory process that his firm had developed. In this, he said, "we have tried to understand and define all of these elements, intangible as well as tangible." The four elements used to construct the inventory were "history, artistic merit, usability, and what we call environmental value."[66]

Over the next two decades, the phrase "sense of place" was used more and more to support cases for designation of historic districts.[67] "There is general agreement," wrote two cultural geographers, Robin E. Datel and Dennis J. Dingemans, in 1988, "that the desire to maintain and enhance a sense of place underlies much contemporary preservation activity."[68] In recent times discussion of the significance of historic districts has been dominated by the sense of place argument. Social and cultural geographers, notably Datel and Dingemans, reacted against what they perceived as the narrow architectural history approach of traditional assessments of why a "historic" district is "historic." Datel appeared to believe that historic preservation, by adopting a wider perspective on historic significance, would be returning to where it began, to its own historic roots. In an article on Charleston, she argued that "regionalism and its attention to sense of place helped give birth to the urban historic district."[69] Some of the problems with the sense of place approach have been acknowledged by its proponents; others have not been or have been skated over. Among the latter are its vagueness and intangibility. It has never been clearly spelled out *how* one discovers it and embodies it concretely in a historic district. Then there is the issue of political conflict over whose history it is and which version(s) of the past should predominate. Once one gets away from the safe ground of architectural history such issues are bound to arise. To reveal history as continual change and adaptation, it is necessary to foster respect for, and a desire to preserve, buildings that have been added to and altered over the generations. An example of what can be done is the interpretation of architecture being adopted at Schenectady. In a walking tour brochure of the Stockade Historic District (NR 1973/1984) issued by the Schenectady Urban Cultural Park the theme is "architecture as a product of a dynamic community." It points out that none of the historic buildings are "pure examples of their original types." While many of the oldest retain their "essential forms," they have all undergone an evolution that "corresponds to the development of the community." The argument is that the recycling of old materials, parts of structures, and even whole buildings "came naturally to people who had to make nearly everything by hand." Therefore, while purists may "deplore their modifications of Schenectady's ancient dwellings, it was those very adaptations that kept so much of the architectural heritage from the ravages of time." Historic preservation is in that tradition: "creatively preserved, these buildings continue to manifest the vitality of the modern community."

It is sometimes necessary to remind advocates of exclusion of new construction of this "normal" feature of urban life. For example, a design manual produced for Beaufort, South Carolina, in 1979 reminded the people of that town, "New construction is a sign of economic health and confidence in Beaufort's future. It is an essential process in a vital community, representing the current phase of an evolution that has been ongoing since the inception of the town."[70]

The challenge of coming to terms with multiple pasts must also be met. As we have seen, the multiple images that arise from the possession by a district of a complex past are formidable barriers to the achievement of some of the community-building goals associated with the creation of historic districts. In the inner city the challenge of creating "historic" districts in areas that have experienced incessant population change has been particularly daunting. The representation of diversity is certainly not an enterprise supported by the predominant models of historic districts. The emphasis has been, as we have seen, on homogeneity and coherence. An example of how the challenge can be met is the South End Landmark District in Boston which was listed on the National Register in 1973 as "the largest urban Victorian neighborhood in the country, representing over 300 acres of land." It secured designation as a Boston landmark district in 1983. The criteria for a landmark district are very general: "any area designated by the commission containing any physical features or improvements or both which are of historical, social, cultural, architectural or aesthetic significance to the city and the commonwealth, the New England region or the nation and cause such area to constitute a distinctive area of the city."[71] The problem with the South End from the point of view of structuring a historic district is summed up well by comparing it with the Back Bay, a much more "obvious" historic district. "Unlike the Back Bay, which was organized around large boulevards and green spaces in the French manner, the South End has no large-scale focus or axis to structure its repetitive blocks."[72] It failed to become the prestige residential area that its developers had hoped for, and it became home instead to a seemingly endless succession of waves of immigrants.

The key to the way the history of this large district was interpreted as meriting designation as a "landmark" is to be found in the justifications advanced in the District Study Committee's report to the Landmarks Commission in 1983. There were two. The architectural justification was placed second: "the largest intact Victorian rowhouse district in the United States." The first reads as follows: "its structures, sites and objects, man made or natural, represent an important aspect of the cultural history of the city, serving once as a first home for many Lebanese, Greek, Russian Jewish,

German, Irish, Canadian and later immigrants and now continues as a multi-ethnic, multi-racial district where various communities continue to co-exist harmoniously." What the narrative in the report does is to tackle head-on the predominance of diversity and complexity in the history of the district and to endeavor to make these the unifying and cohering themes. It presents the South End as the epitome of American social mobility: "Because it is an urban area and because its people worked hard to fulfill the promise of America, it was always in transition. In every instance, the latest arrivals of any ethnic group moved into their community years after the first-comers had left for middle America and the communities outside of the center city." Order, an *American* order, is thus traced through the diversity. "In the South End, all the communities combined to form a kaleidoscope of intermingling and overlapping cultures. It was not Black and White, but Greek, Syrian, Irish, Black, Armenian, Lebanese, Chinese, Jewish, Lithuanian, and so on."[73]

When the report turns to the architecture and planning features, it has to acknowledge both the variety and the absence of focal points and of *apparent* coherence. But these deficiencies are themselves turned into unifying features by being related to the social history as already outlined.

> It is important to note that the physical character of the South End —its street plan and architecture, helped strengthen the neighborhood's social character and provided its residents with a rare, if not unique, experience in American life.
>
> The vast majority of the people who ever lived in the South End started off at the bottom of the social and economic ladder. The neighborhood's small scale side streets made ideal clusters for ethnic enclaves, where immigrants were able to solidify their own identities and ease the shock of social transition.
>
> Scatterings of small parks enhanced the neighborhood feeling and the long avenues became thoroughfares, absorbing major commercial growth and providing commercial "centers" for neighborhoods. Groups came together here and learned the commonality of their problems, which re-affirmed their own self worth. As the similarity of their struggles emerged, so did their cooperation in striving to improve their lives and that of their children. The pattern of stoops and little front yards on many streets further encouraged neighborly communication and the groups learned to share, to respect the rights and dignity of others and to withhold judgement where they could not understand. Most important, they learned to see the common humanity that they shared with all their neighbors in spite of the difference in often seem-

ingly strange culture and customs. It was an experience worth preserving.[74]

The report then goes on to depict the South End as "one of the most racially, ethnically, and economically integrated communities of its size in the nation." It returns to the architecture and planning for reasons for this. In traditional terms what it describes is not a "district." There was created "a series of neighborhoods with no center, no major business or commercial district that could serve as a focal point for the entire community, no one area that dominated all the others." It describes the ravages of urban renewal. But the historic character of the district has survived even these and is enabling people too to survive and cope and rebuild community life. The plain message is that landmark designation will assist this process by highlighting and reinforcing the culturally integrative features of the district's heritage. New immigrant groups have been arriving. There are now several thousand middle-class residents. "Each group contributes a different strand of its culture to the richly-colored fabric that is shared by all who live here." [75]

Another example of how diversity can be confronted is found in Lowell. Its history as a mill town must have seemed relatively straightforward to those who planned the creation of its Historical Park. The diverse backgrounds of the migrants who came to Lowell to work in its mills, although always an important part of the heroic story of industrial enterprise in the city, were essentially subsidiary to it. But by the 1980s, under the impact of new and massive migration into Lowell from Latin America and Asia, the challenge of bringing into the picture the phenomenon of diverse migration began to assume center stage. Interpretations now adapted an appropriate image to emphasize the "common threads" that ran through the experiences of immigrants to Lowell over the years.[76] The *Preservation Plan* presented to Congress in 1980 by the Lowell Historic Preservation Commission explained that there would henceforth be much more emphasis on ethnic festivals. Educational programs would portray cultural diversity, and a multicultural center would be created within the park. In the reactions to the draft plan, the "consistent and most emphatic response" was described as being from local residents who "[saw] the Park as a 'stage' to share and celebrate their traditions and display their skills." As a result, "encouraging the varieties of cultural expression" became one of the commission's major responsibilities.[77]

The invention of meaning for historic districts, especially those in large cities, is bound to be an especially complex and contentious process. This is why the substitution of a long-past, even mythical history that has little relationship to anything in the present except impressive old buildings is often preferred. The apparent simplicities of the tale to be told at Charleston or Marblehead (although that simplicity also usually dissolves on closer scrutiny) is not available in such districts. If there have been multiple pasts, as is almost always the case, there is certain to be a struggle to determine whose history should dominate the interpretation of the district's history. The outcome is not always a South End. Success in synthesizing diversity and then establishing diversity itself as a unifying factor in the community is rare.

The example of the Over-the-Rhine district in Cincinnati may be taken as a contrast to the story of the South End. This district, originally ethnically homogeneous as its name reflects, has seen many ethnic migrant groups come and go. It has had a diverse, largely working-class, population. Local resistance, spurred by fears of gentrification and displacement, attempted to block historic district designation. After a four-year controversy the district was placed on the National Register in 1983. But local designation was rejected at that point (it was finally agreed to in 1994).[78] The struggle over the interpretation of the past of Over-the-Rhine has been examined by Zane Miller. By the early 1980s there were four documents projecting four different futures for the Over-the-Rhine neighborhood. These were based in part on different views of its past or rather different emphases on facets of what had been a complex past. Which of these interpretations prevailed mattered a great deal because each had relevance to current planning and ideas about community development. Each construed the meaning of ethnicity differently. "Yet all of them treated the history of ethnic groups in a way that made control of the past crucial to the control of the future of the neighborhood." One described a pattern of "ethnic group succession"; another, "ethnic group accumulation." With one, the future would belong to only the latest arrivals; with the other, it would belong to all. But one plan "treated ethnicity as essentially irrelevant to the future of Over-the-Rhine and as the least significant aspect of the history of the area."[79] The present state of this district illustrates the paralysis that can ensue when no successful integration or synthesis of conflicting versions of the significance of the past has been achieved.

The issue of the interpretation of diversity in an urban community has been tackled most directly by Dolores Hayden, who argues that ethnic, gender, and many other kinds of diversity have to be taken as starting points. They must be not only acknowledged but also respected as central to human experience in these settings. Her approach is then to reach out to more universal categories of experience to attain unifying themes in historical interpretation. The themes that she favors are similar to those adopted at the South End or, later, at Lowell: the migration experience; the pressures on family structures and how these have been responded to; the search for a new sense of identity.[80] But what is significant is that Hayden looks to modes of historical representation other than the traditional historic district to convey these themes. The work that she and her colleagues did in Los Angeles, for instance, relied heavily on the force of public art to fill in the gaps and render the themes imaginatively in ways that are no longer possible with fragmentary physical remains.

A special problem arises with the representation of history in gentrified districts. Whose history should or can the historic districts created in these places represent? An emphasis on the architectural legacy, especially in its often splendidly restored condition, takes the history back to the original affluent white settlers and screens out the people who lived in the houses in between times. One answer is, as at the South End and at Lowell, to attempt to represent it all, to take the incessant change and in- and out-migration—*including* the gentrifiers themselves—as the history and try to interpret these phenomena in the way the historic district is organized.

The challenge to put back or even remember history that has been neglected, hidden, or suppressed because of a change in the dominant ethnic or social group in a neighborhood has arisen with particular force in connection with African-American history in districts undergoing the kind of historic preservation associated with gentrification. Jackson Ward in Richmond, for example, is an important site in black American history, and the concern in the mid-1970s was that that black history would have no future in this newly designated historic district.[81] The question was asked, Does the concept of preservation embrace the people who are responsible for the historic significance of a street or entire neighborhood? The problem of the underrepresentation of African-American history in the nation's historic districts is, of course, much wider than simply the disappearance of evidence of it in districts that have undergone gentrification. Efforts have been made to widen the scope of historic districts so that they reflect more fully and sensitively African-American dimensions of their history. Not only is the number of historic districts associated with black history increasing, but efforts are also being made to inject an African-American perspective into the interpretation of the history of established historic districts. In some instances, the African-American history, originally ignored or downplayed, is now being highlighted.[82] A notable example of this is Selma, Alabama, under the pressure of the great interest in sites associated with the civil rights struggles of the 1950s and 1960s. Selma, like most older southern cities, has its quota of fine antebellum and late Victorian houses, and these dominate the Historic Districts. But in Selma—and elsewhere—

there has been a considerable recent development of trails linking and commemorating sites significant in African-American history. The most famous of these, almost the prototype, is the Black Heritage Trail in Boston, which commemorates the community of freed slaves that developed on the northern slopes of Beacon Hill.[83] These trails are often overlaid on existing historic district structures. Indeed, the Black Heritage Trail in Boston attracts almost the same attention as the Freedom Trail, inviting through these physical juxtapositions reflections on two interpretations of "freedom" in American history. The experience of walking the Black Heritage Trails can bring out in fascinating ways the tensions between traditional and hidden patterns of historical meaning. There is also a growing emphasis on how blacks have lived in and developed originally Victorian districts, as in Savannah. In such districts the tendency might otherwise be, and indeed often has been, to highlight the architectural legacy of the white originators of the district, the "container" rather than the contents.

The Absence of "Contemporary" History

Critics, with Richard Longstreth in the forefront, have long lamented the failure of historic preservation to find a place for the history of the contemporary world. But what "contemporary" means is forever shifting. In 1966 the fifty-year rule took one back to the era before World War I. By the mid-1990s what many people perceived as a watershed was coming into view: the era after World War II. By then there had been considerable acceptance of districts with a primary significance relating to the 1930s, including Art Deco districts and public housing projects. But for many Americans the "modern" world really begins after World War II. This was an age when there was a conscious rejection of the past in architecture and town planning, for example. The preference was for modernism and an international style that eschewed all reference to historical traditions and motifs. This is the era when urban renewal caused the devastations that spawned the modern historic preservation movement. By the early twenty-first century, that era itself will be "historic" under the fifty-year principle. What historic districts will appear to be its legacy? It is certainly true that nostalgia has been aroused by the media and entertainment industry for recent eras such as the 1960s, and it may be that Americans will be ready to see the concept of the historical applied to these times. But what will it mean in terms of retention of structures from those eras? Historic preservationists are sometimes asked whether they can conceive of being one day as ready to fight for preservation of a business district or commercial strip created in the 1950s or 1960s as they have been to campaign for Main Street preservation. In the historic preservation movement there has been a strong current of antimodernism, which suggests there may be major crises of adjustment ahead.

From the vantage point of the late 1990s the historic district appears as a phenomenon born out of and then nurtured in particular historical circumstances. It emerged in the 1960s from the reactions to the devastations caused to the historic fabric of innumerable urban communities by programs of urban renewal and improvement and the construction of freeways. It took off in the 1970s for a variety of reasons, including the availability of tax credits, the desire of gentrifiers and also longer-term residents of older city districts to protect their environments and properties, the rise of "heritage" tourism stimulated by the 1976 Bicentennial, the growth of concern for the rehabilitation of "neighborhoods" as a basic unit of American society, and the development of the "Main Street" strategy for effecting the revival of older commercial districts. Historic districts were a form of applied and usable history that was particularly well adapted to the requirements of the age. The situations that called forth this particular response still exist. But for the historian—from whose point of view I have endeavored to write this book—what is fascinating about historic districts is the multilayered representation of history they have come to represent. Overlaying the history that is remembered in them and that was the original justification for their being established are both the history of the era in which they were created and the history of their subsequent functioning and use as historic districts. The three are inextricably linked. They are the first, third, and fourth stages in the history of historic districts that have been identified in this book, with only the second stage, the era of survival, suppressed in most interpretations. Historic districts are an ongoing medium for dialogue and intersection between past and present.

Conclusion

Ultimately the history that is in all historic districts is local history. I shall conclude with a focus on one local district in whose history and present-day condition can be found many of the themes of this book: the Harry S. Truman Heritage District in Independence.[84] This is a traditional kind of historic district in one very important respect: it exists as a historic district because of its associations with a famous person who lived there. Everything that has been done to conceptualize, create, promote, and interpret the district has been focused on Truman and his connections with the area. Tourism is important in this regard: the Truman Library is nearby, and a bus takes visitors on a circuit that includes the Truman home, the library, and other sites. Truman was president for nearly eight years during one of

Harry Truman celebrating his sixty-ninth birthday on May 8, 1953, by taking his usual morning walk on the streets adjacent to his home in Independence, Missouri.

the most tumultuous eras in American history. He was responsible for such dramatic decisions as the dropping of the atomic bombs on Hiroshima and Nagasaki, the entry of the United States into the Korean War, and the dismissal of Gen. Douglas MacArthur. The career and achievements of all presidents are of great interest to Americans, and many historic sites are now protected because of their presidential associations. But the Truman District has acquired a vast overlay of additional significance because of the mythology that has become associated with this particular president. The Truman myth has enormous resonance and has indeed grown over the years. It is above all the twentieth-century version of the classic Lincolnian myth of the ordinary man who rose to become president of the United

States. The message that this historic district is designed to convey derives from its very ordinariness. It is remarkable because of the fit between the ordinary—this could be any one of hundreds of similar districts all across the nation—and the extraordinary—one of its residents became president. Nor is the fact that this relationship occurred believed to be a matter of coincidence. The theme that is promoted is that there is a connection: the neighborhood shaped Truman's character and helps to explain how and why he became president. It is a peculiarly American place. David McCullough has likened the area to Emerson's Concord, Mark Twain's Hannibal, and Lincoln's Springfield. The closest resemblance is probably with the last of these. At the heart of Springfield, adjacent to the Lincoln Home, a district of old houses has been constituted and called "Mr. Lincoln's Neighborhood." The way of life that is remembered and indeed celebrated there is summed up in the word "neighborhood," which has resonated through the debates in recent years over what should be done about the Truman district. Such places are interpreted and valued as providing basic clues to understanding and memorializing the underlying values on which American democracy is believed to rest. They are not just "historical." They are a resource for the future. The preservation of neighborhoods is seen as vital for the American democratic system. Their rehabilitation is linked with the maintenance in all its historical integrity of the way of life that has underpinned American democracy.

Through the emphasis that is placed on various stages and rites of passage of Harry Truman's life in Independence the fabric of family-based community is identified. They are retraced for visitors at the various stopping points on the city tour. The story begins with Truman having spent his boyhood in Independence and settled there with his family. He attended Sunday School at a church that is now described as a landmark within the district—a church integrated into the life of the neighborhood, and to which one could walk, as contrasted with the controversial First Baptist Church, which has in recent times been accused of having damaged the neighborhood to provide additional parking space for its worshipers who now come mainly from outside the district. It was at this church that Truman met his future wife. Other landmarks that one is shown include the school they both attended and the home of Truman's aunt and uncle. The nine-year courtship of Harry and Bess is a very important part of the Truman story. The house at 219 N. Delaware, which was their home from 1919 until their deaths, is, of course, the anchor for the entire story. Reference is often made to the many friends within the district whom Truman visited whenever in town. Finally, there is the tremendous significance of the fact that, when he had left the White House, Truman returned "home" to his house on Delaware, and it was there that he died. Stories abound of the way he described the meaning of being back home in Independence. He is frequently quoted as having said of himself, "I'm just a hometown fellow who wants to get along with his neighbors." There are also many anecdotes and recollections of the ways in which he became, and was recognized as, a part of the life of the neighborhood: his early morning strolls, his visits to the railroad depot (another landmark) where he lounged around waiting for the train to arrive, the friends whom he greeted. Everyone in the district has had a story to tell of Truman as "neighbor."

However, the district has undergone enormous change since Harry Truman's death in 1969. That change is history too. It reflects certain trends that are an inescapable feature of urban life in modern-day America, for instance, the conversion of large onetime family homes in inner-city districts to rental accommodation. But, as we have seen, this is not the kind of urban history that is now deemed worthy of remembrance. It is described as "deterioration." The Truman Heritage District was established, shortly after Truman's death, as a local district (the only one in Independence) in 1972. This made alterations to premises within the district subject to review by a heritage commission. The boundaries were quite extensive, coinciding with those of the National Landmark District, which was also designated at this time. However, the protections that this local designation afforded were largely nullified by the exclusion of church properties from the coverage of the ordinance that established the district. The commission decided in 1984 to reduce the boundaries of the district by nearly two-thirds. The church exclusion was removed, but now the churches were outside the district anyway. In effect the boundaries were gerrymandered to ensure that the churches continued to be free to do whatever they wished with their property. The exclusion of churches turned out to be highly deleterious to the Truman era character of the district. One church in particular, the First Baptist, took advantage of the exclusion to demolish six houses to make way for a parking lot. As is often emphasized, the lot is "within view of the Trumans' back porch." "The church expansion will deny the public the right to see Truman's neighborhood—forever," said Norman Reigle, superintendent of the Truman National Site, in 1984. "This could have an adverse effect on tourism. It will cut down on the interpretive potential of the site." [85]

By 1996 deterioration of the Truman Heritage District had become so serious that the National Trust for Historic Preservation accepted it for inclusion on its 11 Most Endangered Historic Places list. [86] This list has become a sort of anti–National Register. Buildings and districts are even nominated to it in a process that echoes—in an almost macabre way—the process of nomination to the National Register. The Jackson County Historical Society's application to have the Truman District placed on the list stressed the need to keep it as the sort of "neighborhood" that helped to shape Truman's character and career. This objective is now being tied in to a more general program of neighborhood revitalization in the city. In Truman's time the majority of houses were middle-class owner-occupied family homes such as his. Now many of the houses are rented to low-income and transient residents.[87] The stresses on the traditional social fabric of the community have been mirrored in the deterioration of its physical fabric. The catalyst for renewed preservationist concern was the collapse in July 1994 of the front of a house—now known as the Choplin House—at 304 N. Delaware, diagonally across from the Truman Home. Its complete demolition was averted, and efforts have since focused on restoring it: it was the scene of a press conference announcing the placing of the district on the 11 Most Endangered Places List. Barbara Potts, executive director of the Jackson County Historical Society, said, "The house is at a major intersection and is visible from the Truman Home. It is a keystone to the historic district."[88] The central argument has been the one that has been used to justify the creation of so many historic districts, the importance of the context of individual buildings. The Truman House will, it is argued, lose much of its meaning if it is deprived of the essential components of its Truman era environment. The view from the house is often mentioned, as are the sights that Truman would have seen as he went on his morning walks. U.S. Rep. Karen McCarthy is quoted as saying, "'We want to feel as if Harry Truman could still stroll down North Delaware Street and take pride in his neighborhood. We owe him that.'"[89]

Above all, North Delaware Street had deteriorated as a "neighborhood." The Choplin House has been given a whole new, or at least revived, significance: it is referred to as a house in which "neighbors" had lived. A contractor who set about stabilizing the House said, "I am from that neighborhood. I used to be Harry Truman's paperboy. It's a sentimental thing with me. I didn't want them to start tearing it down." The houses in the district were described in the following terms: "These homes were not and are not islands, isolated from their surroundings. They are a part of a neighborhood, where Truman knew his neighbors and they knew him." This was why the district should be preserved. It was "a neighborhood which influenced a man who became President of the United States."[90] The subtext is, if neighborhoods like this are allowed to collapse, we will be destroying what in the past have been the seedbeds of American democratic values.

Lisa Vogel and Pratt Cassity, commenting in 1996 on what had been happening at Independence, established a link with wider issues when they wrote that the importance of preserving "districts and neighborhoods—

the historic resources of our daily lives" is now recognized.[91] This sort of thing had been happening in similar districts all over the nation. But hardly any of the others had attracted the same level of attention. The reason was simple: they did not contain the homes of former presidents. So here was a great opportunity. Vogel and Cassity argue that the local decisions of the Independence City Council had affected the entire fabric of American neighborhoods by allowing this particular neighborhood to be diminished. Because of the Truman myth, it had come to stand for all neighborhoods. They acknowledge that many histories are at work in Independence. "All must be respected and all or some may continue to affect the resources of the area. But perhaps paramount over all of them is the history of the neighborhood, plain and simple, because the history of that neighborhood is the history of all our neighborhoods."[92]

Can any implications for the future of historic districts in the American city be read into what has happened in the Truman district, a particular local urban place that has been given such a weight of generic and symbolic significance? The reactions since the near-collapse of the Choplin House in 1994 suggest that historic districts will continue to matter insofar as they are seen to represent permanent archetypal forms of community, the "symbolic landscapes." To judge from what has occurred at Independence, there is still the potential for traumatic changes in communities to revive attachments to these archetypes.

Historic districts will also continue to be valued insofar as Americans want to have examples of communities that embody "symbolic landscapes" available in a protected condition as resources for the benefit of society. That could, of course, be ensured through the medium of museum villages that are sealed off from the public. But most historic districts are not museum villages. They are districts in which people live and work. In the prominence and indeed the formal status assigned to "history" in their management, they are institutionalized forms of influence from the past directed on to the present. They offer a resource as examples of types of communities that have served Americans well in the past. But they do more than that. Because they are still lived in, they also provide models that test the usefulness and relevance of the experience of the past to the circumstances of modern-day living.

Can the model of the community that Truman's Independence is believed to represent serve the country well again? Is it a "usable past"? Or is it now nonrevivable because rooted in a particular and unique set of historical circumstances? In the debate over whether "history" has a role to play in shaping the identities of the communities of today and tomorrow, the answers to questions such as these will be crucial. The contribution of historians cannot be expected to be other than ambivalent. They will be aware of the irredeemable pastness of the past and of how impossible it is to turn the clock back and reinstate in its pristine integrity a form of community that once was. But they will also know that the desire of people to live in a community with values that that community model is perceived as having embodied is a part of the history of our own times.

History is a resource that can be drawn on for all sorts of applications that can benefit our communities today. For example, and perhaps especially, an urban historic district can remind us today of the resourcefulness and imagination of our forebears in creating livable urban environments. Similar qualities are required today to be harnessed to the building of community structures that are appropriate to the needs and use the technologies of the modern world. After all, a historic district is more than just a collection of individual buildings. It constitutes an urban environment, a symbol of the varying ways in which in the past people have effectively come together in the construction and maintenance of livable communities.

The historic districts that have been created in the United States are a distinctively American phenomenon. American area preservation has had broad cultural dimensions, especially as a consequence of having become caught up in the enthusiasm for neighborhood preservation of the 1970s. The vitality of American community life was seen then as being particularly dependent on the health and integrity of the neighborhood, frequently referred to as the most fundamental unit in the community structure. The durability of this belief is seen in the reactions to the disintegration of the Truman district. When I compare historic preservation in my own country, New Zealand, and in the United States, I note the lateness of the emergence of interest in the former country in preservation at the district level. Its emergence in New Zealand during the 1980s coincided with and indeed reflected the growth of a precinct focus in urban design and planning. In the United States by contrast, historic district development began in the 1920s with Charleston, South Carolina, and there had been a half century of maturing of the concept via developments deeply rooted in particular local cultures prior to the post-1966 bureaucratization of procedures via the National Register and then the enmeshing of district preservation in municipal planning.[93]

Historic districts have their roots in American history. They will continue to be viable insofar as they grow from those roots. Artificial creations resulting from gentrification or the desire to gain the advantages of design review and control are much less likely to succeed in the longer run. In part this is because of the strength of historical continuity, which is, after all, what historic districts principally represent. A theme of this study has been historic districts as the outcome of processes of survival. These districts are not artificial creations but the product of unusually great capacities for endurance, often against formidable odds that have meant the disappearance of the historical "integrity" of many similar places. These capacities may have derived from characteristics of the original plan or from the will and determination of successive generations of residents, perhaps threaded together over the years by family links or by elite self-consciousness. The histories of historic districts therefore tell us much about the elements of strength and continuity in the fabric of American urban communities. Communities whose fabric has "deteriorated" or "decayed" are not commemorated and made available as role models through the medium of the historic district. "Frontier" communities characterized by high levels of transience and constant change in land use, for example, are not included in the ranks of historic districts. One could argue that the Truman District in Independence became such a place once more after a period of stability. The tension is between reality and the ideal. Historic districts come down very firmly on the side of the latter. They represent the desire of Americans to aspire to the ideal of "community," even if they are seldom able to achieve it.

Appendix

National Register Criteria for Evaluation

The quality of significance in American history, architecture, archeology, engineering and culture is present in districts, sites, buildings, structures, and objects that possess integrity of location, design, setting, materials, workmanship, feeling, and association, and:

A. that are associated with events that have made a significant contribution to the broad patterns of our history; or
B. that are associated with the lives of persons significant in our past; or
C. that embody the distinctive characteristics of a type, period, or method of construction, or that represent the work of a master, or that possess high artistic values, or that represent a significant and distinguishable entity whose components may lack individual distinction; or
D. that have yielded or may be likely to yield information important in prehistory or history.

Criteria Exceptions

Ordinarily, cemeteries, birthplaces or graves of historical figures, properties owned by religious institutions or used for religious purposes, structures that have been moved from their original locations, reconstructed historic buildings, properties primarily commemorative in nature, and properties that have achieved significance within the last fifty years shall not be considered eligible for the National Register. However, such properties will qualify if they are integral parts of districts that do meet the criteria or if they fall within the following categories:

a. a religious property deriving significance from architectural or artistic distinction or historical importance; or
b. a building or structure removed from its original location, but which is significant primarily for architectural value, or which is the surviving structure most importantly associated with a particular person or event; or
c. a birthplace or grave of a historical figure of outstanding importance if there is no other appropriate site or building directly associated with his productive life; or

d. a cemetery that derives its primary significance from graves of persons of transcendent importance, from age, from distinctive design features, or from association with historic events; or

e. a reconstructed building when accurately executed in a suitable environment and presented in a dignified manner as part of a restoration master plan, and when no other building or structure with the same association has survived; or

f. a property primarily commemorative in intent if design, age, tradition, or symbolic value has invested it with its own historical significance; or

g. a property achieving significance within the past fifty years if it is of exceptional importance.

Notes

Preface

1. Information on National Register Historic Districts is most readily available via the published *National Register of Historic Places*. The dates on which districts came onto the National Register (NR) are supplied in parentheses.

2. Relph, *The Modern Urban Landscape*, 218–19. Relph illustrates the phenomenon of commercial gentrification with a photograph of a historic district, Newburyport, Massachusetts.

Chapter 1

1. The history of which is recounted in Lindgren, *Preserving Historic New England.*

2. Hosmer, *Preservation Comes of Age*, 1:168–69.

3. James A. Glass has written, "Although interest in environmental conservation and aesthetics was common among architects interested in preservation, urban design critics, and neighborhood advocates, it was still rare among the state and local historical societies that made up so much of the preservation movement. For many such societies and the public at large, historic preservation still denoted the commemoration of famous events and personages through operation of museums in historic structures." James A. Glass, *The Beginnings of a New National Historic Preservation Program, 1957 to 1969*, 31.

4. The most detailed account of the development of Colonial Williamsburg is in Hosmer, *Preservation Comes of Age*. For a recent account and critique, see Kammen, *Mystic Chords of Memory*, 359–70.

5. Birch and Roby, "The Planner and the Preservationist," 196.

6. For a critique of Colonial Williamsburg today, see Leon and Piatt, "Living-History Museums."

7. Eddie Nickens, "Delaware Revivalism." See the retort to this from a correspondent in Williamsburg in *Historic Preservation* 47, no. 2 (March–April 1995): 9. The New Castle episode of the late 1930s is described in Hosmer, *Preservation Comes of Age*, 1:67–70.

8. In 1949 a campaign was launched to make Tombstone, Arizona, "the Williamsburg of the West." Hosmer, *Preservation Comes of Age*, 1:371. See below for a Williamsburg reference in connection with Madison, Indiana. The "ultimate goal" of Guthrie, Oklahoma, has been described as "becoming the Victorian architectural 'Williamsburg' of the Southwest." Leider, "Capitol Townsite Historic District," 422.

9. Hosmer, *Preservation Comes of Age*, 1:417.

10. Ibid., 1:350.

11. There are many sources on the history of historic preservation in Charleston. See in particular Datel, "Southern Regionalism and Historic Preservation in Charleston, South Carolina"; Hosmer, *Preservation Comes of Age*, 1:232–79; Silver, "Revitalizing the

Urban South," 70–73; Stipe and Lee, *The American Mosaic*, 115, 159; Weinberg, *Preservation in American Towns and Cities*, 38–42, 77–82.

12. On Frost, see Bland, *Preserving Charleston's Past, Shaping Its Future*.

13. Datel, "Southern Regionalism and Historic Preservation in Charleston, South Carolina," 203.

14. "We are still protecting local historic resources in the method established in 1931." Cassity, "Still Local After All These Years," 25.

15. Hosmer, *Preservation Comes of Age*, 1:274.

16. See below, Chapter 7.

17. On New Orleans, see Sauder and Wilkinson, "Preservation Planning and Geographic Change in New Orleans' Vieux Carré"; Weinberg, *Preservation in American Towns and Cities*, 77–94; Silver, "Revitalizing the Urban South," 73–74; Stipe and Lee, *The American Mosaic*, 115.

18. Murtagh, *Keeping Time*, 105.

19. Silver, "Revitalizing the Urban South," 74.

20. Boyer, *The City of Collective Memory*, 325.

21. Ibid., 330–31.

22. San Antonio, which created one in 1939, was the home of an early conservation society. It took a keen interest in the preservation of entities larger than single houses, in particular because of its concern to preserve the river as the central feature of the city's landscape. Hosmer, *Preservation Comes of Age*, 1:275–90. Alexandria followed in 1946 with its "Charleston ordinance." Murtagh, *Keeping Time*, 106. Residents of Georgetown secured an act of Congress in 1950—the Old Georgetown Act—which required that plans for demolition, renovation, or new construction be approved by a commission. North Carolina created several preservation commissions prior to 1966: Bath in 1959, Edenton in 1961, and Hillsborough in 1963. One of the country's oldest towns received protection in 1959 when the Florida legislature approved the establishment of the St. Augustine Board of Trustees. The Vieux Carré example proved contagious: Texas created an "Old Galveston Quarter" in 1962.

23. Anderson, *Annapolis*, 25–27.

24. The long history of struggle to maintain and protect the special character of Beacon Hill and the reasons for this are explained in Firey, *Land Use in Central Boston*, 87–135.

25. Thurber and Moyer, *State Enabling Legislation for Local Preservation Commissions*, 3–4.

26. For the early history of museum villages in New England, see Lindgren, *Preserving Historic New England*, 169–70.

27. Stipe and Lee, *The American Mosaic*, 116.

28. Grieff, *Independence*, 54–55, 78–79.

29. Ibid., 88–93. Recently tax credits have been used to rehabilitate three landmark buildings on the borders of the park. These commercial structures all derive from eras subsequent to that assigned "significance" in the creation of the park. They are described as "important features of the urban environment surrounding Independence National Historical Park, and their preservation and maintenance continue to help stabilize the park's border areas." Lapsley, "Tax Projects and the National Parks," 16. This reverses the normal pattern of encroachment of "historic" areas onto adjacent territory. For the ste-

rility of the landscape created in the making of Independence Mall, see Dahir, "The Politics of a Public Space."

30. Glaab and Brown, *A History of Urban America,* 283.

31. Stipe and Lee, *The American Mosaic,* 116.

32. Ibid., 166. "Proponents of the measure had assumed that public housing projects would be built on a substantial part of the renewed sites, but of the first fifty-four urban redevelopment projects, only three actually provided public housing for those evicted from the areas." Glaab and Brown, *A History of Urban America,* 282.

33. Merritt, "New Directions: A Local Organization's View," 169.

34. Birch and Roby, "The Planner and the Preservationist," 197–8.

35. Jakle and Wilson, *Derelict Landscapes,* 133.

36. Mulloy, *The History of the National Trust for Historic Preservation 1963–1973,* 83.

37. Stipe and Lee, *The American Mosaic,* 117.

38. Ibid., 118.

39. Ibid.

40. Birch and Roby, "The Planner and the Preservationist," 200. Other legislation also made contributions. For example, the Housing Act of 1961 provided for urban beautification programs, with grants of up to 50 percent of project costs. It was amended in 1966 to provide grants specifically for historic preservation. Section 312 of the Housing Act of 1964 made funds available for housing rehabilitation. Stipe and Lee, *The American Mosaic,* 118.

41. Ibid., 117; Birch and Roby, "The Planner and the Preservationist," 200–202.

42. Mulloy, *The History of the National Trust for Historic Preservation 1953–1973,* 84.

43. The extensive rehabilitation program of Charlestown carried out by the Boston Redevelopment Authority in the early 1970s in which more than 1,000 buildings were rehabilitated and the preservation of forty buildings in Sacramento's Old Town Historic District were both parts of urban renewal projects. Stipe and Lee, *The American Mosaic,* 117.

44. Birch and Roby, "The Planner and the Preservationists," 200.

45. Ibid., 198; Stipe and Lee, *The American Mosaic,* 118.

46. *Preservation News* 17, no. 5 (May 1977): 12.

47. *Auburn Illustrated: A History in Architecture* (catalogue to an exhibition organized by Schweinfurth Memorial Art Center, Auburn, N.Y., 1983), 16.

48. A notable district that escaped urban renewal is Capitol Hill, Washington, D.C. (NR 1976): Scott and Lee, *Buildings of the District of Columbia,* 246–48. The Foggy Bottom Historic District (NR 1987) is a remnant after extensive urban renewal in that area. Ibid., 204–6.

49. Pacyga and Skerrett, *Chicago, City of Neighborhoods,* 369–83, 395–405.

50. Silver, "Revitalizing the Urban South," 76.

51. Johnson and Russell, *Memphis,* 133.

52. Eckert, *Buildings of Michigan,* 79.

53. Freed, *Preserving the Great Plains and Rocky Mountains,* 294–95, 323.

54. *Preservation News* 8, no. 3 (March 1968): 2.

55. *Preservation News* 9, no. 6 (June 1969): 1.

56. Ford, "Urban Preservation and the Geography of the City in the USA," 233.

57. *With Heritage So Rich*, 156.

58. Gratz, *The Living City*, 258–59.

59. Boyer, *The City of Collective Memory*, 54.

60. Olmsted and Watkins, *Here Today*, 108.

61. *Philadelphia Architecture*, 21.

62. Examples are Water Avenue, Selma, Alabama (NR 1972), and Roswell, Georgia (NR 1974).

63. Publicity for Madison, Georgia (NR 1974/1990), states: "Imagine what it must have been like in 1864 when Senator Joshua Hill led a delegation of men to plead with General Sherman to spare Madison from the torch" (brochure issued by the Madison-Morgan County Chamber of Commerce).

64. Murtagh, *Keeping Time*, 70.

65. Archer, "Where We Stand," 27.

66. Stipe and Lee, *The American Mosaic*, 51.

67. Thurber and Moyer, *State Enabling Legislation for Local Preservation Commissions*, 17.

68. For example Tennessee. Ibid.

69. Three percent are nominated by federal agencies, and the rest are National Historic Landmarks designated by the secretary of the interior.

70. A typical entry for a district in the National Register reads as follows: Alabama, Montgomery County: Ordeman-Shaw Historic District, Bounded by McDonough, Decatur, Madison, and Randolph Sts., Montgomery, 5/13/71, B, C, b, 71000105
(the number at the end is the computer reference number). This can be deciphered to indicate that the district was placed on the register in May 1971 and was deemed to satisfy Criteria B and C as well as one of seven listed exceptions to the criteria, in this case exception "b," which allows for acceptance of structures that are no longer on their original location as long as they are "significant primarily for architectural value" or are "the surviving structure most importantly associated with a particular person or event." This particular exception has become increasingly important in allowing the designation of districts into which buildings have been moved from nonhistoric districts for protection. For the full list of the Criteria Exceptions, see the appendix.

71. For a summary of the history and scope of preservation at the local level, see Cassity, "Still Local After All These Years."

72. A local historic district can be an independent entity or have the same dimensions as a National Register historic district. Often a district is first surveyed and processed through the stages of obtaining National Register status, and then a local district is established. Many National Register districts have not become local districts because of various forms of local opposition to establishing the regimes of control that accompany local status. The boundaries of local districts may differ from those of National Register districts, especially when the criteria can be locally developed ones. There tends to be greater emphasis on what the community itself perceives as significant historically.

73. Stipe and Lee, *The American Mosaic*, 85. Enabling legislation has been defined as "the legal authorization of federal or state governing bodies to delegate powers or enact specific measures such as historic district ordinances, taxation, or zoning." Murtagh, *Keeping Time*, 214.

74. Stipe and Lee, *The American Mosaic*, 86, 129.

75. Murtagh, *Keeping Time*, 106.

76. This rapid development of historic districts in New York City appears to have come as a considerable surprise. Writing in 1974, Harmon H. Goldstone and Martha Dalrymple said that when the Landmarks Preservation Law was being drafted, "the idea of Historic Districts came almost as an afterthought. The obvious examples of Greenwich Village and Brooklyn Heights and perhaps a couple of others came to mind, and that was that. But, much to everyone's surprise, after the law was enacted and the Commission set up, pleas came from all over the city for designation not only of individual Landmarks, for which the Commission was prepared, but also of many more Historic Districts than had ever been anticipated." They concluded that this had happened because "ordinary people, even New Yorkers, like the feeling that they belong. They see in the provisions for Historic Districts something that the framers of the law themselves had not foreseen—namely, that the designation of an Historic District would give its residents a sense of identity and of continuity that most of them unconsciously craved. In an era that has become increasingly rootless, people recognize in an Historic District a chance to preserve something of the best from the past and, in preserving it, an opportunity to share in a sense of community pride and achievement." Goldstone and Dalrymple, *History Preserved*, 22-23. See Allison, "Historic Preservation in a Development-dominated City," 372.

77. Stipe and Lee, *The American Mosaic*, 122-23.

78. Ibid., 133.

79. Ibid., 29, 129.

80. These local commissions have a great diversity of names.

81. Historic district or historic preservation commissions are usually composed of a small number of preservation specialists and other lay people who are unpaid volunteers. This means that a "complex regulatory system" is "basically administered by appointed laymen." Their role is to draft regulations and to recommend them and the boundaries of the district to the governing board for adoption. "When adopted, the regulations apply to all properties within the district or to those designated as individual landmarks, and these may not thereafter be altered, demolished or moved without approval of the commission. Such approval is in the form of a certificate attesting to the appropriateness of the owner's plans and proposals, usually required before other zoning and building permits may be applied for." Stipe and Lee, *The American Mosaic*, 29.

82. For an overview, see Davis, *State Systems for Designating Historic Properties and the Results of Designation*.

83. Thus we shall see, for instance, the revival of the concept of the "park" as an appropriate setting for preservation at the district level. See below, Chapter 7.

Chapter 2

1. Neasham, *Old Sacramento*, 32.

2. "In this fast-moving nation, we run the risk of having *no* past against which to measure the present." Adler and Adler in *Preservation News* 26, no. 7 (July 1986): 4.

3. Hamer, *New Towns in the New World*, chaps. 4, 5.

4. *Plan and Program for the Preservation of the Vieux Carre*, 1, 3.

5. Russo, *Keepers of Our Past*.

6. Hamer, *New Towns in the New World*, 172-74.

7. See also Wilson, "Old Sacramento."

8. Datel and Dingemans, "Historic Preservation and Urban Change," 238.

9. Schwarzer, "Myths of Permanence and Transience in the Discourse on Historic Preservation in the United States," 2.

10. Biddle, "Saving our Cities Through Preservation," 31. On the cyclical interpretation of history and its application to towns and cities, see Hamer, *New Towns in the New World,* 120–30.

11. The authors of a book on Minneapolis see temporariness as the dominant theme of American urban history and the reason so little of the past has survived. "The continuous change in land use — not only in the substitution of different activities for what formerly existed, but in sheer density of activities — has all but erased whole episodes of the past for many communities." While some of the past does survive, there is no consistent pattern. "The classic pattern of a landscape, creation, stability, decay, and then eventual replacement, never occurs consistently throughout any urban environment. In some areas of a city, remnants of the past exist side-by-side with the new, while other areas may appear as encapsulated moments of the past." Particularly prone to disappearance are the mansion areas near to downtowns. Some districts can be read with ease; in others change has been such that we can no longer respond to them as readable artifacts of the past. Borchert et al., *Legacy of Minneapolis,* 109–10, 122.

12. "Neighborhoods may be ignored because the costs of conversion exceed the rent anticipated through private development. This can give an area a breathing period during which, ignored by the active speculators and challenged only by the rain, wind, and poor, it can survive, to one day 'come back' as an architectural gem, yielding higher rents than anyone ever dreamed." Logan and Molotch, *Urban Fortunes,* 122–23.

13. For example, Heartside, Grand Rapids, Michigan. But even it shows considerable signs of wear and tear.

14. David Lanegan explains thus why certain parts of cities have survived: "They are not as accessible as other parts of the city, and they have commonly been preserved because the commercial and industrial areas of the city expanded in other directions. They have not been dissected or seriously impacted by major transportation corridors like freeways. This eliminated serious competition for space so that the land values in these neighborhoods were never high enough to make clearance economical." Lanegan, *Urban Dynamics in Saint Paul,* 40.

15. Examples of rehabilitated warehouse districts are Morris Avenue, Birmingham (NR 1973); Leather District, Boston (NR 1983); Heartside, Grand Rapids (NR 1982); SoHo, New York (NR 1978); South Street Seaport, New York (NR 1978); Westend, Dallas (NR 1978); Union Depot–Warehouse, Tacoma (NR 1980). Warehouse districts and their restoration are discussed in Wood, "Nothing Should Stand for Something that Never Existed." Wood has argued that in the case of warehouse districts this should be accepted and welcomed as preferable to a fake historicizing. His Omaha example — Old Market (NR 1979) — is one that appears to have successfully blended modern uses with a retention of general historic ambience. For a critique of what has been done at South Street Seaport, see Boyer, "Cities for Sale," and *The City of Collective Memory,* 421–50.

16. The District Program at Nashville is modeled on the Main Street Program of the National Trust. Three downtown National Register districts were combined as

the focus for an economic revitalization program. *History-Gram* (Nashville Metropolitan Commission), no. 53 (Fall 1990): 1–3.

17. For example, Elizabeth Collins Cromley has argued that too many features of a district's history are left out of the story. The actual historical uses of buildings are usually not restored—nor can they be. New architecture is required to conform to the "spirit of the district" and will not therefore show itself as part of the history of rebuilding that characterizes all working cities. Zoning of this type, she argues, is very new and does not reflect the way the development of an area was shaped. Late-twentieth-century zoning restricts variety of scale and use and acts to purify a district of intrusive nineteenth-century variety. The history that is conveyed is one of pure residentiality, a twentieth-century formulation imposed on nineteenth-century districts. Our landmark vision of the past, according to Cromley, is one in which people lived at ground level, a far cry from the life experience of many people today in high-rise blocks. The preservation district in her view is truthful about how some want to see history—as a clean, neat, expensive portrait of our own current needs and desires. Cromley, "Public History and the Historic Preservation District," 30–36.

18. Wallace, *Mickey Mouse History*, 92–3.

19. Richard Longstreth argues that such a change "would not undermine the recognition of a given time span that may be the seminal one for a district; it would, however, recognize the fact that significant work seldom ceased altogether in subsequent years. Thus proposals made for modifications to *all* properties would be evaluated on a consistent basis, irrespective of date. . . . Under current practice, historic districts tend to become artificially homogeneous over time, with many small pieces that are not of the 'right' period removed or altered beyond recognition." Richard Longstreth, "When the Present Becomes the Past." The National Register Criteria state that "properties that have achieved significance within the last fifty years shall not be considered eligible for the National Register." However, they are allowed to qualify if "they are integral parts of districts that do meet the criteria." Criteria exception "g" also allows for a property to achieve significance "within the past fifty years if it is of exceptional importance."

20. Gratz, *The Living City*, 253–54, 258.

21. *Preservation News* 17, no. 12 (November 1977): 16. This is one of the very few references to the urban historian as an at least potentially interested party in these matters. Old Sacramento was created in the 1960s on 6 blocks out of the more than 700 blocks which comprise what is known as Old City, Sacramento. Datel and Dingemans, "Historic Preservation and Social Stability."

22. Neasham, *Old Sacramento*, 25.

23. Datel and Dingemans, "Historic Preservation and Urban Change," 238–40.

24. "Guidebook for the Old and Historic Districts of Nantucket and Siasconset" (Nantucket, Mass., Historic Districts Commission, 1967, 4), in Williams, Kellogg, and Gilbert, *Readings in Historic Preservation*, 144.

25. Weinberg, *Preservation in American Towns and Cities*, 27–28.

26. Bartlett, "Miami Beach Bets on Art Deco," 8.

27. Examples of a stress on homogeneity are the references to the Central Park West and Cobble Hill Historic Districts, New York, in Goldstone and Dalrymple, *History Preserved*, 336, 427–33.

28. *National Register Bulletin* 15, 5.

29. Ibid., 46.

30. Eckert, *Buildings of Michigan*, 320.

31. Francaviglia, *Hard Places*, 81.

32. Ralph W. Richardson, *Historic Districts: New England*, 34.

33. Richardson, *Historic Districts of America: The West*, 255.

34. Greenwood, "Ohio Renaissance," 37.

35. Datel and Dingemans, "Historic Preservation and Urban Change," 232, 235.

36. Comp, "Introduction."

37. Bennett, *Oxford County, Maine*, 17.

38. Eric Stoehr, *Bonanza Victorian*.

39. Woodbridge and Montgomery, *A Guide to Architecture in Washington State*, 296–98; Kirk and Alexander, *Exploring Washington's Past*, 498–501.

40. Kirk and Alexander, *Exploring Washington's Past*, 124.

41. Examples are Centerville and Metamora, Ind.; Kensington and New Market, Md.

42. Burke, "Port Townsend," 17.

43. *Historic Preservation* 46, no. 4 (July–August 1994): 32–39.

44. Hosmer and Williams, *Elsah*, 4.

45. Gebhard and Mansheim, *Buildings of Iowa*, 103, tell of Guttenberg, Iowa, where the tracks were laid three blocks away from the river and so a River Park Drive was subsequently established.

46. Examples of this are Allegan and Manistee in Michigan. The relationships between the river and Main Street in river towns are explored in Francaviglia, *Main Street Revisited*, 92.

47. Examples are Bellows Falls, Vt. (NR 1982), Lockport, Ill. (NR 1975), Lockport, N.Y. (1973/1975), and Metamora, Ind., where the Whitewater Canal Historic District was placed on the National Register in 1973 and the Metamora Historic District in 1992.

48. For example, Homer, N.Y. (NR 1973).

49. For example, Poolesville, Md. (NR 1975).

50. On Attica, see Taylor et al., *Indiana*, 304–5.

51. Ibid., 112–13. The Brookville Historic District is described in Grannis et al., *Visiting the Midwest's Historic Preservation Sites*, 238.

52. Taylor et al., *Indiana*, 101–2.

53. Washington, Ark. (NR 1972), is an example of a town of this kind.

54. Nickens, "Delaware Revivalism."

55. Grannis et al., *Visiting the Midwest's Historic Preservation Sites*, 234. Taylor et al., *Indiana*, 97–8.

56. Taylor et al., *Indiana*, 215.

57. Gebhard and Martinson, *A Guide to the Architecture of Minnesota*, 292.

58. See in particular "Historic Albany: Seems Like Old Times: A Guide to Historic Albany Oregon" (the Historic District Signage Publications Committee, Albany), 3, 16. There seems to have been a boosting tradition to draw on: that Albany was known as the "Hub City" of the Willamette Valley at the turn of the century is referred to in modern publicity material concerning the historic districts.

59. On Las Vegas, see Freed, *Preserving the Great Plains and Rocky Mountains*, 66.

60. An example is Evansville, Wisc. (NR 1978). See Grannis et al., *Visiting the Midwest's Historic Preservation Sites*, 31.

61. Described in Hudson, "Main Streets of the Yellowstone Valley."

62. For example, Garrett, Ind. (NR 1983): Taylor et al., *Indiana*, 33.

63. "Historical Landscapes — Livingston."

64. An example is Valdosta, Ga. Spector, *The Guide to the Architecture of Georgia*, 41.

65. The former seat of Sibley County. "Today it is only a small village with a few impressive remains of its past." Gebhard and Martinson, *A Guide to the Architecture of Minnesota*, 236.

66. *Historic Buildings of Centre County, Pennsylvania*, 11.

67. Rifkind, *Main Street*, 207.

68. Reps, *Cities of the American West*, 167. Another example of this phenomenon is Galena, Ill.

69. Olmert, "Delaware's Colonial Hideaway," 61.

70. Francaviglia, *Hard Places*, 178.

71. Ibid., 177–78. Francaviglia, "Learning From America's Preserved Historic Mining Landscapes," 12. On Tombstone's earlier preservation history, see Hosmer, *Preservation Comes of Age*, 1:365–71.

72. Ittleson, "Gambling." The impact of the Colorado constitutional amendment legalizing limited gambling in towns such as Cripple Creek and Central City is discussed in *Colorado History News* (July 1991). Other towns such as Telluride, Colo. (NR 1966), have to cope with the impact of mass tourism associated with skiing and festivals.

73. Fine examples of Victorian commercial architecture are to be found in such districts as the Idaho Springs Downtown Commercial District, Colo. (NR 1984); Victor, Colo. (NR 1985); and Silverton, Colo. (NR 1966).

74. Richardson, *Historic Districts of America: The West*, 305.

75. Roslyn is described in Francaviglia, *Hard Places*, 110–11; Kirk and Alexander, *Exploring Washington's Past*, 131–2; Woodbridge and Montgomery, *A Guide to Architecture in Washington State*, 370; Richardson, *Historic Districts of America: The West*, 292.

76. Richardson, *Historic Districts of America: The Mid-Atlantic*, 290.

77. Brochure issued by the Pennsylvania Historical and Museum Commission.

78. Francaviglia, *Hard Places*, 190–92; idem, "Learning From America's Preserved Historic Mining Landscapes," 13.

79. Eckert, *Buildings of Michigan*, 470.

80. Examples are Manistee, Mich. (NR 1982); Skamokawa, Wash. (NR 1976); College Avenue Historic District, Appleton, Wisc. (NR 1982); Hudson, Wisc. (NR 1984); West Main Street Historic District, Oconto, Wisc. (NR 1979).

81. Eckert, *Buildings of Michigan*, 526.

82. Information from the Hudson Walking Tour brochure.

83. Information from a walking tour guide prepared by Huntingdon Revitalization and Development.

84. An example in New York State is Cortland (NR 1975/1982), which flourished industrially after the Civil War.

85. Another example of this is Keeseville, N.Y.

86. Information from a walking tour brochure issued by Marietta Restoration Associates.

87. For example, Newton Lower and Upper Falls, Newton, Mass. (NR 1986).

88. Oyster Point, New Haven, Conn. (NR 1989), an oystering community that developed before the Civil War. It is still a detached boating district. Brown, *New Haven*, 89–92.

89. Reiff and Hirsch, "Pullman and Its Public."

90. Richardson, *Historic Districts of America: The Mid-Atlantic*, 248.

91. Garner, *The Model Company Town*, 49.

92. Richardson, *Historic Districts of America: The Mid-Atlantic*, 45.

93. Garner, *The Model Company Town*, 30–3. See also Stilgoe, *Borderland*, 252–53.

94. Attebery, *Building Idaho*, 77; Richardson, *Historic Districts of America: The West*, 115.

95. Kirk and Alexander, *Exploring Washington's Past*, 350.

96. Richardson, *Historic Districts of America: The Mid-Atlantic*, 291.

97. Eckert, *Buildings of Michigan*, 482.

98. Kirk and Alexander, *Exploring Washington's Past*, 390-93; Woodbridge and Montgomery, *A Guide to Architecture in Washington State*, 25, 52, 353–55. Other company towns that are now incorporated into historic districts include Bay View, Milwaukee, Wisc. (NR 1982), and DuPont Village, DuPont, Wash. (NR 1987). For the latter, described as "one of the state's most architecturally intact company towns," see Kirk and Alexander, *Exploring Washington's Past*, 304–5. Richardson, *Historic Districts of America: The West*, 285.

99. Richardson, *Historic Districts: The Mid-Atlantic*, 74.

100. Taylor et al., *Indiana*, 585.

101. *New City on the Merrimack*, 19–20; Richardson, *Historic Districts: New England*, 89.

102. Eckert, *Buildings of Michigan*, 337–38.

103. Information derived from the National Register nominations. See also Richardson, *Historic Districts: The Mid-Atlantic*, 128.

104. Information derived from a brochure issued in 1989 by the City of Bethlehem.

105. Richardson, *Historic Districts: The Mid-Atlantic*, 216.

106. Ibid., 45.

107. Ibid., 170.

108. Dolkart, *Guide to New York City Landmarks*, 99.

109. Jackson, *Crabgrass Frontier*, 46.

110. A good example of this kind of district is the Westwood Town Center Historic District, Cincinnati (NR 1974).

111. Woodbridge and Montgomery, *A Guide to Architecture in Washington State*, 189.

112. Eckert, *Buildings of Michigan*, 130. Three districts in Monroe were placed on the National Register in 1982. The phenomenon is also commented on in Kreisman, *Historic Preservation in Seattle*, 45. Michael Wallace has written on how local historians have reminded people of the onetime independent status of their districts and how this has sometimes led to the seeking of historic district status. *Mickey Mouse History*, 194.

113. Miller, "History and the Politics of Community Change in Cincinnati," 28–29. Clifton Avenue became a National Register Historic District in 1978.

114. Spector, *The Guide to the Architecture of Georgia*, 138.

Chapter 3

1. Greiber, "Secrets of Great Old Neighborhoods," 32.

2. Jackson, *Crabgrass Frontier*, 71–73. An example of the "picturesque" suburb whose origins can be traced to the 1850s is Lake Forest near Chicago (NR 1978).

3. Information from the National Register nomination and a walking tour brochure issued by the Brookline Preservation Commission. Other examples of this type of suburb, incorporating in particular the planning principles of Frederick Law Olmsted and Andrew Jackson Downing, are Short Hills Park, Millburn, N.J. (NR 1980), Llewellyn Park, West Orange, N.J. (NR 1986), and Roland Park, Baltimore (NR 1974).

4. The substantial masonry row houses, interspersed with institutional buildings of exceptional quality, reflect Harlem's development as "an affluent residential community following the extension of transit lines into the area around 1880." Dolkart, *Guide to New York City Landmarks*, 148. Examples of commuter and streetcar suburbs from the late nineteenth and early twentieth century are Baynard Boulevard and Delaware Avenue, Wilmington, Del.; Kensington, Md. (NR 1980); Mount Pleasant, Washington, D.C. (NR 1987); Stuart Neighborhood, Kalamazoo, Mich. (NR 1983); and Mount Morris Park, New York (NR 1973).

5. See Historic Newton's publication "Discover Historic Waban." The Pine Ridge Road–Plainfield Street Historic District at Waban was placed on the National Register in 1990.

6. Examples are Takoma Park, Washington, D.C. (NR 1983), Haddon Heights, N.J. (NR 1989), Hamilton Heights, New York (NR 1983), and Newton Highlands (NR 1986/1990) and Waban, Newton, Mass. A railroad was built out to the Newton Highlands area in the 1850s, but commuter trains were run infrequently, especially when trains were needed in the 1860s to work around the clock for the filling of Back Bay. In the 1870s, when that project was finished and a more regular service established, the area began to go ahead rapidly. Information derived from Historic Newton's publication "Discover Historic Newton Highlands."

7. Information from the National Register nomination and from the Historic Neighborhood Brochures for High Street Hill/Pill Hill prepared by the Brookline Preservation Commission.

8. All these features are now gone. Scott and Lee, *Buildings of the District of Columbia*, 366–67.

9. Hudson, "Main Streets of the Yellowstone Valley," 63–64.

10. Attebery, *Building Idaho*, 78.

11. For example, East River Road, Grosse Ile, Mich. (NR 1974), where a fine array of Gothic Revival houses were built between 1840 and 1870 for Detroit's elite. Eckert, *Buildings of Michigan*, 121.

12. Wiberg, *Rediscovering Northwest Denver*, 51.

13. Hunter, "From the Development Commission."

14. Moore, Becker, and Campbell, *The City Observed*, 275.

15. Scott and Lee, *Buildings of the District of Columbia*, 294.

16. Pacyga and Skerrett, *Chicago*, 104, 122.

17. Dolkart, *Guide to New York City Landmarks*, 179; White and Wilensky, *AIA Guide to New York City*, 330.

18. Information derived from the "Fabric of Pittsburgh" walking tour brochure issued by the Pittsburgh Historic Review Commission.

19. Dolkart, *Guide to New York City Landmarks,* 206.

20. Ibid., 153.

21. Goldstone and Dalrymple, *History Preserved,* 438.

22. Ibid., 330–32. Dolkart, *Guide to New York City Landmarks,* 146.

23. White and Wilensky, *AIA Guide to New York City,* 122. See also Dolkart, *Guide to New York City Landmarks,* 94.

24. Clay, "Townscape and Landscape," 38.

25. Examples are Edgewood Park, New Haven, Conn. (NR 1986); Cool Spring Park, Wilmington, Del. (NR 1983); Fort Greene, New York (NR 1983/1984).

26. A notable example is Grant Park, Atlanta (NR 1979).

27. *A Brief History of the Irvine Park District,* 10–11.

28. Eckert, *Buildings of Michigan,* 219–21.

29. Details from *DeWitt Park Historic District and Downtown Ithaca.*

30. Brown, *New Haven,* 184.

31. Gebhard et al., *A Guide to Architecture in San Francisco and Northern California,* 181. Richardson, *Historic Districts of America: The West,* 66. Reps, *Cities of the American West,* 168–72.

32. Examples are Boonville, Ind.; Albia Square and Central Commercial HD, Iowa; Courthouse Square HD, Bloomington, Ind.; Delaware County Courthouse Square HD, Delhi, N.Y.; Chenango County Courthouse District, Norwich, N.Y.; Courthouse Square HD, Mason, Mich. (see description in Eckert, *Buildings of Michigan,* 289); Hood County Courthouse HD, Granbury, Texas (significant as a historic district in relation to the development of the National Trust's Main Street Program: see Freed, *Preserving the Great Plains and Rocky Mountains,* 202–8).

33. Warner, *Streetcar Suburbs,* 158–59.

34. Cf. Frederick Law Olmsted's reason for favoring a curvilinear street system for neighborhood development: "It will be observed, that . . . while the roads are so laid out as to afford moderately direct routes of communication between the different parts of the neighborhood, they would be inconvenient to be followed for any purpose of business beyond the mere supplying of the wants of the neighborhood itself,—that is to say, it would be easier for any man wishing to convey merchandise from any point a short distance on one side of your neighborhood to a point a short distance on the other side, to go around it rather than go through it." Olmsted, Vaux & Co., *Report Upon a Projected Improvement of the Estate of the College of California* (New York, 1886), 19, quoted in Reps, *The Making of Urban America,* 344.

35. Taylor et al., *Indiana,* 491.

36. Examples are the May's Island Historic District at Cedar Rapids, Iowa (Gebhard and Mansheim, *Buildings of Iowa,* 172–73, 182); Washington Boulevard, Detroit (Eckert, *Buildings of Michigan,* 70); Civic Center, San Francisco (Olmsted and Watkins, *Here Today,* 90); Civic Center, Denver, Colo. (Leonard and Noel, *Denver,* 148); Duluth Civic Center, Duluth, Minn.

37. Richardson, *Historic Districts of America: The Mid-Atlantic,* 51.

38. *Built in Milwaukee,* 161.

39. Herman Day, *Historical Collections of the State of Pennsylvania*, 1843, quoted in *Historic Buildings of Centre County Pennsylvania*, 122.

40. Grannis et al., *Visiting the Midwest's Historic Preservation Sites*, 61.

41. Schroeder, "Types of American Small Towns and How to Read Them," *Order and Image in the American Small Town*, 125.

42. Datel and Dingemans, "Historic Preservation and Social Stability in Sacramento's Old City," 583–84.

43. Goldstone and Dalrymple, *History Preserved*, 464–67. Another example is Cato Hill, Woonsocket, R.I. (NR 1976), which is defined topographically by steep slopes and major arterial thoroughfares and is described as "untroubled by noise and traffic." *Woonsocket, Rhode Island: Statewide Historic Preservation Report P-W-1* (Rhode Island Historical Preservation Commission, 1976), 17.

44. Morse, "Neighborhood Spirit Shapes a City."

45. Examples are Irvington, Indianapolis, and Palmer Park Apartments, Detroit.

46. Reps, *The Making of Urban America*, 456. On Zoar, see also Horstman, "Defining a Role for Professionals in Small Town Preservation."

47. For example, Enfield, N.H. (NR 1979), Shakertown at Pleasant Hill, Kentucky (NR 1971), and Watervleit Shaker, Colonie, N.Y. (NR 1973).

48. Such as Greenbelt, Md. (NR 1980), Greenhills, Ohio (NR 1989—another "greenbelt" town), and Jersey Homesteads, Roosevelt, N.J. (NR 1983). Richardson, *Historic Districts of America: The Mid-Atlantic*, 100–1.

49. Cf. this comment on Browne's Addition, Spokane, Wash. (NR 1976): "Dramatically situated on a bluff rising above the river, the very geography contributed to the exclusive nature of this early residential area." Woodbridge and Montgomery, *A Guide to Architecture in Washington State*, 406.

50. Examples in smaller towns are University Courts, Bloomington, Ind.; North End, Colorado Springs, Colo.; Near Westside, Elmira, N.Y.; Green Street-Brenau, Gainesville, Ga.; Riverview HD, Kankakee, Ill.; Chapin Park and West Washington HDs, South Bend, Ind.; Las Vegas High School Neighborhood, Las Vegas, Nev.; Heritage Hill, Grand Rapids, Mich.; East Elm–North Macomb Street, Monroe, Mich.; Barnard Park, Fremont, Neb.; Rucker Hill, Everett, Wash.

51. For example, Kalorama, Washington D.C.; Hyde Park–Kenwood, Chicago; Northside, Indianapolis; Boston-Edison, Detroit; Upper East Side, New York; Prospect Avenue, Milwaukee (at one time known as Milwaukee's Gold Coast). *Built in Milwaukee*, 186.

52. Clark, " 'Ramcat' and Rittenhouse Square," 125.

53. Warner, *The Living and the Dead*, 44, 50, 153.

54. Starr, *Southern Comfort*, 5–7.

55. Information from the *City of Bloomington Interim Report* of the Indiana Historic Sites and Structures Inventory (second printing, Feb. 1988), 8. Unfortunately, the Walnut Street homes of the Showers brothers were subsequently razed.

56. Southworth and Southworth, *A.I.A. Guide to Boston*, 466.

57. Richardson, *Historic Districts of America: The Mid-Atlantic*, 13.

58. Details from a walking tour brochure issued by the Schenectady Urban Cultural Park.

59. Cigliano and Landau, *The Grand American Avenue 1850–1920*, xiii.
60. *Hartford Architecture*, 1:122.
61. Brown, *New Haven*, 134–36.
62. On Prairie Avenue, see Cigliano and Landau, *The Grand American Avenue*, 129–52.
63. Clubbe, *Cincinnati Observed*, 238. Other grand avenues that are now represented by historic districts include

- Baynard Boulevard, Wilmington, Del. (NR 1979). Richardson, *Historic Districts of America: The Mid-Atlantic*, 10.
- Delaware Avenue, Buffalo (NR 1974). *Buffalo Architecture*, 140; Cigliano and Landau, *The Grand American Avenue*, chap. 2.
- Park Avenue, Minneapolis (NR 1978), some of the mansions in which (few are left) can be seen in the Washburn-Fair Oaks Mansion District. Kane and Ominsky, *Twin Cities*, 271; Millett, *Lost Twin Cities*, 115.

64. Pacyga and Skerrett, *Chicago*, 195–97.
65. White and Wilensky, *AIA Guide to New York City*, 227.
66. Richardson, *Historic Districts of America: The Mid-Atlantic*, 163.
67. Cigliano and Landau, *The Grand American Avenue*, xvi.
68. White and Wilensky, *AIA Guide to New York City*, 306.
69. Attebery, *Building Idaho*, 60.
70. Brown and Dorsett, *K.C.*, 161.
71. Ehrlich, *Kansas City, Missouri*, 206.
72. Brown, *New Haven*, 54.
73. Richardson, *Historic Districts: The Mid-Atlantic*, 109.
74. Freed, *Preserving the Great Plains and Rocky Mountains*, 376–80.
75. Other examples of gatepost markers at the entrance to historic districts of this exclusive enclave type are White Place Historic District, Bloomington, Ill. (NR 1988), and Highland Historic District, Waterloo, Iowa (NR 1984). For the history of gates and other boundary markers and defensive devices in suburban developments, see Stilgoe, *Borderland*, 55. Mary Corbin Sies has drawn attention to "boundary-marking strategies" in the development of planned, exclusive suburbs. "Designers might make the physical borders visibly distinct by surrounding the suburb with fences, walls, a buffer zone of land, or a distinguishing landscape effect. In Kenilworth [near Chicago], for example, stone pillars crowned by monumental urns filled with flowers were added at all three principal entrances to the community." Sies, "Paradise Retained," 178–79.
76. Savage, *African American Historic Places National Register of Historic Places*, 141.
77. Southworth and Southworth, *A.I.A. Guide to Boston*, 171. Other examples are the 1850s development of Hamilton Park, Jersey City, N.J. (NR 1979/1982), and the later Van Vorst Park in the same city (NR 1980/1984). Richardson, *Historic Districts: The Mid-Atlantic*, pp. 86–87.
78. Dolkart, *Guide to New York City Landmark*, 56; Goldstone and Dalrymple, *History Preserved*, 233–37.
79. Richardson, *Historic Districts: The Mid-Atlantic*, 201.
80. Starr, *Southern Comfort*, 5.
81. *Preservation News* 33, no. 1 (January 1993): 8.

82. Brown, *New Haven*, 36, 44.

83. Weeks, *A Guide to the Architecture of Washington, D.C.*, 119, 129.

84. *Buffalo Architecture: A Guide*, 100.

85. Information derived from a walking tour brochure issued by the City of Covington (1991).

86. Peters and McCue, *A Guide to the Architecture of St. Louis*, 96; Primm, *Lion of the Valley*, 361-62.

87. He added, "Ordinarily poor white and poor black people couldn't give less than a darn about the historical significance of something." Myers and Binder, *Neighborhood Conservation*, 22.

88. Pacyga and Skerrett, *Chicago*, 269-99.

89. Burns, "The Enduring Affluent Suburb."

90. Sies, "Paradise Retained," 166-80.

91. Information from the National Register nomination.

92. Quoted in the Historic Neighborhood Brochure for High Street Hill/Pill Hill issued by the Brookline Preservation Commission. A New York City historic district where restrictive covenants have contributed to its distinctive character today is Riverside-West 105th Street, New York. Dolkart, *Guide to New York City Landmarks*, 129.

93. *A Guide to the Older Neighborhoods of Dallas*, 22.

94. Dorsey and Dilts, *A Guide to Baltimore Architecture*, xlii-xlv.

95. Fishman, *Bourgeois Utopias*, 145-46.

96. Gebhard and Martinson, *A Guide to the Architecture of Minnesota*, 120.

97. Taylor et al., *Indiana*, 402-3.

98. Information derived from the National Register nomination.

99. For example, Durango, Colo.

100. Kaplan, *The Historic Architecture of Cabarrus County, North Carolina*, 99.

101. According to Patricia Mooney Melvin, neighborhoods emerged as identifiable units in the cityscape at the point when urban centers underwent a transformation from the pedestrian city of the eighteenth and early nineteenth century to the expanded and differentiated urban structure of the early twentieth century. The walking city had inhibited the development of a neighborhood consciousness based on the specialization of land uses along commercial, manufacturing, and residential lines. But in the late nineteenth century the internal structure of cities became characterized by distinct units that included residential areas that became known as "neighborhoods." Melvin, "The Neighborhood-City Relationship," 257-59.

102. Beale Street, Memphis, is perhaps the worst example of this.

103. For examples, see the entries for the North Lawrence-Monroe Street Historic District, Montgomery, Ala. (NR 1984), Pleasant Street, Gainesville, and Northwest, West Palm Beach, Fla. (NR 1989; 1992), Merrehope, Meridian, Miss. (NR 1988), and Waverly, Columbia, S.C. (NR 1989). Savage, *African American Historic Places*, 100-1, 153, 164, 309, 452-53.

104. Ibid., 166.

105. Eckert, *Buildings of Michigan*, 400-1; Savage, *African American Historic Places*, 285.

106. Savage, *African American Historic Places*, 88-89.

107. Ibid., 184-85.

108. Ball et al., *Indianapolis Architecture*, 87.

109. Savage, *African American Historic Places*, 85.

110. See the discussions of the Fort Hill and Pleasant Hill Historic Districts in Macon (NR 1993; 1986). Ibid., 172.

111. Ibid., 192. Note also the entry for the East Russell Street Area Historic District, Orangeburg, S.C. (NR 1985). Ibid., 445.

112. *Historic Preservation* 47, no. 1 (January-February 1995): 34.

113. Savage, *African American Historic Places*, 148, 358.

114. For examples, see ibid., 91, 153, 172, 176.

115. See the comment on Northwest, West Palm Beach (NR 1992). Ibid., 164.

116. Miller, *Reclaiming the Past. CRM* 20, no. 3 (1997) was devoted to "Placing Women in the Past." There are few references to historic districts.

117. See also Kazickas and Scherr, *Susan B. Anthony Slept Here.*

118. Information derived from a brochure on the South Wayne Historic District prepared by the Division of Community and Economic Development of the City of Fort Wayne.

119. Information from a brochure on the Smithfield Historic District prepared by the Birmingham Historical Society.

Chapter 4

1. Among other historic districts with associations with famous literary figures is Nook Farm and Woodland Street District, Hartford, Conn. (NR 1979; Mark Twain and Harriet Beecher Stowe).

2. Neither the National Park Service headquarters nor the local historical society was able to find information for me on, or appeared to know anything about, the small Baxter Street Historic District, an enclave of distinctive working-class housing.

3. Kay, "Salem," 20.

4. Devlin, *Handbook for Connecticut Historical District and Historic Properties Commissions and Report of the Historian-in-Residence Project to the Connecticut Association of Historic District Commissioners,* 7:78-82; 9:4-5. The requirement has been eased.

5. An example of this is Lewes, Del.

6. On the remembering of the witchcraft episode in Salem, see Foote, *Shadowed Ground*, 2-5, 27, 187-91.

7. Meinig, "Symbolic Landscapes."

8. Meinig, "Symbolic Landscapes," 164. See also Hummon, *Commonplaces.*

9. Wood, " 'Build, Therefore, Your Own World,' " 46. See also Wood and Steinitz, "A World We Have Gained."

10. *Handbook for Connecticut Historical District and Historic Properties Commissioners,* 7:41.

11. Ibid., 27.

12. Meinig, "Symbolic Landscapes," 167.

13. Rifkind, *Main Street*, xi-xiii, 63.

14. Ibid., 14.

15. Ibid., 174-190.

16. For a comprehensive survey of attitudes to small towns and their Main Streets, see Lingeman, *Small Town America.*

17. Works that analyze the architecture of Main Street include Longstreth, *The Buildings of Main Street.*

18. *Main Street, Ohio,* 72; Rifkind, *Main Street,* 149–51.

19. The stereotyping of the small town is analyzed in Jakle, *The American Small Town.*

20. The removal of these false fronts to reveal the original Italianate facades beneath was a major theme of restoration work in Main Street, Madison, Ind. See Skelcher, "Preserving Main Street in the Heartland." Ironically, the coverings have functioned as a protection for the original facades. Notable other examples of this form of facade restoration can be found in Syracuse, New York, and in Baker City, Oregon: see Cole, "Baker City, Oregon, Develops Tourism as a Springboard for Economic Development," 6.

21. Spector, *The Guide to the Architecture of Georgia,* 14.

22. This is a major theme in Connecticut. It is discussed in the Devlin Handbook.

23. See Wilson, *The City Beautiful Movement,* 41–44; Rifkind, *Main Street,* 149.

24. Rifkind, *Main Street,* 149.

25. Dorsey and Dilts, *A Guide to Baltimore Architecture,* 195–97. Another example of this is Albion, R.I. (NR 1984). "Today Albion is a pleasant village—tidy and neat, its modest houses surrounded by lawns. . . . Like Lincoln's other mill villages, Albion is attractive, so much so that it is easy to forget how much less salubrious life in a mill village was even a hundred years ago." Albion underwent a beautification and renovation campaign from 1908, led by the Valley Falls Company and its superintendent. *Lincoln, Rhode Island,* 30.

26. *Historic Preservation* 21, no. 4 (October-December 1969): 14. George Kramer has argued vigorously for the toleration within historic districts of commercial signs of the kind appropriate to modern commercialism. "Signs." "The gold and silver towns of the West were noisy, bustling communities with garish signs. Every shopkeeper was out to take the miners for their money. In some respects, then, Virginia City may be more evocative of the 19th-century West than an outdoor village museum would be. The fine line between appropriate atmosphere and tasteless commercialism is not always an easy one to draw." John L. Frisbee, *Preservation in the West* (Washington, D.C.: National Trust, 1972, 2, 22–24), in Williams, Kellogg, and Gilbert, *Readings in Historic Preservation,* 47–50.

27. Pat Ross, in *Remembering Main Street,* 36, comments on the strict controls over signs in Lexington, Virginia, that it has become "difficult to tell which signs are made to look old and which are truly old" and cites the sign put up for the film *Sommersby* and not subsequently removed.

28. Cawley, "Fort Worth Rides Again," 15–16.

29. Ibid.

30. Ford, "Urban Preservation and the Geography of the City in the USA," 224.

31. "Utility lines were installed underground [on Church Street] in the 1920's to avoid their intrusion into the scene." National Register nomination for Dorset, Vt.

32. Murtagh, *Keeping Time,* 35, shows the wires still there in a photograph of Rockefeller and others examining plans for the restoration.

33. *Water Street Historic District,* 28.

34. Woodbridge and Montgomery, *A Guide to Architecture in Washington State,* 202.

35. Jacobs, "A Current View of Area Preservation," 50.

36. Boslough, "Is This the Williamsburg of the Rockies?" *A Guide to Delineating Edges,* 64–5.

37. In 1976 Lynch called for the development of "methods for analyzing the environmental image of time, which may be even more important to our emotional well-

being than that of space. . . . While the historic associations of certain special spaces are a common subject of planning attention, the usual aim is to save a few old places just as they 'used to be.' How an entire working landscape might connect us to the present time, or to the recent past, or to the future—indeed, to the unending *passage* of time—still seems a remote question." Lynch, *Managing the Sense of a Region*, 27–28.

38. "The frequent stress on associating historical importance with an organic and static representation of the city overlooks, to some degree, the continual renewal of both buildings and cities, the successive waves of alterations and inhabitants." Schwarzer, "Myths of Permanence and Transience," 8.

39. Hamer, *New Towns in the New World*, 166–67.

40. Stipe and Lee, *The American Mosaic*, 199.

41. Williams, *Upscaling Downtown*, 131.

42. Breen, *Imagining the Past*, 288–95.

43. *Information Series*, no. 65 (1992): "Cultural and Ethnic Diversity in Historic Preservation," 3, 12.

44. Tomlan, "Who Will Care in the 1990s?"

45. Ortega, "Unwanted," 43.

46. Mattox, "As I See It."

47. Olson, *Baltimore*, 6.

48. Janka, "An Old-West Mining Town Copes with Growth."

Chapter 5

1. Roderick S. French, director of the Division of Experimental Programs at George Washington University, quoted in *Preservation News* 18, no. 12 (December 1978): 5.

2. Kidney, "Small History," 5.

3. Hunter, *Symbolic Communities*, 160.

4. Ibid., 161.

5. Richard V. Francaviglia has written that "Bodie is preservation as theater." Francaviglia, "Learning from America's Preserved Historic Mining Landscapes," 11. This article includes a useful discussion of ghost towns and the arguments about what they are and what should be preserved in them.

6. *Ghost Towns and Mining Camps*, 5–8, 11–13, 25; Huston and Tilgham, "Bodie, California."

7. *Preservation News* 21, no. 12 (December 1991): 4. On the preservation of ghost towns, see also John L. Frisbee, *Preservation in the West* (Washington, D.C.: National Trust, 1972), 2, 22–24, in Williams, Kellogg, and Gilbert, *Readings in Historic Preservation*, 47–50.

8. *Values of Residential Properties in Urban Historic Districts*, 15.

9. Information supplied by the Weston Development Company.

10. The impressiveness of this statistic is somewhat offset when another is taken into account. At the beginning of the 1990s Philadelphia had only one locally designated district, and that was not in the Center City. It is only through the designation of such districts that there can be any real protection against the demolition of historic buildings. Collins, Waters, and Dotson, *America's Downtowns*, 92–93, 97–98.

11. Ibid., 97–98.

12. Based on material put out by the City of Harrisburg and the Historic Harrisburg Association.

13. The most frequently expressed objections are summarized—and rebutted—in *Maintaining Community Character*, 19–20. The reasons why historic preservation is often opposed and resisted are also well set out in Gay, "Urban Treasures or Urban Nightmares?"

14. Silver, "Revitalizing the Urban South," 78–79.

15. Miller, "History and the Politics of Community Change in Cincinnati," 32; footnote 19.

16. Miller, "Planning and the Politics of Ethnic Identity."

17. *Preservation News* 22, no. 11 (November 1982): 11.

18. Ortega, "Unwanted," 43.

19. Levy and Cybriwsky, "The Hidden Dimensions of Culture and Class: Philadelphia," 147–48.

20. Local pride and the importance of the status conferred by National Register listing are referred to in Velt, "Local Preservation Activities."

21. Not many writers on modern urban preservationism have commented on possible links with boosting traditions or with modern-day boosting. One who does put emphasis on the interest of modern boosters in historic districts is Wallace, *Mickey Mouse History*, 203. Changing attitudes of southern boosters to historic preservation are referred to in Cassity and Crimmins, "Local Historic Preservation Ordinances and Cultural Resource Protection Strategies in the Mid-South," 7. One of the very few studies of modern urban boosterism in this context is an article on Syracuse, New York: Short et al., "Reconstructing the Image of an Industrial City." Another article has looked at the search of business communities in Iowa towns for a pseudohistorical theme: Engler, "Drive-Thru History." Numerous articles over the years in *Small Town* have described how towns have sought to change their image through historic preservation. A good example is Greenwood, "Ohio Renaissance: A New Image Makes Good Business Sense for Medina's Public Square" (Medina is in Ohio).

22. For example, Neighborhood Housing Services at Bridgeport, Conn. Kay with Chase-Harrell, *Preserving New England*, 107–9.

23. For example, at Manitou Springs, Colorado, designation as one of the 30 Main Street towns in the United States in 1981 was followed by Historic District designation in 1983.

24. Frantz, "Okmulgee, Oklahoma."

25. Datel and Dingemans, "Why Places Are Preserved," 45, 50.

26. Usually they can also vote for the termination of Historic District designation. Thurber and Moyer, *State Enabling Legislation*, 21–2.

27. Eckert, *Buildings of Michigan*, 260.

28. Examples of the institutional threat are the Colorado Springs North End district and the College Hill district at Providence. Freed, 366–69; Kay with Chase-Harrell, 98.

29. Freed, *Preserving the Great Plains and Rocky Mountains*, 285–87.

30. Leider, "Capitol Townsite Historic District," 398–400.

31. An example is Georgetown–Silver Plume near Denver.

32. Steilacoom's preservation history is described in *CRM* (1994): 26.

33. An example is the restoration of the city hall in the Church Street East Historic District in Mobile (NR 1971/ 1984). *Maintaining Community Character*, 5.

34. Taylor et al., *Indiana*, 90-1. The Union Station is also the focus of a historic district at Indianapolis (NR 1982).

35. On Granbury, see Freed, *Preserving the Great Plains and Rocky Mountains*, 202-8.

36. Examples are Elmira and Corning, New York.

37. Gratz, *The Living City*, 226.

38. Cramm, *Historic Ellicott City*, 23.

39. *Historic Preservation News* 34, no. 5 (October-November 1994): 11-12. The impact of disasters on small towns is analyzed in Francaviglia, *Main Street Revisited*, 59-64.

40. H. Briavel Holcomb and Robert A. Beauregard have written, "Revitalization efforts consciously try to remold the image of the city. . . . Another key dimension of revitalization, as seen from a phenomenological perspective, focuses on recapturing and reusing images of the past. Forms of historic preservation, adaptive reuse, and reconstruction of formerly bustling waterfront areas and 'Main Streets' link an ostensibly glorious past with a much-desired vibrant future. . . . Waterfronts and old main streets receive particular attention in the hope of regenerating their former vigor and ambiance." The aim is to provide "societal memory of times past, times when the city flourished and its people prospered." Holcomb and Beauregard, *Revitalizing Cities*, 51-53, 58.

41. For example, Old Colorado City near Colorado Springs received a major "historical" face-lift at the time of the Colorado centennial and national bicentennial in 1976.

42. Purdy, "The Anatomy of Creating a Local Historic District," 9.

43. Information from a brochure issued by the society. See also Grannis et al., *Visiting the Midwest's Historic Preservation Sites*, 209.

44. The quotations are from an undated brochure, "Historic Weston: Mid-America's Most Historic City," issued by the Weston Development Company.

45. Taylor et al., *Indiana*, 54-65.

46. Gene Bunnell, ed., *A Future from the Past* (Washington, D.C.: U.S. Department of Housing and Urban Development and Massachusetts Department of Community Affairs, 1978), 21-22, 67, 75-79, in Williams, Kellogg, and Gilbert, *Readings in Historic Preservations*, 61.

47. A prominent theme in Glisson, *Main Street*.

48. Weeks, *The Buildings of Westminster in Maryland*, 85, 119.

49. Salwen, *Upper West Side Story*, 295.

50. For a case study of divided attitudes in business communities, see Stanwood, "Coupeville's Historic District Dilemma."

51. *Historic Preservation* 21, no. 4 (October-December 1969): 32.

52. *Preservation News* 32, no. 1 (February 1992): 2.

53. Ide, "St. Joseph, Mo." St. Joseph had been a principal station for the Pony Express. A Main Street study of Hot Springs, South Dakota, refers to a major problem in midwestern downtowns: "a general lack of appreciation for 'that old stuff' around town." *Hot Springs, South Dakota, Main Street Study*, 7.

54. Letter to author, January 18, 1994.

55. Brochure issued by the Office of the Mayor of Harrisburg entitled "History and Heritage Are Alive and Well in Harrisburg: A Guide to the City's Historic Preservation Program."

56. *Salmon Falls — The Mill Village*, 15.

57. Glisson, *Main Street*, 52.

58. *CRM* 17, no. 2 (1994): 26.
59. Glisson, *Main Street*, 103.
60. Galbreath, "Communities Benefit from a Sense of History," 7.
61. *Conserve Neighborhoods*, no. 2 (August-September 1978).
62. *Building the Future from Our Past*, 20–21.
63. Comp, "Introduction," 2–3.
64. *Lowell, Massachusetts*, 23.
65. Helfgot et al., *Lowell, Massachusetts*, 5, 193–94.
66. Bunnell, *A Future from the Past*, in Williams, Kellogg, and Gilbert, *Readings in Historic Preservation*, 61.
67. Gittell, *Renewing Cities*, 72.
68. Hamer, *New Towns in the New World*, 173–74.
69. Gittell, *Renewing Cities*, 71.
70. Ibid.
71. Ibid., 72.
72. Ibid., 73.
73. Ibid., 94.
74. *Lowell*, 90–91.
75. Collins, "Progress and Profit through Blending Past and Present."
76. Ortega, "Unwanted," 41–43.
77. The quotations are from an undated brochure, "Walking Tour of Belle Grove Historic District."
78. The quotations are from an undated brochure, "Madison, Indiana," issued by the Madison Area Chamber of Commerce.
79. Lyle and Lynn, "Lexington, Virginia." See also Ross, *Remembering Main Street*, 22–46.
80. Quoted in Hosmer, *Preservation Comes of Age*, 1:256.
81. Kay with Chase-Harrell, 87–88.
82. Schwarzer acknowledges that the dilemma is that if one attacks historic preservation's myth of permanence one can end up sounding antihistorical and prodevelopment. . . . "[O]vercoming the opposition between myths of permanence and transience invites further rethinking of the focus of the preservation movement. . . . [T]he myth of permanence represents built culture through opposed categories: old and new, high and low, lasting and ephemeral, historic and unhistoric. These oppositions encourage a belief that historic buildings and districts are those whose historic elements have been restored to original form with period constructive techniques and equivalent materials. It advocates the isolation of historic districts from the modern city or suburb and their transportation and communications systems. Finally, it implies that unpreserved buildings and sites are not of historical importance." Schwarzer, "Myths of Permanence and Transience," 2–10.
83. Lanegan, *Urban Dynamics in Saint Paul*, 39–40.
84. Biddle, "Saving Our Cities Through Preservation," 31. See also Neil Smith, "New City, New Frontier," 69.
85. Kidney, "Small History," 5.
86. Tise, "Saving our Towns," 6.
87. *With Heritage So Rich*, 190.

88. Ibid., 193.

89. Bender, *Community and Social Change in America,* 5.

90. Ibid., 93.

91. Ibid., 144.

92. Scherzer, *The Unbounded Community,* 1. Subjective and idealized conceptions of neighborhood have, according to Scherzer, secured a strong hold on the modern imagination. Historians, especially labor historians with their nostalgic allusions to a golden age of working-class communities, have contributed substantially to this in his view.

93. "Old West Side," *Historic Preservation* 25, no. 3 (July-September 1973): 21.

94. Winters, "The Social Identity of Evolving Neighborhoods."

95. *Preservation Is Progress,* 3–6.

96. Harry E. White, Jr., in *Columbia Law Review* (April 1963), quoted in Christopher Tunnard, "Landmarks of Beauty and History," in *With Heritage So Rich,* 133.

97. Birch and Roby, "The Planner and the Preservationist," 200.

98. Melvin, "The Neighborhood-City Relationship," 263–64.

99. Ibid., 257.

100. Savery, "Instability and Uniformity," 193.

101. Ibid., 195.

102. Firey, *Land Use in Central Boston.*

103. Hunter, *Symbolic Communities,* 7.

104. *Preservation News* 16, no. 12 (December 1976): 9.

105. Ziegler, *Historic Preservation in Inner City Areas,* 55–57.

106. Suttles, *The Social Construction of Communities,* 9–10.

107. Ziegler, *Historic Preservation in Inner City Areas,* 57.

108. Scherzer, *The Unbounded Community,* 138.

109. Ehrlich, *Kansas City, Missouri,* 206–8.

110. Freed, *Preserving the Great Plains and Rocky Mountains,* 376–80.

111. As happened in German Village in Columbus, Ohio. Ford, "Urban Preservation and the Geography of the City in the USA," 227–28.

112. From information supplied by the neighborhood associations in these districts. On the history of the preservation movement and the creation of historic districts in Lynchburg, see *Lynchburg,* 485.

113. Datel and Dingemans, "Why Places Are Preserved," 43. For an exploration of the consequences for the appreciation of the history of a district of the attitudes and emphases associated with gentrification, see Datel, "Preservation and a Sense of Orientation for American Cities," 133–34.

114. Stipe and Lee, *The American Mosaic,* 29.

115. These include orientation, setback, spacing, and site coverage of buildings; height, width, and massing of buildings; size, shape, and proportion of building fenestration; materials, textures, colors, and details of facades; roof forms and cornice lines; open spaces; unique features of the area. *Landmark Yellow Pages,* 19. Incentives are described in *Maintaining Community Character,* 12.

116. Schoenberg and Rosenbaum, *Neighborhoods that Work,* 67–68.

117. Morris, "A Neighborhood Grows in Charlotte," 64–65.

118. *Preservation Forum* 1, no. 1 (Fall 1987): 7.

119. Beasley, "Reviewing New Design in Historic Districts," 28.

120. John A. Jakle and David Wilson have referred to the ambivalent attitudes of most Americans to "the evidence of decline about them." "Mindsets operate to obscure the implications of decay, dereliction being discounted as abnormal and a deviation from prevailing norms of growth. Vacancy and abandonment are believed transitional. Americans have an extraordinary penchant to ignore dereliction." Jakle and Wilson, *Derelict Landscapes*, 11.

121. The phenomenon of the blotting out of a vast in-between period in a community's historical consciousness is studied in Miller, "History and the Politics of Community Change in Cincinnati," pp. 28–29; and Shapiro and Miller, *Clifton*, 43.

122. Lynch, *Managing the Sense of a Region*, 72, 189–91.

123. Miller, "Planning and the Politics of Ethnic Identity," 248–65.

Chapter 6

1. Glass, *The Beginning of a New National Historic Preservation Program*, 31.

2. Murtagh, "Historic Districts," 15.

3. Paul Sprague, a leading midwestern preservationist, saw preservationists as "beginning to realize that the key to saving historic cultural properties is through the conservation of sympathetic environments." This meant that "efforts are presently being directed at preventing or, at the least, controlling change in those sub-areas of communities that are being designated historic districts. The theory is that if a compatable [*sic*] environment remains, and does not decline in quality or change markedly in use, the ordinary economic pressures for alteration or replacement of important historic sites and structures will not arise. If urban districts can thus be stabilized, the owners of historic sites and structures will be encouraged to continue maintaining and using their properties, with the result that costly rehabilitations and restorations will never be necessary. Although there will certainly always be a need for conserving isolated sites and structures, as museums if necessary, because of the unavoidable loss of their original environments, it is probable, nonetheless, that most historic properties will be more easily and more economically preserved by becoming parts of historic districts." Sprague and Lerner, *Historic Districts*, 2–3.

4. *Historic Preservation News* 34, no. 3 (June–July 1994): 20.

5. "Marshall, Mich.: Preserving Our Town," in *Preservation in Your Town*, 10.

6. The area is roughly bounded by East Drive and Plum, Forest and Hanover streets. Eckert, *Buildings of Michigan*, 209.

7. On Strawbery Banke, see Chase and Garvin, *Portsmouth*; Candee, *Building Portsmouth*, 49–60.

8. Sprague observed, "Until recently conservationists have concentrated on preserving individual structures and sites of historic, architectural and cultural significance. Such a selective approach has not worked in many cases because of changes in neighboring properties which, through physical deterioration or alterations in use, have made it economically unfeasible to preserve the historic site or structure in its changed setting. . . . [Properties] have frequently become so isolated in their surroundings that it becomes all but impossible for the average person to understand and appreciate their historic significance." Sprague and Lerner, *Historic Districts*, 2.

9. In 1975 Sprague explained that while he was director of the Illinois Historic Structures Survey he "gradually came to the conclusion that the most effective means

for preserving important works of architecture was through the device of the Historic District. Only by encouraging the stabilization of entire urban areas, and thus insuring the continuity of sympathetic environments for buildings of special architectural merit, would it ever be possible to ease—and perhaps even eliminate—the pressures for change, usually to higher density, that have led to the loss of so many of our fine older buildings." Sprague, *Defining and Describing Historic Districts*, [4]. See also Sprague's contribution to the 1979 Forum on Architectural Preservation reprinted in *Controversies in Historic Preservation: Understanding the Preservation Movement Today*, ed. Pamela Thurber, 57–58 (National Trust for Historic Preservation: Preservation Policy Research Series N. PPR-RO3, Fall 1985).

10. "A district . . . may even be considered eligible if all of the components lack individual distinction, provided that the grouping achieves significance as a whole within its individual context." *National Register Bulletin 15: How to Apply the National Register Criteria for Evaluation*, rev. ed. (1991), 5.

11. *Preservation News* 15, no. 8 (August 1975): 5.

12. "There appear to be regional differences in public attitudes about districting. Since New England was settled in towns and villages earlier than most of the rest of the country, it is not surprising that there are more potential districts there than elsewhere. These districts tend to be locally generated since there is often more historical consciousness and local awareness of the benefits of districts." *A Guide to Delineating Edges of Historic Districts*, 87.

13. Quoted in *Maintaining Community Character*, 1.

14. Lindgren, *Preserving Historic New England*, 173.

15. Massachusetts Historical Commission, *Establishing Local Historic Districts*, 29.

16. Ibid., 1.

17. At the local level the way in which traditional concern to protect a single property widened into a campaign to save an entire district can be illustrated by the case of the Third Ward in Rochester, New York. The Landmark Society had been founded there in 1937 to save and operate a single house. Gradually the "neighborhood context" of this house began to become a concern. According to a history of preservation in Rochester, there were "several other houses of significance in the Third Ward, and many of a historic character that seemed to warrant preservation." Concern for protection of the whole district began to emerge for other reasons: "Some older residents still found the neighborhood a good place to live, and it was thought that many younger people in the community might be attracted by an improved neighborhood, convenient to the city center." But the change in strategy caused some strain in the society as preservationists found themselves involved in issues that were very different from those they had hitherto associated with historic preservationism. "Not without some dissent, the organization began to shift the focus of its concern from individual historic buildings to broader problems of area preservation, environmental quality, and neighborhood vitality." Malo, *Landmarks of Rochester and Monroe County*, 138–39.

18. Lee-Thomas Associates, *Historic Preservation in California*, 6.

19. Datel and Dingemans, "Why Places Are Preserved," 43.

20. Pohl, "Visual Aspects of an Historic District," 6.

21. Birch and Roby, "The Planner and the Preservationist," 200–2.

22. Sauder and Wilkinson, "Preservation Planning and Geographic Change," 50–51.

23. Borchert et al., *Legacy of Minneapolis*, 182.

24. The North End district in Colorado Springs again provides an example. Freed, *Preserving the Great Plains and Rocky Mountains*, 366–69.

25. Something of the very personal world of historic preservation in the older self-consciously historic communities has been recorded in John Berendt's best-selling book, *Midnight in the Garden of Good and Evil*.

26. To counter this, much time is spent at National Trust conferences extolling the work of individual preservationists and upholding the importance of the role of the heroic and committed individual in historic preservation. The National Trust is an organization whose lobbying effectiveness depends in considerable part on its being seen as having substantial grassroots support. It must therefore show that individuals still matter in the work of preservation.

27. Datel and Dingemans, "Why Places Are Preserved," 45.

28. For example, McAlester and McAlester, *A Field Guide to American Houses;* Klein and Fogle, *Clues to American Architecture;* Rifkind, *A Field Guide to American Architecture;* and the numerous publications of the Preservation Press.

29. Pomada and Larsen, *Daughters of Painted Ladies*. Another such book is Sinclair, *Victorious Victorians*.

30. For example, Thomas, "Architectural Patronage and Social Stratification in Philadelphia between 1840 and 1920."

31. Archer, "Where We Stand," 25.

32. Ibid.

33. Sprague and Lerner, *Historic Districts*, 3.

34. Edwards, "Two Virginia Historic Districts."

35. From information supplied by Historic York.

36. From information supplied by the Near Westside Neighborhood Association.

37. Freed, *Preserving the Great Plains and Rocky Mountains,*106–7.

38. However, Mary C. Means has commented that far too often local historical societies "think that preservation is not their bailiwick and concern themselves with local history or genealogy. Historical societies should recognize that they are quite often the only organized groups that can lead the preservation vanguard and that as custodians of the community's past they are also responsible for its retention in the future." "Town Preservation in the Midwest."

39. Munsell, "Historic Home Tours Awaken Interest."

40. Skelcher, "Main Street Mid-America,"

41. In 1990 Steven Fischer, planner with the Town of Steilacoom, attacked the idea that historic districts *"must* be preserved as museum pieces." "The problem with this method arises from the simple fact that these are living, not dead, segments of our community. People live here; business takes place here, and change will take place as growth takes place here. The best examples of districts preserved in time are ghost towns and museum pieces set aside for show, not living communities." "What Is Preservation All About?"

42. Collins et al., *America's Downtowns*, 22–23.

43. Kay with Chase-Harrell, *Preserving New England*, 104.

44. Toft, *St. Louis: Landmarks & Historic Districts*, 25. A similar fate appears to be befalling the downtown commercial buildings in the Dayton Terra Cotta District, Ohio (NR 1984), in spite of the strenuous efforts of the Living City Project there to arouse interest in the city's splendid terra cotta legacy. Commercial buildings of that era (early twentieth century) are particularly unwanted these days and susceptible to demolition.

45. Freed, *Preserving the Great Plains and Rocky Mountains*, 347–53. On Jobbers Canyon see also *Preservation News* 27, no. 12 (December 1987): 15, and White, "Lessons from the Loss of Omaha's Jobbers Canyon," *Preservation Forum* 3, no. 1 (Spring 1989): 8–12.

46. The issue of how new buildings are introduced into a historic district was discussed in *Historic Preservation* 23, no. 1 (January-March 1971): 19. One of the participants in this discussion was Harmon Goldstone, a leading New York preservationist and former chairman of the New York City Landmarks Preservation Commission. For his views, see also his article, "Aesthetics in Historic Districts," *Law and Contemporary Problems* 36 (1971): 378–85, reprinted in Williams, Kellogg, and Gilbert, *Readings in Historic Preservation*.

47. Williams, Kellogg, and Lavigne, *Vermont Townscape*, 123.

48. "A district can contain buildings, structures, sites, objects, or open spaces that do not contribute to the significance of the district. The number of noncontributing properties a district can contain yet still convey its sense of time and place and historical development depends on how these properties affect the district's integrity." *How to Apply the National Register Criteria for Evaluation*, 5. "A district is not eligible if it contains so many alterations or new intrusions that it no longer conveys the sense of a historic environment." Ibid., 46.

49. *Preservation News* 23, no. 11 (November 1983): 1. In 1989 William Seale, a local historian and resident and former member of the Board of Architectural Review, wrote an essay critical of what had happened in Alexandria. Alexandria's desired "architectural image" since the 1930s had, he said, been the "colonial," "even if it represented only a small part of the total architectural picture of a town whose genesis had taken 200 years." The problem was that many people moving to Old Town demanded it, "and if a house did not match up, it could be converted." The result, in his view, was that "whole blocks today are virtually unrecognizable in old photographs taken from the 1920's through the 1950's, although the original houses—at the core—are still there." The character of the town had been "slowly transformed to something quite different from what it had been—buildings and populace alike. . . . Endless pastiching of what is already there will turn a town into an indecipherable mixture of real and fake, with the result that the real is devalued and the meaning of the town is drowned in later bastardizations of itself." This essay originated as "Notes on the Restoration Movement in Alexandria" in the catalog of the 1989 Historic Alexandria Antiques Show. It was then published in *Preservation Law Update* (1989): 44 and was reprinted in numerous local preservation journals. See, for instance, *Buffalo Preservation Report* 13, no. 2 (June 1991): 13.

50. Sauder and Wilkinson write, "At the time of its historic-district designation, the Vieux Carré was a vibrant, historic neighborhood. Distinctive architecture, dense, low-scale streetscapes, and the work and family relationships of Creoles, blacks, and Italians all helped inspire the desire for preservation. But 'design preservation,' practiced by the Vieux Carré Commission since the 1940s, has resulted in a significant alteration in the traditional Vieux Carré character. . . . [P]ristine renovations and sign controls have

modified the sense of an aged and used environment. . . . And while visual harmony has been retained by designers of new buildings who have been required to copy old Vieux Carré styles, the sense of historical continuity has been disrupted. Natural architectural infusions were abruptly halted in the Vieux Carré beginning in the 1940s. Since that time, a one-dimensional, 'official,' sanitized past has been encouraged." They condemn a preservation that "operates solely within the context of architectural specifications." Sauder and Wilkinson, "Preservation Planning and Geographic Change," 51–59.

51. Howley, "Community Profile: Concord Works Hard to Protect Its Legacy," *Boston Globe*, Real Estate section (June 26, 1994).

52. Millett, *Lost Twin Cities*, 277. See also the extensive literature on the rehabilitation of Lowertown, St. Paul (NR 1983): ibid., pp. 52, 277. Collins, Waters, and Dotson, *America's Downtowns*, 117–30. Eaton, *Gateway Cities and Other Essays*, 3–17.

53. Kammen, *Mystic Chords of Memory*, 583–84.

54. Hosmer, *Preservation Comes of Age*, 1:54.

55. Ibid., 369.

56. Ross, *Remembering Main Street*, 35–36.

57. Ross tells of how an overscale millinery sign painted on a historic building was thought to be so attractive that it remains a town showpiece. Ibid., 36.

58. The mining town of Roslyn, Wash., has become known, for instance, as the location for the series "Northern Exposure." One of the best-known aspects of the history of Wallace, Idaho, has become the use of its railroad station in the movie *Heaven's Gate*.

59. Beasley, "Reviewing New Design," 20–30.

60. "Historic housing styles, preserved and renovated in the inner city, have begun to show up in new tract development in the suburbs [of Canadian cities]. Such neo-traditional forms run the gamut from straight revival to the incorporation of symbolic elements such as, in suburban Toronto, the inclusion of red-brick detailing and gable ends, reminiscent of the renovated Victorian dwellings in the inner city." Ley, *The New Middle Class and the Remaking of the Central City*, 359.

61. For an example of the rejection of innovative contemporary design, see Samuel Wilson, "Evolution in a Historic Area's 'Tout Ensemble,'" 159.

62. Weinberg, *Preservation in American Towns and Cities*, 166. The impacts of preservation guidelines on architecture in historic districts and beyond are discussed in *Preservation* 49, no. 1 (January-February 1997): 24–25.

63. For which see Francaviglia, *Main Street Revisited*, 50–51.

64. Jacobs, *The Death and Life of Great American Cities*, 127–32, 264.

65. Lynch, *The Image of the City*, 22–25, 47–49.

66. Ibid., 103–4.

67. Ibid., 22–25.

68. Ibid., 103–4.

69. Goldstone and Dalrymple, *History Preserved*, 369–71.

70. Dolkart, *Guide to New York City Landmarks*, 143.

71. The Grand Central Subdistrict in New York has been announced: *Preservation News* 33, no. 1 (January 1993): 21. Miles, "Pioneer Square."

72. Ford, "Urban Preservation and the Geography of the City in the USA," 228.

73. *A Guide to Delineating Edges of Historic Districts*, 77–79.

74. Ibid., 16–17.

75. Ibid., 44–5.

76. *Information Series*, no. 50: "From Visitors to Volunteers: Organizing a Historic Homes Tour," 2.

77. Freed, *Preserving the Great Plains and Rocky Mountains*, 365.

78. Examples are Waterford, Virginia, and Shirley, Massachusetts. See Dehart, *Rural Historic Village Protection in Maryland*.

79. *Values of Residential Properties in Urban Historic Districts*, 12.

80. *Guide to Delineating the Edges of Historic Districts*, 45.

81. Ford and Fusch, "Historic Preservation and the Inner City," 111.

82. Beasley, "New Construction in Residential Historic Districts," 231.

83. Greider, "Secrets of Great Old Neighborhoods," 32.

84. *Guide to Delineating the Edges of Historic Districts*, 29–30.

85. Ibid., 42.

86. Ibid., 15.

87. Davis, *Contested Ground*, 225.

88. *Preservation News* 18, no. 12 (December 1978): 5.

89. Bennett, *Fragments of Cities*, 46, 75–76.

90. Hunter, *Symbolic Communities*, 67–68, 71–81, 196.

91. Suttles, *The Man-Made City*, 87–89.

92. Ibid., 89. On the history of the invention of names in Chicago, see also Suttles, *The Social Construction of Communities*, 52–53.

93. Hamer, *New Towns in the New World*, 115, 178.

94. Lingeman, *Small Town America*, 286.

95. Warner, "Slums and Skyscrapers." In his study of nineteenth-century New York, Scherzer has shown the immense complexity of the names that people gave informally to districts. He discusses how and when names defining district characteristics and reputations developed. Scherzer, *The Unbounded Community*, 137–41, 158–60.

96. There is a Quality Hill in Pawtucket, Rhode Island, and a Millionaire's Row in Danville, Virginia. Examples of Silk Stocking Rows are Columbia City, Ind. (Taylor et al., *Indiana* 552–54); Old Silk Stocking, Kokomo, Ind.; Lewistown Silk Stocking, Lewistown, Mont.; Talladega, Ala. (NR 1979). There is a Mansion Row Historic District in New Albany, Ind. (NR 1983) and a Mansion Hill at Newport, Ky. (NR 1980/1985).

97. Perhaps the best-known Pill Hills are in Rochester, Minn., and Brookline, Mass.

98. Zorbaugh, *The Gold Coast and the Slum*.

99. Schneider, "Skid Row as an Urban Neighborhood, 1880–1960."

100. White and Wilensky, *AIA Guide to New York City*, 306. For the coinage and acceptance of new, "more charming" names for Philadelphia neighborhoods see Levy and Cybriwsky, "The Hidden Dimensions of Culture and Class," 142–43.

101. Johnson and Russell, *Memphis*, 207, 225.

102. *College Hill*, 10, 126.

103. Jacobs, *The Death and Life of Great American Cities*, 129.

104. *Historic Preservation League of Oregon Newsletter*, no. 60 (Spring 1991): 8–9.

105. New Bedford, Mass., Redevelopment Authority, *Preservation and Rehabilitation of a Historic Commercial Area* (1973), 31–32.

106. *Lincoln, Rhode Island,* 18.

107. Kay with Chase-Harrell, *Preserving New England,* 133.

108. Reps, *The Making of Urban America,* 484–90. In 1994 the Pickaway County Historical Society issued a walking tour guide that helps the visitor to re-create the dimensions of the circle. Circleville became a National Register historic district in 1978. On Circleville, see also Francaviglia, *Main Street Revisited,* 83–84.

109. Information from a walking tour brochure prepared by the Emmitsburg Historical Society.

110. Hosmer, *Preservation Comes of Age,* 1:257–58. The slowness of the development of concern about the adverse impacts of the automobile in New England's historic towns is revealed in Lindgren, *Preserving Historic New England,* 121.

111. *Establishing an Historic District,* 29.

112. There is a nostalgic account of Chestertown in Ross's *Remembering Main Street,* 5–21.

113. This is taken to an extreme in ghost towns such as Hill End and Coolgardie in Australia where photographs at strategic points showing what the area once looked like are virtually all that now exists to be seen. A city in the United States where photographs are exhibited around town to advantage is Rochester, N.Y.

114. Barnett, *The Fractured Metropolis,* 122–24.

Chapter 7

1. Francaviglia, *Main Street Revisited,* 142–76.

2. Lindgren, *Preserving Historic New England,* 129. Appleton used the argument that a house was in "parklike surroundings" to support a case for its retention. Ibid., 130.

3. "The cleared zone would have included not only houses designed by well-known architects Alexander Parris and Cornelius Coolidge in the 1820s but a cultural fabric that interwove human spirit and material form in the neighborhood." Ibid., 132.

4. *Preservation News* 11, no. 7 (July 1971): 1–2.

5. *Lowell, Massachusetts,* 9.

6. Boyer, *The City of Collective Memory,* 54.

7. On the connections between history and theme parks, see also Edward Ball, "To Theme or Not to Theme."

8. Engler, "Drive-Thru History."

9. *Preservation News* 22, no. 11 (November 1982): 2.

10. Cawley, "Company Town Works on Its Future," 14.

11. *Guide to Delineating Edges of Historic Districts,* 59.

12. *Plan and Program for the Preservation of the Vieux Carre,* 4.

13. McNulty et al., *The Return of the Living City,* 296.

14. Weinberg, *Preservation in American Towns and Cities,* 62–63.

15. *Historic Preservation News* 34, no. 1 (February-March 1994): 21.

16. The information in this section is derived from *A Brief History of the Irvine Park District.* There is also a St. Paul Heritage Preservation District, which has somewhat more extended boundaries. The National Register form for the White Place Historic District in Brookline indicates that when Samuel A. Walker, a real estate auctioneer, laid out White Place in 1848, he bought some older homes and had them moved to the

property that was being developed "in an effort to encourage development in this new residential area."

17. A subsidiary strengthening structure is the Forepaugh-Hammond House, which has attracted attention well beyond the district both through the remarkable quality of its rehabilitation and as a result of the fame of the restaurant operating in it.

18. "Wild West Side," *Historic Preservation* 25, no. 3 (July-September 1973): 21.

19. McGregor, "Historic Preservation in New York State."

20. Jakle, *The Tourist*, 284.

21. Ibid., 275, 286.

22. Morris, "A Neighborhood Grows in Charlotte."

23. *Preservation News* 11, no. 5 (May 1971): 2.

24. *Great Falls Newsletter of the S.U.M. Historic District, Paterson, N.J. America's First Planned Industrial City* (Winter 1993): 1–3.

25. See Gossman and Curtis, "Sketching Back to the Future" (on what was similarly done for Wilmington, Ohio).

26. For an example, see Skelcher, "Main Street Mid-America," 8.

27. A group of preservationists who were visiting the town at this time were horrified. They brought to bear a preservationist attitude, explaining that "to restore the town according to today's tastes would date it within 10 years, and tourists would flock to more authentic areas." Means, "Town Preservation in the Midwest."

28. *Preservation News* 20, no. 8 (July 1980): 3.

29. The 1976 National Trust publication, *A Guide to Delineating Edges of Historic Districts,* was unsure whether the word "historic" ought to be used. "In considering historic districts, it is necessary from the outset to emphasize the broad definition of the term *historic.* Districts are generally groupings of buildings or structures, but not just of historical significance. Districts can and do include groups of buildings with visual, architectural and environmental significance. Districting can therefore be used for the preservation of basic amenities and as a means of stabilizing the desirability and aesthetic qualities of an area. This broad use of the term *historic* should be stressed and explained in order to gain local understanding of and support for the concept. It is perhaps appropriate to give further consideration to the use of the term *historic district* in view of the range of objectives intended to be accomplished through this process" (86).

30. *Historic Zoning Handbook: A Guide to Historic Preservation and Neighborhood Conservation Zoning in Nashville* (Nashville: Metropolitan Historic Zoning Commission, 1985).

31. Business interests got even this watered down. Clubbe, *Cincinnati Observed,* 104.

32. *Landmarks Preservation Council of Illinois* (newsletter) 21, no. 2 (May 1992): 4.

33. "Conservation Districts as an Alternative to Historic Districts." See also Kelly and Goodman, *Conservation District Project Research Report.*

34. Birch and Roby, "The Planner and the Preservationist," 204.

35. *Trust News* (Washington Trust for Historic Preservation) (Summer 1991): 2.

36. The author noted this in connection with downtown Muncie, Indiana, and Leadville, Colorado.

37. Hosmer, *Preservation Comes of Age,* 1:318.

38. Murtagh, *Keeping Time,* 122.

39. Hayden, *The Power of Place,* 57–59. On the Women's Rights National Historical Park at Seneca Falls, see also Rose, "Preserving Women's Rights History."

40. Ziegler, *Historic Preservation in Inner City Areas*, 64.

41. Datel, "Preservation and a Sense of Orientation for American Cities," 133–34.

42. Hayden, *The Power of Place*, xi.

43. Tuan, *Space and Place*, 174.

44. Moul, "Santa Fe Styles and Townscapes."

45. For an example, see the brochure "Discovering Green Spaces in Roxbury's Highland Park Neighborhood: A Walker's Guide to Parks, Gardens, and Urban Wilds." This was prepared as part of Hawthorne Youth and Community Center's Mural Project at Marcella Park and developed by the center and the Old South Meeting House.

46. Napoli, "Historic Preservation in Point Arena, California."

47. Comp, "Learning from Heritage Development."

48. For an account of this development at Sackets Harbor, see Lamme, *America's Historic Landscapes*, 120–23.

49. There are also UCPs at New York City ("Maritime and Immigration"), Kingston ("Transportation"), Albany ("Business and Capital"), the communities of Troy, Cohoes, Colonie, Green Island, Waterford, and Watervliet combined into the Hudson-Mohawk UCP ("Labor and Industry"), Schenectady (also "Labor and Industry"), Saratoga Springs ("Natural Environment"), Sackets Harbor ("Defense"), Syracuse ("Business and Capital" and "Transportation"), Seneca Falls ("Reform Movements"), Whitehall ("Defense"), the communities of Binghamton, Johnson City, and Endicott combined into the Susquehanna UCP ("Labor and Industry"), Rochester ("Natural Environment"), and Buffalo ("Flowering of Culture").

50. Exceptions would include the Truman Historic District in Independence and districts identified with great architects.

51. Brochure issued by the New York State Office of Parks, Recreation and Historic Preservation.

52. 1977 Lowell Report to Congress, 9.

53. *Preservation News* 33, no. 8 (December 1993–January 1994): 6.

54. Cronon, *Nature's Metropolis*.

55. Lefevre, "Historic District Designation: Panacea or Placebo." But see also the spirited reply by Mark C. McDonald, director of the Mobile Historic Development Commission, Mobile, Alabama: *CRM* 18, no. 6 (1995): 26.

56. See the comments by Stephen A. Morris, Certified Local Government Coordinator, National Park Service, on Lefevre's article: *CRM* 18, no. 4 (1995): 25.

57. Hosmer, *Preservation Comes of Age*, 2:883–85.

58. Thurber and Moyer, *State Enabling Legislation*, 10.

59. There have been some contrasting views on the involvement of historians in historic preservation. At one extreme are the views of Alan Mayne, who attaches much of the blame to historians themselves: "City as Artifact," 155–56, 169. A considerably more optimistic point of view, at least as regards recent trends, is expressed in Lee, "Historians Then, Historians Now."

60. *"We urge the major national associations of professional historians to give attention to preservation in their regional and national conferences, to include preservation in their job placement and counseling services, to maintain lists of members willing to consult with local preservation committees, and to routinely list meetings on historic preservation along with notices about other conferences"* (italics in the original). *Living Cities*, 16. In 1987 the Office of Technology Assessment issued a

report, *Technologies for Prehistoric and Historic Preservation,* that came to the conclusion that "there is not enough history in preservation." It saw a need for more research into "the historical context which establishes the significance of the structure, landscape, site or sites in question." "The holistic view which a historical perspective can bring is central to the creation of the context in which human activities took place." Warren-Findley, "Historians and Historic Preservation."

61. This alliance had become sufficiently established by the early 1980s to be the subject of an article in an academic journal: Birch and Roby, "The Planner and the Preservationist."

62. Sprague, "Why Form Historic Districts?" 3.

63. Gowans, *Styles and Types of North American Architecture.*

64. Archer, "Where We Stand," 30.

65. Frank, "Defining Historic Districts," 7.

66. Ibid., 7-8.

67. E.g., "Preservationists Make Strong Case to Planning Board for Takoma Park Historic District," *The Preservationist* (Montgomery County Historic Preservation Commision) 5, no. 2 (November-December 1989): 1, 6.

68. Datel and Dingemans, "Why Places Are Preserved," 49.

69. Datel, "Southern Regionalism and Historic Preservation in Charleston, South Carolina," p. 198.

70. *Beaufort Preservation Manual,* 41.

71. "South End Landmark District: Standards and Criteria" (Boston Landmarks Commission).

72. Southworth and Southworth, *A.I.A. Guide to Boston,* 307-8.

73. "The South End District Study Committee Report" (revised copy, November 14, 1983), 11, 13.

74. Ibid., 17-18.

75. Ibid., 18-24.

76. *Lowell,* 91.

77. *Preservation Plan,* 3-5.

78. Gratz, *The Living City,* 67-68. The history and character of Over-the-Rhine are discussed in Clubbe, *Cincinnati Observed,* chaps. 7 and 8.

79. Miller, "Planning and the Politics of Ethnic Identity," 248-65.

80. Hayden, *The Power of Place,* 8-9, 39, passim.

81. Rhinehart, "Preservation's Best Interests."

82. Abundant evidence of this is provided in Savage, *African American Historic Places.*

83. Hayden, *The Power of Place,* 54-57.

84. This account of the Truman Heritage District is based on the following sources: Taylor, "Preserving a President's Community"; Vogel and Cassity, "The Buck Stops . . . Where?"; 1996 11 Most Endangered Nomination Form submitted to the National Trust for Historic Preservation by the Jackson County Historical Society on February 15, 1996; Statement regarding the application for Designation of the Harry S. Truman District as "Most Endangered" released by the Jackson County Historical Society on June 3, 1996; press releases by the National Trust for Historic Preservation on their 1996 11 Most Endangered Historic Places List, June 17, 1996; Statement by Ken Apschnikat, superintendent of the Harry S. Truman National Historic Site, at

the press conference announcing the listing of the Truman Heritage District on the National Trust's 1996 11 Most Endangered Historic Places List, June 17, 1996; Statement by Mayor Rondell F. Stewart on the status of the Truman Landmark District, June 17, 1996; National Historic Landmark Status Report Update on the Truman Historic District, August 1, 1996; extracts from local newspapers dealing with the Choplin House, etc., in the *Examiner* (Independence) July 18, August 9, September 1, 1994; June 17, 18, July 17, 1996; *Kansas City Star*, July 21, 1994; June 18, 23, 1996.

I am most grateful to Christina A. Leakey, Historic Preservation Technician with the City of Independence, for assistance with getting access to this information.

85. *Preservation News* 24, no. 4 (April 1984): 6.

86. The district became a political issue in 1996 when Secretary of the Interior Bruce Babbitt used it to dramatize the impacts of Republican cutbacks in funding for the National Park Service. *Examiner*, June 17, 1996. Truman was a Democratic president but has become something of an icon with an appeal that transcends party divisions, standing for the lost integrity of the American democratic system.

87. The mayor's statement of June 17, 1996, referred to the poverty of many of the people in the district.

88. Quoted in the *Kansas City Star*, July 21, 1994.

89. *Kansas City Star*, June 18, 1996.

90. Quotations from statement by Ken Apschnikat, superintendent of the Harry S. Truman National Historic Site, at the press conference on June 17, 1996.

91. Vogel and Cassity, "The Buck Stops . . . Where?" 19.

92. Ibid., 22. The publicity given to the Truman Heritage District has indeed been an at least short-term stimulus to the renewal of neighborhood consciousness. Long-dormant networks of neighborhood associations have begun to stir into life again, and new organizations have been formed.

93. An example is the use of the word "district" itself. In my own country, New Zealand, for instance, it tends to be avoided in favor of such terms as "area," which is much more vague, and "precinct," which has a bureaucratic ring appropriate to the dominance of planning considerations. Another example is the "Main Street" concept. The American Main Street Program has attracted a great deal of international attention. New Zealand is but one of the countries where numerous local authorities have been starting, or at least giving thought to starting, Main Street programs. There is a strong emphasis in New Zealand as in the United States on restoring the buildings whose frequently flamboyant and richly detailed architecture embodies the confidence and optimism of the business communities in their heyday, usually in the late nineteenth and early twentieth century. But "Main Street" introduces terminology that is far more familiar to Americans than it is to New Zealanders. Indeed, it is a term that has a resonance in American discourse that has been largely absent in the antipodean context. "Main Street" is more than just a very common street name in the United States. It is also short hand for an idealized way of life and, in its physical form, embodies a "symbolic landscape." In the United States the imagery and nostalgic associations have provided powerful themes on which to base the restoration of small town commercial districts. It remains to be discovered how much of this exists in New Zealand culture and can be drawn on for this kind of exercise.

Bibliography

When the National Register was introduced, not a great deal of thought seems to have been given to the uses to which it might be put. Information about historic districts is still not readily available. National Register nominations are not published and there is no consolidated collection of them. For many years there was little or no effort to prepare publications based on the National Register that would enable it to be used for educational purposes, or that provided information on its contents and their significance. In 1976 one writer called historic districts a "neglected resource" (Bailey, "Historic Districts"). The situation has not changed a great deal since. The National Register itself has been published for some time, but it consists only of a listing of the buildings and districts with addresses and letters indicating which of the criteria have been met in respect of each entry. There is no description of any listing. That state of affairs is now beginning to be remedied. For instance, in 1993 the Preservation League of New York State sponsored the publication of a book entitled *The National Register of Historic Places in New York State* which contains brief but informative descriptions of each listing, including districts, in the state. The consultant who prepared this publication, Peter D. Shaver, read the vast number of nomination submissions and condensed each into a paragraph of fewer than fifty words. Appendixes classify the listings in various categories. In 1994 the National Park Service, the National Trust for Historic Preservation, and the National Conference of State Preservation Officers collaborated in the production of *African American Historic Places*, a series of descriptions (longer than those in the New York book) of listings on the National Register that relate to African American history. Another book, *Reclaiming the Past*, has surveyed sites associated with women's history, although in the form of essays on different facets of the subject rather than the catalog or encyclopedia format used in the other publications. Heritage Books has been publishing a five-volume series of information on historic districts, compiled by Ralph W. Richardson. The information is derived substantially from National Register nominations, and there is advice on the location of local sources such as walking tour brochures. Some evaluation is attempted, but the entries vary considerably in the amount and quality of the information. One problem with such guidebooks is that the information in them quickly becomes out of date. The challenge now obviously is to get as much information as possible into computer-accessible formats. Architectural guidebooks often include descriptions and tour guides of districts as well as individual buildings. For larger cities in particular a variety of guidebooks are now available which provide detailed accounts of architecture and information on historic districts. It should be noted that most of these publications are architectural in emphasis. Social geographers have been slow to provide examples of how a "sense of place" approach could be used to create a different kind of guidebook. (A notable exception, although it provides a driving rather than a walking tour, is *Megalopolis: Washington, D.C., to Boston* by John R. Borchert, a professor of geography at the University of Minnesota.)

The agencies responsible for interpreting a historic district vary greatly, and the style of the interpretation and information offered depends on their own backgrounds and agendas. For instance, the approach likely to be taken by chambers of commerce, the agencies to which many visitors turn first for information (they often run the visitors' centers), will likely be very different from that adopted by a historical society. If a historical society has been active in a community for a long time and has house museums in its care and open to the public, it is likely to have a prominent, sometimes even dominant, role in the interpretation of a district. Traditional historical society themes tend to be less architectural than social, with a heavy emphasis, for instance, on the lives of the early settlers in the district and on the families who have lived in the houses. However, many guides are published by preservation organizations as part of their strategy of developing informed awareness and appreciation of the architectural heritage of a community. These guides may be the outcome of architectural resource surveys that have been the prelude to the preparation of National Register nominations.

Allison, Eric William. "Historic Preservation in a Development-dominated City: The Passage of New York City's Landmark Preservation Legislation." *Journal of Urban History* 22, no. 3 (March 1996): 350–76.

Anderson, Elizabeth B. *Annapolis: A Walk Through History*. Centreville, Md.: Tidewater, 1984.

Archer, Madeline Cirillo. "Where We Stand: Preservation Issues in the 1990s." *Public Historian* 13, no. 4 (Fall 1991): 25–40.

Atherton, Lewis. *Main Street on the Middle Border*. New York: Quadrangle/New York Times Book Co., 1966. Originally published in 1954.

Attebery, Jennifer Eastman. *Building Idaho: An Architectural History*. Moscow: University of Idaho Press, 1991.

Back to the City: A Guide to Urban Preservation. New York: Brownstone Revival Committee of New York, 1975.

Bailey, Walter L. "Historic Districts: A Neglected Resource." *North Dakota History* 43 (1976): 22–24.

Ball, Edward. "To Theme or Not to Theme: Disneyfication without Guilt." In *The Once and Future Park*, edited by Deborah Karasov and Steve Waryan, 31–38. New York: Princeton Architectural Press, 1993.

Ball, Rick A., et al. *Indianapolis Architecture*. Indianapolis: Indiana Architectural Foundation, 1975.

Barnett, Jonathan. *The Fractured Metropolis: Improving the New City, Restoring the Old City, Reshaping the Region*. New York: HarperCollins, 1995.

Bartlett, Ellen. "Miami Beach Bets on Art Deco." *Historic Preservation* 33, no. 1 (January–February 1981): 8–15.

Beasley, Ellen. "New Construction in Residential Historic Districts." In *Old and New Architecture: Design Relationship*, 229–56. Washington, D.C.: Preservation Press, 1980.

———. "Reviewing New Design in Historic Districts." In *Design Review: Challenging Urban Aesthetic Control*, edited by Brenda Case Scheer and Wolfgang F. E. Preiser, 20–30. New York: Chapman & Hall, 1994.

Bibliography

The Beaufort Preservation Manual. Beaufort: Prepared for the City of Beaufort, South Carolina, by John Milner Associates, West Chester, Pennsylvania, August 1979.

Bender, Thomas. *Community and Social Change in America*. Baltimore: Johns Hopkins University Press, 1982.

Bennett, Larry. *Fragments of Cities: The New American Downtowns and Neighborhoods*. Columbus: Ohio State University Press, 1990.

Bennett, Randall H. *Oxford County, Maine: A Guide to Its Historic Architecture*. Bethel, Maine: Oxford County Historic Resource Survey, 1984.

Benson, Susan Porter, Stephen Brier, and Roy Rosenzweig, eds. *Presenting the Past: Essays on History and the Public*. Philadelphia: Temple University Press, 1986.

Berendt, John. *Midnight in the Garden of Good and Evil: A Savannah Story*. New York: Random House, 1994.

Biddle, James. "Saving our Cities Through Preservation." *Back to the City: A Guide to Urban Preservation*, pp. 31-33. Brownstone Revival Committee of New York, 1975.

Birch, Eugenie Ladner, and Douglas Roby. "The Planner and the Preservationist: An Uneasy Alliance." *Journal of the American Planning Association* 50 (1984): 194-207.

Bland, Sidney R. *Preserving Charleston's Past, Shaping Its Future: The Life and Times of Susan Pringle Frost*. Westport, Conn.: Greenwood Press, 1994.

Blatti, Jo, ed. *Past Meets Present: Essays about Historic Interpretation and Public Audiences*. Washington, D.C.: Smithsonian Institution Press, 1987.

Bluestone, Daniel. "Preservation and Renewal in Post-World War II Chicago." *Journal of Architectural Education* 47, no. 4 (May 1994): 210-23.

Borchert, John R. *Megalopolis: Washington, D.C., to Boston*. New Brunswick, N.J.: Rutgers University Press, 1992.

Borchert, John R., David Gebhard, David Lanegan, and Judith A. Martin. *Legacy of Minneapolis: Preservation amid Change*. Bloomington, Minn.: Voyageur Press, 1983.

Boslough, John. "Is this the Williamsburg of the Rockies?" *Historic Preservation* 36, no. 6 (December 1984): 32-37.

Boyer, M. Christine. "Cities for Sale: Merchandising History at South Street Seaport." In *Variations on a Theme Park: The New American City and the End of Public Space*, edited by Michael Sorkin, 181-204. New York: Noonday Press, 1992.

————. *The City of Collective Memory: Its Historical Imagery and Architectural Entertainments*. Cambridge, Mass.: MIT Press, 1994.

Breen, T. H. *Imagining the Past: East Hampton Histories*. Reading, Mass.: Addison-Wesley, 1989.

A Brief History of the Irvine Park District: The People and Architecture of an Extraordinary Neighborhood. St. Paul: Historic Irvine Park Association, n.d.

Brown, A. Theodore, and Lyle W. Dorsett. *K.C.: A History of Kansas City, Missouri*. Boulder, Colo.: Pruett, 1978.

Brown, Elizabeth Mills. *New Haven: A Guide to Architecture and Urban Design*. New Haven: Yale University Press, 1976.

Brown, Patricia Leigh. "Main Streets Get Street-Wise." *Historic Preservation* 31, no. 1 (March-April 1979): 29-34.

Buffalo Architecture: A Guide. Cambridge, Mass.: MIT Press, 1981.

Building the Future from Our Past: A Report on the Saint Paul Historic Hill District Planning Program. St. Paul: Old Town Restorations, 1975.

Built in Milwaukee: An Architectural View of the City. Prepared for the City of Milwaukee by Landscape Research and published by the City, 1980.

Burke, Padraic. "Port Townsend: Preservationists Stir Political Row in Their Efforts to Save Historic Homes." *American Preservation* 1, no. 4 (April-May 1978): 9-19.

Burns, Elizabeth K. "The Enduring Affluent Suburb." *Landscape* 24, no. 1 (1980): 33-41.

Candee, Richard M. *Building Portsmouth: The Neighborhoods and Architecture of New Hampshire's Oldest City.* Portsmouth, N.H.: Portsmouth Advocates, 1992.

Cassity, Pratt. "Still Local After All These Years." *CRM* 19, no. 6 (1996): 25-29.

Cassity, Pratt, and Timothy J. Crimmins. "Local Historic Preservation Ordinances and Cultural Resource Protection Strategies in the Mid-South." In *The Best of Both Worlds: The Challenge of Growth Enhancement in the Mid-South*, part 2, edited by Carroll Van West. A report prepared by the Center for Historic Preservation, Middle State University, Murfreesboro, Tenn, as a Critical Issues Fund Project of the National Trust for Historic Preservation, 1988. Part II: 4-9.

Cawley, Peter. "Company Town Works on Its Future." *Historic Preservation* 29, no. 3 (July-September 1977): 10-15.

———. "Fort Worth Rides Again." *Historic Preservation* 32, no. 1 (January-February 1980): 10-16.

Chambers, S. Allen. *Lynchburg: An Architectural History.* Charlottesville: University Press of Virginia, 1981.

Chase, Robert S., and James L. Garvin. *Portsmouth: An Architectural Evolution, 1664–1890.* Reprinted from *New Hampshire Profiles*, December 1970. Portsmouth Preservation, Inc. No date indicated.

Cigliano, Jan, and Sarah Bradford Landau. *The Grand American Avenue, 1850–1920.* San Francisco: Pomegranate Artbooks, 1994.

Clark, Dennis. " 'Ramcat' and Rittenhouse Square: Related Communities." In *The Divided Metropolis: Social and Spatial Dimensions of Philadelphia, 1800–1975*, edited by William W. Cutler III and Howard Gillette, Jr., 125-40. Westport, Conn.: Greenwood Press, 1980.

Clay, Grady. "Townscape and Landscape: The Coming Battleground." *Historic Preservation* 24, no. 1 (January-March 1972): 34-43.

Clubbe, John. *Cincinnati Observed: Architecture and History.* Columbus: Ohio State University Press, 1992.

Cole, Brian D. "Baker City, Oregon, Develops Tourism as a Springboard for Economic Development." *Small Town* 24, no. 6 (May-June 1994): 4-9.

College Hill: A Demonstration Study of Historic Area Renewal Conducted by the Providence City Plan Commission in Cooperation with the Providence Preservation Society and the Department of Housing and Urban Development. 2d ed. Providence, R.I.: City Plan Commission, 1967.

Collins, Richard C., Elizabeth B. Waters, and A. Bruce Dotson. *America's Downtowns: Growth Politics and Preservation.* Washington D.C.: Preservation Press, 1991.

Collins, Robertson. "Progress and Profit through Blending Past and Present: Preservation, Politics and People." *Small Town* 5, no. 9 (March 1975): 10.

Comp, T. Allan. "Introduction: History outside the Historical Museum, or, My Peculiar Torture." In *Interpreting Local Culture and History*, edited by J. Sanford Rixoon and Judith Austin, 1-10. Moscow: University of Idaho Press, 1991.

————. "Learning from Heritage Development: Whole Places, New Possibilities." *Historic Preservation Forum* 5, no. 6 (November–December 1991): 7.

"Conservation Districts as an Alternative to Historic Districts: Viable Planning Tools for Maintaining the Character of Older Neighborhoods." *Historic Preservation Forum* 7, no. 5 (September–October 1993): 6–14.

Cramm, Joetta. *Historic Ellicott City: A Walking Tour.* Sykesville, Md.: Greenberg, 1990.

Craycroft, Robert. "Small Town Public Policy: Strategies for Downtown Revitalization." In *Order and Image in the American Small Town*, edited by Michael W. Fazio and Peggy Whitman Prenshaw, 15–29. Jackson: University Press of Mississippi, 1981.

Cromley, Elizabeth Collins. "Public History and the Historic Preservation District." In *Past Meets Present: Essays about Historic Interpretation and Public Audiences*, edited by Jo Blatti, 30–36. Washington, D.C.: Smithsonian Institution Press, 1987.

Cronon, William. *Nature's Metropolis: Chicago and the Great West.* New York: W. W. Norton, 1991.

Cutler, William W., III, and Howard Gillette, Jr., eds. *The Divided Metropolis: Social and Spatial Dimensions of Philadelphia, 1800–1975.* Westport, Conn.: Greenwood Press, 1980.

Dahir, Mubarak S. "The Politics of a Public Space." *Preservation* 48, no. 5 (September–October 1996): 30–31.

Datel, Robin E. "Preservation and a Sense of Orientation for American Cities." *Geographical Review* 75, no. 2 (April 1985): 125–41.

————. "Southern Regionalism and Historic Preservation in Charleston, South Carolina." *Journal of Historical Geography* 16 (1990): 197–215.

Datel, Robin E., and Dennis J. Dingemans. "Environmental Perception, Historic Preservation, and Sense of Place." In *Environmental Perception and Behavior: An Inventory and Prospect*, edited by Thomas F. Saarinen, David Seamon, and James L. Sell, 131–44. Chicago: Department of Geography, University of Chicago Research Paper No. 209, 1984.

————. "Historic Preservation and Social Stability in Sacramento's Old City." *Urban Geography* 15, no. 6 (1994): 565–91.

————. "Historic Preservation and Urban Change." *Urban Geography* 1, no. 3 (July–September 1980): 229–53.

————. "Why Places Are Preserved: Historic Districts in American and European Cities." *Urban Geography* 9, no. 1 (January–March 1988): 37–52.

Davis, John Emmeus. *Contested Ground: Collective Action and the Urban Neighborhood.* Ithaca: Cornell University Press, 1991.

Davis, Margaret. *State Systems for Designating Historic Properties and the Results of Designation.* Washington, D.C.: National Trust for Historic Preservation, 1987.

Dehart, H. Grant. *Rural Historic Village Protection in Maryland.* Washington, D.C.: National Trust for Historic Preservation, 1990.

Devlin, William E. *Handbook for Connecticut Historical District and Historic Properties Commissions and Report of the Historian-in-Residence Project to the Connecticut Association of Historic District Commissioners.* Hartford: Connecticut Historical Commission, 1988.

DeWitt Park Historic District and Downtown Ithaca: An Architectural Walking Tour. Ithaca: Historic Ithaca and Tompkins County, n.d.

Dolkart, Andrew S. *Guide to New York City Landmarks.* Washington, D.C.: Preservation Press, 1992.

Dorsey, John, and James D. Dilts. *A Guide to Baltimore Architecture.* 2d ed. Centreville, Md.: Tidewater, 1981.

Eaton, Leonard K. *Gateway Cities and Other Essays.* Ames: Iowa State University Press, 1989.

Eckert, Kathryn Bishop. *Buildings of Michigan.* New York: Oxford University Press, 1993.

Edwards, David. "Two Virginia Historic Districts: A Study in Collaborative Effort." *Notes on Virginia* 27 (Fall 1985): 29–33.

Ehrlich, George. *Kansas City, Missouri: An Architectural History 1826–1990.* Rev. ed. Columbia: University of Missouri Press, 1992.

Engler, Mira. "Drive-Thru History: Theme Towns in Iowa." *Landscape* 32, no. 1 (1993): 8–18.

Establishing an Historic District: A Guideline for Historic Preservation. Raymond, Parish, Pine & Plavnick for the Maryland Historical Trust, and the Department of Economic and Community Development, Maryland Department of State Planning, 1973.

Fazio, Michael W., and Peggy Whitman Prenshaw, eds. *Order and Image in the American Small Town.* Jackson: University Press of Mississippi, 1981.

Firey, Walter. *Land Use in Central Boston.* New York: Greenwood Press, 1968.

Fischer, Steven. "What Is Preservation All About?" Local Preservation Programs Newsletter (Office of Archaeology and Historic Preservation, a Division of the Washington State Department of Community Development), issue 20, November 1990. P. 7.

Fishman, Robert. *Bourgeois Utopias: The Rise and Fall of Suburbia.* New York: Basic Books, 1987.

Foote, Kenneth E. *Shadowed Ground: America's Landscapes of Violence and Tragedy.* Austin: University of Texas Press, 1997.

Ford, Larry R. "Urban Preservation and the Geography of the City in the USA." *Progress in Human Geography* 3, no. 2 (June 1979): 211–38.

Ford, Larry R., and Richard Fusch. "Historic Preservation and the Inner City: The Perception of German Village by Those just Beyond." *Proceedings of the American Association of Geographers* 8 (1976): 110–14.

Francaviglia, Richard V. *Hard Places: Reading the Landscape of America's Historic Mining Districts.* Iowa City: University of Iowa Press, 1991.

———. "Learning from America's Preserved Historic Mining Landscapes: Some New Perspectives on Community Historic Preservation." *Small Town* 25, no. 1 (July-August 1994): 8–21.

———. *Main Street Revisited: Time, Space, and Image Building in Small-Town America.* Iowa City: University of Iowa Press, 1996.

Frank, Richard C. "Defining Historic Districts." In *Historic Districts: Summary of a Conference at Oak Park, Illinois, February 9, 1994.* Pp. 7–10.

Frantz, Ronald H., Jr. "Okmulgee, Oklahoma: Bust to Boom." *Historic Preservation Forum* 5, no. 3 (May-June 1991): 35–36.

Freed, Elaine. *Preserving the Great Plains and Rocky Mountains.* Albuquerque: University of New Mexico Press, 1992.

Galbreath, Carol G. "Communities Benefit from a Sense of History. Small Town Preservation: A Systemic View." *Small Town* 5, no. 9 (March 1975): 6–8.

Bibliography

Gale, Dennis E. "The Impacts of Historic District Designation: Planning and Policy Implications." *Journal of the American Planning Association* 57 (1991): 325–40.

Garner, John S. *The Model Company Town: Urban Design through Private Enterprise in Nineteenth-Century New England.* Amherst: University of Massachusetts Press, 1984.

Gay, Patricia H. "Urban Treasures or Urban Nightmares?" *CRM* 19, 6 (1996): 39–41.

Gebhard, David, and Gerald Mansheim. *Buildings of Iowa.* New York: Oxford University Press, 1993.

Gebhard, David, and Tom Martinson. *A Guide to the Architecture of Minnesota.* Minneapolis: University of Minnesota Press, 1977.

Gebhard, David, Roger Montgomery, Robert Winter, John Woodbridge, and Sally Woodbridge. *A Guide to Architecture in San Francisco and Northern California.* 2d ed. Salt Lake City: Peregrine Smith, 1976.

Ghost Towns and Mining Camps: Selected Papers from the Ghost Towns and Mining Camps Preservation Conferences in Boise, Idaho, May 1974, and in Flagstaff, Arizona, April 1975, and the Developing Historic Districts in Small Towns and Cities Workshop in Salt Lake City, Utah, March 1975. Washington, D.C.: Preservation Press, 1977.

Gillette, Howard, Jr., and Zane L. Miller, eds. *American Urbanism: A Historiographical Review.* New York: Greenwood Press, 1987.

Gittell, Ross J. *Renewing Cities.* Princeton: Princeton University Press, 1992.

Glaab, Charles N., and A. Theodore Brown. *A History of Urban America.* 2nd ed. New York: Macmillan, 1976.

Glass, James A. *The Beginnings of a New National Historic Preservation Program, 1957 to 1969.* Nashville: American Association for State and Local History; Washington, D.C.: National Conference of State Historic Preservation Officers, 1989.

Glisson, Linda S. *Main Street: Open for Business.* Washington, D.C.: National Trust Main Street Center/National Trust for Historic Preservation, 1984.

Goldstone, Harmon H., and Martha Dalrymple. *History Preserved: A Guide to New York City Landmarks and Historic Districts.* New York: Simon and Schuster, 1974.

Gossman, Craig E., and Rhonda Curtis. "Sketching Back to the Future." *Historic Preservation Forum* 7, no. 5 (September–October 1993): 25–31.

Gowans, Alan. *Styles and Types of North American Architecture: Social Function and Cultural Expression.* New York: Icon Editions, 1992.

Grannis, Marjory, and Uri Grannis, and Rosemary Hale, and George Hale. *Visiting the Midwest's Historic Preservation Sites.* Ottawa, Ill.: Jameson Books, 1991.

Gratz, Roberta Brandes. *The Living City: How America's Cities Are Being Revitalized by Thinking Small in a Big Way.* Washington D.C.: Preservation Press, 1994.

Greenwood, Fred M., III. "Ohio Renaissance: A New Image Makes Good Business Sense for Medina's Public Square." *Small Town* 3:3 (November-December 1982): 36–42.

Greider, Linda. "Secrets of Great Old Neighborhoods." *Historic Preservation* 38, no. 1 (February 1986): 28–35.

Grieff, Constance M. *Independence: The Creation of a National Park.* Philadelphia: University of Pennsylvania Press, 1987.

A Guide to Delineating Edges of Historic Districts. Washington, D.C.: Preservation Press, 1976.

A Guide to the Older Neighborhoods of Dallas. Dallas: Historic Preservation League, 1986.

Hall, Donna. "The Role of Local Planning in the Preservation of Historic Districts: Case

Studies from Washington State." *Small Town* 21, no. 4 (January-February 1991): 12–24.

Hamer, David. "Historic Preservation in Urban New Zealand: An Historian's Perspective." *New Zealand Journal of History* 31, no. 2 (October 1997): 251–69.

———. *New Towns in the New World: Images and Perceptions of the Nineteenth-Century Urban Frontier.* New York: Columbia University Press, 1990.

Hartford Architecture. Vol. 1: *Downtown.* Hartford, Conn.: Hartford Architecture Conservancy Survey, 1978.

Hayden, Dolores. *The Power of Place: Urban Landscapes as Public History.* Cambridge, Mass.: MIT Press, 1995.

Helfgot, Joseph H., et al. *Lowell, Massachusetts: Living with Adversity. A Community Social Profile.* Community Sociology Monograph Series, vol. 4. Department of Sociology, Boston University, 1977.

Historic Buildings of Centre County, Pennsylvania. Historic Restoration Project of Centre County Library; Keystone Books, 1980.

"Historical Landscapes—Livingston: Railroad Town on the Yellowstone." *Montana: The Magazine of Western History* 35, no. 4 (Autumn 1985): 84–86.

Holcomb, H. Briavel, and Robert A. Beauregard. *Revitalizing Cities.* Washington, D.C.: Association of American Geographers, 1981.

Horstman, Neil. "Defining a Role for Professionals in Small Town Preservation." *Small Town* 13:3 (November-December 1982): 43–47.

Hosmer, Charles B., Jr. *Preservation Comes of Age: From Williamsburg to the National Trust, 1926–1949.* 2 vols. Charlottesville: University Press of Virginia, 1981.

Hosmer, Charles B., Jr., and Paul O. Williams. *Elsah: A Historic Guidebook.* Elsah, Ill.: Historic Elsah, 1967.

Hot Springs, South Dakota, Main Street Study: A Project of the National Trust for Historic Preservation. Ann Arbor, Mich.: Preservation/Urban Design Incorporated, 1978.

Hudson, John C. "Main Streets of the Yellowstone Valley: Town-building along the Northern Pacific in Montana." *Montana: The Magazine of Western History* 35, no. 4 (Autumn 1985): 64–65.

Hummon, David M. *Commonplaces: Community Ideology and Identity in American Culture.* Albany: State University of New York Press, 1990.

Hunter, Albert. *Symbolic Communities: The Persistence and Change of Chicago's Local Communities.* Chicago: University of Chicago Press, 1974.

Hunter, Kevin A. "From the Development Commission: Ashland Place Historic District." *Landmark Letter* (Historic Mobile Landmark Preservation Society) 20, no. 2 (Fall 1987): 6, 7, 14.

Huston, Ann, and B. Noah Tilgham. "Bodie, California: Preserving a Historic Mining Landscape." *CRM* 20, no. 9 (1997): 41–45.

Ide, Barbara. "St. Joseph, Mo.: Preservation or Demolition?" In *Preservation in Your Town* (Theme Handbook 1 of the 1973 Annual Meeting and Preservation Conference of the National Trust), 13–15.

Ittleson, Ellen. "Gambling: Boom or Bust for Preservation. The Impact on Four Western Communities." *Historic Preservation Forum* 5, no. 6 (November–December 1991): 16.

Jackson, Kenneth T. *Crabgrass Frontier: The Suburbanization of the United States.* New York: Oxford University Press, 1987.

Jacobs, Jane. *The Death and Life of Great American Cities.* New York: Vintage Books, 1961.

Jacobs, Stephen W. "A Current View of Area Preservation." *AIA Journal* 42, no. 6 (December 1964): 49–53.

Jakle, John A. *The American Small Town: Twentieth-Century Place Images.* Hamden, Conn.: Archon Books, 1982.

———. *The Tourist: Travel in Twentieth-Century North America.* Lincoln: University of Nebraska Press, 1985.

Jackle, John A., and David Wilson. *Derelict Landscapes: The Wasting of America's Built Environment.* Savage, Md.: Rowman & Littlefield, 1992.

Janka, Katherine. "An Old-West Mining Town Copes with Growth." *Historic Preservation* 35, no. 6 (November-December 1983): 24–29.

Johnson, Eugene J., and Robert D. Russell, Jr. *Memphis: An Architectural Guide.* Knoxville: University of Tennessee Press, 1990.

Kammen, Michael. *Mystic Chords of Memory: The Transformation of Tradition in American Culture.* New York: Vintage Books, 1993.

Kane, Lucile M., and Alan Ominsky. *Twin Cities: A Pictorial History of Saint Paul and Minneapolis.* St. Paul: Minnesota Historical Society Press, 1983.

Kaplan, Peter R. *The Historic Architecture of Cabarrus County, North Carolina.* Concord: Historic Cabarrus, 1981.

Karasov, Deborah, and Steve Waryan, eds. *The Once and Future Park.* New York: Princeton Architectural Press, 1993.

Kay, Jane Holtz. "Salem." *American Preservation* 1, no. 2 (December 1977-January 1978): 9–20.

Kay, Jane Holtz, with Pauline Chase-Harrell. *Preserving New England: Connecticut, Rhode Island, Massachusetts, Vermont, New Hampshire, Maine.* New York: Pantheon Books, 1986.

Kazickas, Jurate, and Lynn Scherr. *Susan B. Anthony Slept Here.* New York: Times Books, 1994.

Keister, Kim. "Main Street Makes Good." *Historic Preservation* 42, no. 5 (September-October 1990): 44–50.

Kelly, Deborah Marquis, and Jennifer B. Goodman. *Conservation District Project Research Report.* Washington, D.C.: National Trust for Historic Preservation, 1991.

Keune, Russell V., ed. *The Historic Preservation Yearbook: A Documentary Record of Significant Policy Developments and Issues.* 1st ed. Bethesda, Md.: Adler & Adler, 1985.

Kidney, Walter C. "Small History: What the Books Will Never Know." *PH & LF News* (Pittsburgh History and Landmarks Foundation), no. 117 (Spring 1991): 4–5.

Kirk, Ruth, and Carmela Alexander. *Exploring Washington's Past: A Road Guide to History.* Seattle: University of Washington Press, 1990.

Klein, Marilyn W., and David P. Fogle. *Clues to American Architecture.* Washington, D.C.: Starrhill Press, 1986.

Kramer, George. "Signs: Preserving a Sense of Place." *Heritage* (Summer 1990): 20–23.

Kreisman, Lawrence. *Historic Preservation in Seattle.* Seattle: Historic Seattle Preservation and Development Authority, 1985.

Lamme, Ary J., III. *America's Historic Landscapes: Community Power and the Preservation of National Historic Sites.* Knoxville: University of Tennessee Press, 1989.

Landmark Yellow Pages: Where to Find All the Names, Addresses, Facts, and Figures You Need. Washington, D.C.: Preservation Press, 1993.

Lanegan, David. *Urban Dynamics in Saint Paul.* St. Paul: Old Town Restorations, Inc., 1977.

Lapsley, Guy. "Tax Projects and the National Parks." *CRM* 20, no. 6 (1997): 14–16.

Laska, Shirley Bradway, and Daphne Spain, eds. *Back to the City: Issues in Neighborhood Renovation.* New York: Pergamon Press, 1980.

Lee, Antoinette J. "Historians Then, Historians Now." *CRM* 19, no. 6 (1996): 45–47.

Lee, Antoinette, J., ed. *Past Meets Future: Saving America's Historic Environments.* Washington, D.C.: Preservation Press, 1992.

Lee-Thomas Associates. *Historic Preservation in California: A Handbook for Local Communities.* Sacramento: California Office of Historic Preservation, December 1986.

Lefevre, Michel R. "Historic District Designation: Panacea or Placebo." *CRM* 18, no. 4 (1995): 26.

Leider, Charles L. W. "Capitol Townsite Historic District: Guthrie, Oklahoma. A Case Study, 1980–1986." *Chronicles of Oklahoma* 68 (Winter 1990–91): 396–423.

Leon, Warren, and Margaret Piatt. "Living-History Museums." In *History Museums in the United States: A Critical Assessment,* edited by Warren Leon and Roy Rosenzweig, 65–78. Urbana: University of Illinois Press, 1989.

Leon, Warren, and Roy Rosenzweig, eds. *History Museums in the United States: A Critical Assessment.* Urbana: University of Illinois Press, 1989.

Leonard, Stephen J., and Thomas J. Noel. *Denver: Mining Camp to Metropolis.* Niwot: University Press of Colorado, 1990.

Levy, Paul R., and Roman A. Cybriwsky. "The Hidden Dimensions of Culture and Class: Philadelphia." In *Back to the City: Issues in Neighborhood Renovation,* edited by Shirley Bradway Laska and Daphne Spain, 138–55. New York: Pergamon Press, 1980.

Ley, David. *The New Middle Class and the Remaking of the Central City.* Oxford: Oxford University Press, 1996.

Lindgren, James M. *Preserving Historic New England: Preservation, Progressivism, and the Remaking of Memory.* New York: Oxford University Press, 1995.

Lingeman, Richard. *Small Town America: A Narrative History 1620–The Present.* Boston: Houghton Mifflin, 1981.

Living Cities: Report of the Twentieth Century Fund Task Force on Urban Preservation Policies. New York: Priority Press Publications, 1985.

Logan, John R., and Harvey L. Molotch. *Urban Fortunes: The Political Economy of Place.* Berkeley: University of California Press, 1987.

Longstreth, Richard. *The Buildings of Main Street: A Guide to American Commercial Architecture.* Washington, D.C.: Preservation Press, 1987.

————. "When the Present Becomes the Past." In *Past Meets Future: Saving America's Historic Environments,* edited by Antoinette J. Lee, 213–25. Washington, D.C.: Preservation Press, 1992.

Lowell, Massachusetts: Report of the Lowell Historic Canal District to the Ninety-fifth Congress of the United States of America. Lowell: The Lowell Historic Canal District Commission, 1977.

Lowell: The Story of an Industrial City. A Guide to Lowell National Historical Park and Lowell Heritage State Park Lowell, Massachusetts. Washington, D.C.: Division of Publications, National Park Service, 1992.

Lyle, Royster, Jr., and Michael A. Lynn. "Lexington, Virginia: Linking Preservation Planning and Tourism." *Small Town* 13:3 (November-December 1982): 22–26.

Bibliography

Lynch, Kevin. *The Image of the City*. Cambridge, Mass.: MIT Press, 1960.

————. *Managing the Sense of a Region*. Cambridge, Mass.: MIT Press, 1976.

————. *What Time Is this Place?* Cambridge, Mass.: MIT Press, 1972.

McAlester, Virginia, and Lee McAlester. *A Field Guide to American Houses*. New York: Alfred A. Knopf, 1991.

McGregor, Robert Kuhn. "Historic Preservation in New York State." *Public Historian* 7, no. 4 (Fall 1985): 71-78.

McNulty, Robert H., R. Leo Penne, Dorothy R. Jacobson, and Partners for Livable Spaces. *The Return of the Living City: Learning from America's Best*. Washington, D.C.: Acropolis Books, 1986.

Main Street, Ohio: Opportunities for Bringing People Back Downtown. Columbus, Ohio: Department of Economic and Community Development, State of Ohio, 1981.

Maintaining Community Character: How to Establish a Local Historic District. National Trust for Historic Preservation Information Series no. 58, 1992.

Malo, Paul. *Landmarks of Rochester and Monroe County: A Guide to Neighborhoods and Villages*. Syracuse: Syracuse University Press, 1974.

Massachusetts Historical Commission. *Establishing Local Historic Districts*. Boston: Massachusetts Historical Commission, 1994.

Mattox, Joe Louis. "As I See It: Ghetto or Gold Mine—Hold on to that Old House." *American Preservation* 1, no. 3 (February-March 1978): 3-4.

Mayne, Alan. "City as Artifact: Heritage Preservation in Comparative Perspective." In *Urban Public Policy: Historical Modes and Methods*, edited by Martin V. Melosi, 153-88. University Park: Pennsylvania State University Press, 1993.

Means, Mary C. "Town Preservation in the Midwest." In *Preservation in Your Town: 1973 Annual Meeting and Preservation Conference*, 9. Washington, D.C.: National Trust for Historic Preservation, 1973.

Meinig, D. W. "Symbolic Landscapes: Models of American Community." In *The Interpretation of Ordinary Landscapes: Geographical Essays*, edited by D. W. Meinig, 164-94. New York: Oxford University Press, 1979.

Meinig, D. W., ed. *The Interpretation of Ordinary Landscapes: Geographical Essays*. New York: Oxford University Press, 1979.

Melosi, Martin V., ed. *Urban Public Policy: Historical Modes and Methods*. University Park: Pennsylvania State University Press, 1993.

Melvin, Patricia Mooney. "The Neighborhood-City Relationship." In *American Urbanism: A Historiographical Review*, edited by Howard Gillette, Jr., and Zane L. Miller, 257-70. New York: Greenwood Press, 1987.

Merritt, Louise McAllister. "New Directions: A Local Organization's View." In National Trust for Historic Preservation, *Preservation: Toward an Ethic in the 1980s*, 167-75. Washington D.C.: Preservation Press, 1980.

Miles, Don C. "Pioneer Square: A Case Study." *Critical Issues* (Spring 1989): 8-11.

Miller, Page Putnam. *Reclaiming the Past: Landmarks of Women's History*. Bloomington: Indiana University Press, 1992.

Miller, Zane. "History and the Politics of Community Change in Cincinnati." *Public Historian* 5, no. 4 (Fall 1983): 17-35.

————. "Planning and the Politics of Ethnic Identity: Making Choices for Over-the-Rhine, 1971-85." In *Ethnic Diversity and Civic Identity: Patterns of Conflict and Cohesion in*

Cincinnati since 1820, edited by Henry D. Shapiro and Jonathan D. Sarna, 248–65. Urbana: University of Illinois Press, 1992.

Millett, Larry. *Lost Twin Cities*. St. Paul: Minnesota Historical Society Press, 1983.

Moore, Charles, Peter Becker, and Regula Campbell. *The City Observed: Los Angeles, a Guide to Its Architecture and Landscapes*. New York: Random House, 1984.

Morrill, Dan L. "Keeping History in Historic Preservation." In *The Historic Preservation Yearbook: A Documentary Record of Significant Policy Developments and Issues*, edited by Russell V. Keune, 481–82. 1st ed. Bethesda, Md.: Adler & Adler, 1985.

Morris, Phillip. "A Neighborhood Grows in Charlotte." *Architecture* 72, no. 8 (October 1983): 64–65.

Morse, Susan. "Neighborhood Spirit Shapes a City." *Historic Preservation* 40, no. 4 (July-August 1988): 24–31.

Moul, Harry. "Santa Fe Styles and Townscapes: The Search for Authenticity." In *Design Review: Challenging Urban Aesthetic Control*, edited by Brenda Case Scheer and Wolfgang F. E. Preiser, 95–110. New York: Chapman & Hall, 1994.

Mulloy, Elizabeth D. *The History of the National Trust for Historic Preservation, 1963–1973*. Washington, D.C.: Preservation Press, 1976.

Munsell, Ken. "Historic Home Tours Awaken Interest." *Small Town* 13, no. 3 (November-December 1982): 59–60.

Murtagh, William J. "Historic Districts: Aesthetic and Social Dimensions." In *Historic Districts: Summary of a Conference at Oak Park, Illinois, February 9, 1974*, edited by Paul Sprague and Linda Lerner, 11–15.

———. *Keeping Time: The History and Theory of Preservation in America*. New York: Sterling, 1993.

Myers, Phyllis, and Gordon Binder. *Neighborhood Conservation: Lessons from Three Cities*. Washington, D.C.: Conservation Foundation, 1977.

Napoli, Donald S. "Historic Preservation in Point Arena, California: A Model for Context-based Planning." *Small Town* 21, no. 5 (March-April 1991): 4–9.

National Register Bulletin 15: How to Apply the National Register Criteria for Evaluation. Rev. ed. Washington, D.C.: National Park Service, 1991.

National Trust for Historic Preservation. *Preservation: Toward an Ethic in the 1980s*. Washington, D.C.: Preservation Press, 1980.

Neasham, V. Aubrey. *Old Sacramento: A Reference Point in Time*. Rev. ed. Sacramento: Sacramento Historic Landmarks Commission in cooperation with the Redevelopment Agency of the City of Sacramento, 1968.

New Architecture-Design Relationship. Washington, D.C.: Preservation Press and National Trust for Historic Preservation, 1981.

New City on the Merrimack: Prints of Lawrence 1845–1876. Merrimack Valley Textile Museum Occasional Reports no. 2, 1974.

Nickens, Eddie. "Delaware Revivalism." *Historic Preservation* 47, no. 1 (January-February 1995): 21.

Old and New Architecture: Design Relationship. Washington, D.C.: Preservation Press, 1980.

Olmert, Michael. "Delaware's Colonial Hideaway." *Historic Preservation* 37, no. 3 (June 1985): 58–63.

Olmsted, Roger, and T. H. Watkins. *Here Today: San Francisco's Architectural Heritage*. San Francisco: Chronicle Books, n.d.

Olson, Sherry. *Baltimore.* Cambridge, Mass.: Ballinger, 1976.

Ortega, Richard I. "Unwanted: Historic District Designation." *Historic Preservation* 28, no. 1 (January-March 1976): 41–43.

Pacyga, Dominic A., and Ellen Skerrett. *Chicago, City of Neighborhoods: Histories and Tours.* Chicago: Loyola University Press, 1986.

Peters, Frank, and George McCue. *A Guide to the Architecture of St. Louis.* Columbia: University of Missouri Press, 1989.

Philadelphia Architecture: A Guide to the City. Cambridge, Mass.: MIT Press, 1984.

Plan and Program for the Preservation of the Vieux Carre. Historic District Demonstration Study Conducted by the Bureau of Governmental Research, New Orleans, Louisiana, for the City of New Orleans, December 1968.

Pohl, Jon. "Visual Aspects of an Historic District." In *Historic Districts: Summary of a Conference at Oak Park, Illinois, February 9, 1974,* edited by Paul Sprague and Linda Lerner, 4–6.

Pomada, Elizabeth, and Michael Larsen. *Daughters of Painted Ladies: America's Resplendent Victorians.* New York: E. P. Dutton, 1987.

Preservation in Your Town: 1973 Annual Meeting and Preservation Conference. Washington, D. C.: National Trust for Historic Preservation, 1973.

Preservation in Your Town. Theme Handbook 1 of the 1973 Annual Meeting and Preservation Conference of the National Trust.

Preservation Is Progress: New Orleans. A report prepared for presentation to the Conference of Great Cities of the World in Boston, September 1980. Mostly done by the City Planning Department.

Primm, James Neal. *Lion of the Valley: St. Louis, Missouri.* Boulder, Colo.: Pruett, 1981.

Purdy, Lisa A. "The Anatomy of Creating a Local Historic District." *Urban Design and Preservation Quarterly* 13, no. 2 (Spring 1990): 8–11.

Reiff, Janice L., and Susan E. Hirsch. "Pullman and Its Public: Image and Aim in Making and Interpreting History." *Public Historian* 11, no. 4 (Fall 1989): 99–112.

Relph, Edward. *The Modern Urban Landscape.* Baltimore: Johns Hopkins University Press, 1992.

Reps, J. W. *Cities of the American West : A History of Frontier Urban Planning.* Princeton: Princeton University Press, 1979.

———. *The Making of Urban America: A History of City Planning in the United States.* Princeton: Princeton University Press, 1965.

Rhinehart, Raymond P. "Preservation's Best Interests." *Preservation News* 16, no. 10 (October 1976): 5.

Richardson, Ralph W. *Historic Districts: New England: Connecticut—Maine—Massachusetts—New Hampshire—Rhode Island—Vermont.* Bowie, Md.: Heritage Books, 1992.

———. *Historic Districts of America: The Mid-Atlantic: Delaware—District of Columbia—Maryland—New Jersey—New York—Pennsylvania—West Virginia.* Bowie, Md.: Heritage Books, 1991.

———. *Historic Districts of America: The South: Alabama—Florida—Georgia—Kentucky—Louisiana—Mississippi—North Carolina—South Carolina—Tennessee—Virginia.* Bowie, Md.: Heritage Books, 1987.

———. *Historic Districts of America: The West: Arizona—California—Colorado—Idaho—Mon-*

tana—Nevada—New Mexico—North Dakota—Oklahoma—Oregon—South Dakota—Texas—Utah—Washington—Wyoming. Bowie, Md.: Heritage Books, 1993.

Rifkind, Carole. *A Field Guide to American Architecture.* New York: New American Library, 1980.

———. *Main Street: The Face of Urban America.* New York: Harper & Row, 1977.

Rixoon, J. Sanford, and Judith Austin, eds. *Interpreting Local Culture and History.* Moscow: University of Idaho Press, 1991.

Rodwin, Lloyd, and Robert M. Hollister, eds. *Cities of the Mind: Images and Themes of the City in the Social Sciences.* New York: Plenum Press, 1984.

Rose, Vivien. "Preserving Women's Rights History." *CRM* 20, no. 3 (1997): 25–28.

Ross, Pat. *Remembering Main Street: An American Album.* New York: Penguin Books, 1994.

Russo, David J. *Keepers of Our Past: Local Historical Writing in the United States, 1820s-1930s.* New York: Greenwood Press, 1988.

Saarinen, Thomas F., David Seamon, and James L. Sell, eds. *Environmental Perception and Behavior: An Inventory and Prospect.* Chicago: Department of Geography, University of Chicago Research Paper no. 209, 1984.

Salmon Falls—The Mill Village: Historic District Study for the Town of Rollinsford, New Hampshire. Dover, N.H.: Strafford Regional Planning Commission, 1974.

Salwen, Peter. *Upper West Side Story: A History and Guide.* New York: Abbeville Press, 1989.

Sauder, Robert A., and Teresa Wilkinson. "Preservation Planning and Geographic Change in New Orleans' Vieux Carré." *Urban Geography* 10, no. 1 (January-February 1989): 41–61.

Savage, Beth L., ed. *African American Historic Places: National Register of Historic Places.* Washington, D.C.: Preservation Press, 1994.

Savery, Meredith. "Instability and Uniformity: Residential Patterns in Two Philadelphia Neighborhoods, 1880-1970." In *The Divided Metropolis: Social and Spatial Dimensions of Philadelphia, 1800–1975,* edited by William W. Cutler III and Howard Gillette, Jr., 193–226. Westport, Connecticut: Greenwood Press, 1980.

Scheer, Brenda Case, and Wolfgang F. E. Preiser, eds. *Design Review: Challenging Urban Aesthetic Control.* New York: Chapman & Hall, 1994.

Scherzer, Kenneth A. *The Unbounded Community: Neighborhood Life and Social Structure in New York City, 1830–1875.* Durham: Duke University Press, 1992.

Schneider, John C. "Skid Row as an Urban Neighborhood, 1880-1960." *Urbanism Past & Present* 9, no. 17 (Winter-Spring 1984): 10–20.

Schoenberg, Sandra Perlman, and Patricia L. Rosenbaum. *Neighborhoods that Work: Sources for Viability in the Inner City.* New Brunswick, N.J.: Rutgers University Press, 1980.

Schroeder, Fred E. H. "Types of American Small Towns and How to Read Them." In *Order and Image in the American Small Town,* edited by Michael W. Fazio and Peggy Whitman Prenshaw, 104–35. Jackson: University Press of Mississippi, 1981.

Schuler, Jill R., Robert B. Kent, and Charles B. Monroe. "Neighborhood Gentrification: A Discriminant Analysis of a Historic District in Cleveland, Ohio." *Urban Geography* 13, no. 1 (January-February 1992): 49–67.

Schwarzer, Mitchell. "Myths of Permanence and Transience in the Discourse on Historic Preservation in the United States." *Journal of Architectural Education* 48, no. 1 (September 1994): 2–11.

Bibliography

Scott, Pamela, and Antoinette J. Lee. *Buildings of the District of Columbia.* New York: Oxford University Press, 1993.

Shapiro, Henry D., and Zane L. Miller. *Clifton: Neighborhood and Community in an Urban Setting. A Brief History.* Cincinnati: Laboratory in American Civilization, 1976.

Shapiro, Henry D., and Jonathan D. Sarna, eds. *Ethnic Diversity and Civic Identity: Patterns of Conflict and Cohesion in Cincinnati since 1820.* Urbana: University of Illinois Press, 1992.

Shaver, Peter D. *The National Register of Historic Places in New York State.* New York: Rizzoli, 1993.

Short, J. R., L. M. Benton, W. B. Luce, and J. Walton. "Reconstructing the Image of an Industrial City." *Annals of the Association of American Geographers* 83, no. 2 (June 1993): 207–24.

Sies, Mary Corbin. "Paradise Retained: An Analysis of Persistence in Planned, Exclusive Suburbs, 1880–1980." *Planning Perspectives* 12, no. 2 (April 1997): 165–92.

Silver, Christopher. "Neighborhood Planning in Historical Perspective." *APA Journal* 51 (Spring 1985): 161–74.

———. "Revitalizing the Urban South: Neighborhood Preservation and Planning since the 1920s." *APA Journal* 69 (1991): 69–84.

Sinclair, Peg B. *Victorious Victorians: A Guide to the Major Architectural Styles.* New York: Holt, Rinehart & Winston, 1985.

Skelcher, Bradley. "Main Street Mid-America: An Historical Overview of the Main Street Pilot Project in Galesburg, Illinois." *Small Town* 21, no. 1 (July-August 1990): 4–13.

———. "Preserving Main Street in the Heartland: The Main Street Pilot Project in Madison, Indiana." *Small Town* 22, no. 2 (September-October 1991): 4–13.

Smith, Neil. "New City, New Frontier: The Lower East Side as Wild, Wild West." In *Variations on a Theme Park: The New American City and the End of Public Space,* edited by Michael Sorkin, 61–93. New York: Noonday Press, 1992.

Sorkin, Michael, ed. *Variations on a Theme Park: The New American City and the End of Public Space.* New York: Noonday Press, 1992.

Southworth, Susan, and Michael Southworth. *A.I.A. Guide to Boston.* 2d ed. Chester, Conn.: The Globe Pequot Press, 1992.

Spector, Tom. *The Guide to the Architecture of Georgia.* Columbia: University of South Carolina Press, 1993.

Sprague, Paul E. "Why Form Historic Districts?" In *Historic Districts: Summary of a Conference at Oak Park, Illinois, February 9, 1974,* edited by Paul Sprague and Linda Lerner, 2–3.

———. *Defining and Describing Historic Districts: Methods, Techniques and Time Studies for Making Verbal and Visual Descriptions and Analyses of Visual Resources in Historic Districts for Preservation Planning.* 1975.

Sprague, Paul E., and Linda Lerner, eds. *Historic Districts: Summary of a Conference at Oak Park, Illinois, February 9, 1974.*

Stanwood, Les. "Coupeville's Historic District Dilemma." *Historic Preservation* 33, no. 6 (November-December 1981): 24–29.

Starr, S. Frederick. *Southern Comfort: The Garden District of New Orleans, 1800–1900.* Cambridge, Mass.: MIT Press, 1989.

Stilgoe, John R. *Borderland: Origins of the American Suburb, 1820–1939.* New Haven: Yale University Press, 1988.

Stipe, Robert E., and Antoinette J. Lee, eds. *The American Mosaic: Preserving a Nation's Heritage.* Washington, D.C.: US/ICOMOS, 1987.

Stoehr, C. Eric. *Bonanza Victorian: Architecture and Society in Colorado Mining Towns.* Albuquerque: University of New Mexico Press, 1975.

Strauss, Anselm L. *Images of the American City.* New Brunswick, N.J.: Transaction Books, 1976.

Suttles, Gerald D. *The Man-Made City: The Land-Use Confidence Game in Chicago.* Chicago: University of Chicago Press, 1990.

———. *The Social Construction of Communities.* Chicago: University of Chicago Press, 1972.

Taylor, Jon E. "Preserving a President's Community." *CRM* 20, no. 9 (1997): 16–18.

Taylor, Robert M., Jr., Errol Wayne Stevens, Mary Ann Ponder, and Paul Brockman. *Indiana: A New Historical Guide.* Indianapolis: Indiana Historical Society, 1989.

Thomas, George E. "Architectural Patronage and Social Stratification in Philadelphia between 1840 and 1920." In *The Divided Metropolis: Social and Spatial Dimensions of Philadelphia, 1800–1975,* edited by William W. Cutler III and Howard Gillette, Jr., 85–123. Westport, Conn.: Greenwood Press, 1980.

Thurber, Pamela, ed. *Controversies in Historic Preservation: Understanding the Preservation Movement Today.* Preservation Policy Research Series No. PPR-RO3. Washington, D.C.: National Trust for Historic Preservation, Fall 1985.

Thurber, Pamela, and Robert Moyer. *State Enabling Legislation for Local Preservation Commissions.* Preservation Policy Research Series No. SLP-001, Order No. 5236. Washington D.C.: National Trust for Historic Preservation, 1984.

Tise, Larry E. "Saving Our Towns: A Strategy for Protecting and Preserving the Historic Character of Towns and Cities in the Mid-South Region." In *The Best of Both Worlds: The Challenge of Growth Enhancement in the Mid-South,* pt. 3, edited by Carroll Van West. A report prepared by the Center for Historic Preservation, Middle State University, Murfreesboro, Tenn., as a Critical Issues Fund Project of the National Trust for Historic Preservation, 1988.

Toft, Carolyn Hewes. *St. Louis: Landmarks and Historic Districts.* St. Louis: Landmarks Association of St. Louis, 1988.

Tomlan, Michael. "Who Will Care in the 1990s?" *Preservation Forum* 3, no. 4 (Winter 1990): 20–21.

Tuan, Yi-Fu. *Space and Place: The Perspective of Experience.* Minneapolis: University of Minnesota Press, 1977.

———. *Topophilia: A Study of Environmental Perception, Attitudes, and Values.* Englewood Cliffs, N.J.: Prentice-Hall, 1974.

Values of Residential Properties in Urban Historic Districts: Georgetown, Washington, D.C., and Other Selected Districts. Washington, D.C.: National Trust for Historic Preservation, 1977.

Van West, Carroll, ed. *The Best of Both Worlds: The Challenge of Growth Enhancement in the Mid-South.* A report prepared by the Center for Historic Preservation, Middle State University, Murfreesboro, Tenn., as a Critical Issues Fund Project of the National Trust for Historic Preservation, 1988.

Velt, Tanya M. "Local Preservation Activities." *CRM* 17, no. 2 (1994): 24.

Vogel, Lisa, and Pratt Cassity. "The Buck Stops . . . Where?" *Historic Preservation Forum* (Summer 1996): 15–23.

Wallace, Michael. *Mickey Mouse History and Other Essays on American Memory.* Philadelphia: Temple University Press, 1996.

Warner, Sam Bass, Jr. *Streetcar Suburbs: The Process of Growth in Boston, 1870–1900.* New York: Atheneum, 1976.

———. "Slums and Skyscrapers: Urban Images, Symbols, and Ideology." In *Cities of the Mind: Images and Themes of the City in the Social Sciences,* edited by Lloyd Rodwin and Robert M. Hollister, 181–96. New York: Plenum Press, 1984.

Warner, W. Lloyd. *The Living and the Dead: A Study of the Symbolic Life of Americans.* Westport, Conn.: Greenwood Press, 1975. Originally published in 1959.

Warren-Findley, Jannelle. "Historians and Historic Preservation." *OAH Newsletter* (February 1988): 16–17.

Water Street Historic District: Port Townsend, Washington. Field Report by the National Trust for Historic Preservation, 1977.

Weeks, Christopher. *The Buildings of Westminster in Maryland: A Socio-architectural Account of Westminster's First 250 Years, including an Illustrated Inventory of over 200 Historic Structures.* 2d ed. Annapolis, Md.: Fishergate Publishing Company for the City of Westminster, 1979.

———. *A Guide to the Architecture of Washington, D.C.* Baltimore: Johns Hopkins University Press, 1994.

Weinberg, Nathan. *Preservation in American Towns and Cities.* Boulder, Colo.: Westview Press, 1979.

White, Norval, and Elliot Wilensky, eds. *AIA Guide to New York City.* New York: Macmillan, 1968.

White, Thomas M. "Lessons from the Loss of Omaha's Jobbers Canyon." *Preservation Forum* 3, no. 1 (Spring 1989): 8–12.

Wiberg, Ruth Eloise. *Rediscovering Northwest Denver: Its History, Its People, Its Landmarks.* Boulder, Colo.: Pruett, 1976.

Williams, Brett. *Upscaling Downtown: Stalled Gentrification in Washington, D.C.* Ithaca: Cornell University Press, 1988.

Williams, Norman, Jr., Edmund H. Kellogg, and Frank B. Gilbert, eds. *Readings in Historic Preservation: Why? What? How?* New Brunswick, N.J.: Center for Urban Policy Research, 1983.

Williams, Norman, Jr., Edmund H. Kellogg, and Peter M. Lavigne. *Vermont Townscape.* New Brunswick, N.J.: Center for Urban Policy Research, 1987.

Wilson, David Scofield. "Old Sacramento: Place as Presence, Palimpsest, and Performance." *Places* 5, no. 2 (1988): 54–63.

Wilson, Richard Guy. "Old West Side." *Historic Preservation* 25, no. 3. (July-September 1973): 16–21.

Wilson, Samuel, Jr. "Evolution in a Historic Area's 'Tout Ensemble.' " In *New Architecture-Design Relationship.* Washington, D.C.: Preservation Press and National Trust for Historic Preservation, 1981.

Wilson, William H. *The City Beautiful Movement.* Baltimore: Johns Hopkins University Press, 1989.

Winters, Christopher. "The Social Identity of Evolving Neighborhoods." *Landscape* 23, no. 1 (1979): 8–14.

With Heritage So Rich. Washington, D.C.: Preservation Press, 1983. Originally published in 1966.

Wood, Joseph S. "'Build, Therefore, Your Own World': The New England Village as Settlement Ideal." *Annals of the Association of American Geographers* 81, no. 1 (March 1991): 32–50.

———. "Nothing Should Stand for Something that Never Existed." *Places* 2, no. 5 (1985): 81–87.

Wood, J. S., and M. Steinitz. "A World We Have Gained: House, Common, and Village in New England." *Journal of Historical Geography* 18, no. 1 (1992): 105–20.

Woodbridge, Sally B., and Roger Montgomery. *A Guide to Architecture in Washington State: An Environmental Perspective.* Seattle: University of Washington Press, 1980.

Ziegler, Arthur P., Jr. *Historic Preservation in Inner City Areas: A Manual of Practice.* Pittsburgh: Allegheny Press, 1971.

Zorbaugh, Harvey M. *The Gold Coast and the Slum.* Chicago: University of Chicago Press, 1929.

Index

The abbreviation HD is used for Historic District.

URBAN LIFE AND URBAN LANDSCAPE SERIES
Zane L. Miller *and* Henry D. Shapiro, *General Editors*

*The series examines the history of urban life
and the development of the urban landscape through works
that place social, economic, and political issues in the intellectual
and cultural context of their times.*

Designing Modern America: The Regional Planning Association and Its Members
    EDWARD K. SPANN

Hopedale: From Commune to Company Town, 1840–1920
    EDWARD K. SPANN

Visions of Eden: Environmentalism, Urban Planning, and City Building in St. Petersburg, Florida, 1900–1995
    R. BRUCE STEPHENSON

Welcome to Heights High: The Crippling Politics of Restructuring America's Public Schools
    DIANA TITTLE

Washing "The Great Unwashed": Public Baths in Urban America, 1840–1920
    MARILYN THORNTON WILLIAMS